THE PARISH BOOK OF
CERNE ABBAS

THE PARISH BOOK OF
CERNE ABBAS

ABBEY AND AFTER

VIVIAN AND PATRICIA VALE

HALSGROVE

First published in Great Britain in 2000

British Library Cataloguing-in-Publication Data
A CIP record for this title is available from the British Library

ISBN 1 84114 055 4

HALSGROVE
PUBLISHING, MEDIA AND DISTRIBUTION

Halsgrove House
Lower Moor Way
Tiverton, Devon EX16 6SS
Tel: 01884 243242
Fax: 01884 243325
email: sales@halsgrove.com
website: http://www.halsgrove.com

Printed and bound in Great Britain by Bookcraft Ltd, Midsomer Norton.

PROLOGUE

Cerne Abbas, with a history stretching back time out of mind and so often since the Dissolution reported to be dead or dying (when it was noticed at all), is now the home of a thriving, vigorous community. For a long time dignified with the title of Cerne Town, it is probably Dorset's best known village. Tucked away in a steep valley, straddling its little river, its hills topped with banks and ditches labelled 'British Settlement' on local maps, Cerne's fortunes have followed national trends of good times and bad despite its apparent isolation. And yet, it has always quietly survived. Even those visitors who thought it to be fading away have succumbed to its charm.

Cerne Abbas sits among downs to the east, west and north. The Coombes to the east and west were hollowed out by receding waters millennia ago as they made their way to the sea. Now there are trees; there is grazing for sheep and cattle; there are blackberries and sloes, bluebells and cowslips, primroses and violets, and the fauna to go with them – including foxes and badgers, deer and water voles, trout and too much birdlife to list.

Fortunately, much of the surrounding land has been designated SSSI, although that is little enough protection these days. There is good arable land in the valley and although miles of hedges have been ripped out during the last 30 years a new wooded area has recently been planted down in the meadows.

There were certainly people in the area before the founding of the Abbey. Worked flints and arrowheads have been found; Celtic field shapes and lynchets abound; pottery shards turn up and a Roman coin has been discovered. The Abbey enjoys a chapter of its own in this volume, but it is worth quoting Domesday.

LAND OF ST PETER'S OF CERNE (ABBAS)

St Peter's Church, Cerne, holds CERNE (Abbas). Before 1066 it paid tax for 22 hides. Land for 20 ploughs, of which 3 hides are in lordship; 3 ploughs there; 5 slaves; 26 villagers and 32 small-holders with 14 ploughs and 15 hides. A mill which pays 20s.; meadow, 20 acres; pasture 2 leagues long and 8 furlongs wide; woodland 1 league long and 8 furlongs wide. 3 cobs; 6 cattle; 14 pigs; 500 sheep.

Brictwin holds 4 hides of this land from the Abbott he has 4 ploughs there. He held them likewise before 1066; he could not withdraw from the Church, nor can he. The value of the Church's lordship was and is £21; for Brictwin's 100s.

The Domesday Book survey shows Cerne as having the second highest income of Dorset's abbeys, only Shaftesbury being richer. It is mentioned as owning land in Little Piddle, Radipole, Bloxworth, Affpuddle (one of the first endowments), Poxwell, Woodsford, Hethfelton, Worgret, Little Bredy, Winterborne, Long Bredy, Nettlecombe, Milton (West, not Abbas), Kimmeridge, Renscombe and Symondsbury. By the end of the 1200s it was still second richest, marginally better off than Milton and Sherborne. Near the time of the Dissolution it was fourth richest out of five, although it was wealthy enough to be still building. After 1539 matters changed, but the Crown did not dispose of all the Abbey lands. A survey of 1617 made the following report:

... the town is most inorderly governed for all the officers are weak men. There are many absentee landlords who have let their property to base people, mere mendicants – in one near a dozen lousy people, and yet these houses stand in the principal part of the town. [The Guildhall]... wherein the courts of the manor have been used to meet, is now so decayed that none dare stay in it [and the Abbey is]... wholly ruinated.

In 1930 a traveller declared Cerne 'not merely dead but buried'. Even a recent tourist guide suggested that Cerne 'went dead in the winter'. Wrong again! The real survivor and the cause of Cerne's present fame is the Giant, so he has a chapter to himself in this book. As the newspaper sellers used to cry, 'Read all about it!'

Known as Priest's Walk, this track climbs Giant Hill to the top Sherborne-Dorchester road.

The ancient Piddle Lane, climbing from the village between St Catherine's and Black Hill Barn.

CONTENTS

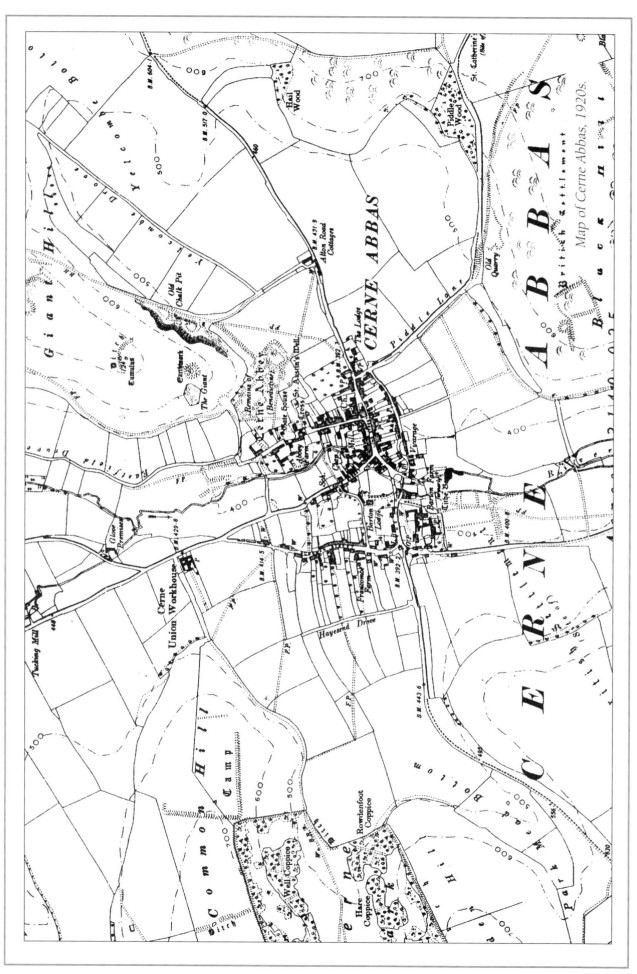

Map of Cerne Abbas, 1920s.

ACKNOWLEDGEMENTS

Any would be historian of Cerne Abbas must immediately confront a temporal problem – how to represent to the 21st century a community which reached its zenith in the 14th or 15th century? Hence the unique merit of Halsgrove's photographic enterprise in swinging the camera as it were across the panorama of time. Hence also our primary indebtedness as authors to the very many (too numerous to be listed individually) who have loaned us all sorts of illustrative material with permission to copy. They include the Syndics of the Cambridge University Press who allowed us to reproduce pages from our great predecessor, the medieval *Book of Cerne*, and the magazine *Dorset Life* for permission to use photographs. As many again by their oral reminiscences brought the folk memory to life.

Secondly, our fellow contributors, Mr and Mrs John Turner and Mr and Mrs Gordon Bartlet, who gave generously from their specialised knowledge, while Mr and Mrs Eric Fox and Miss Prudence Pile added to our stores of information on nonconformity and the local transport system. We are indebted to Messrs R. Stenhouse and F. Hamblin (churchwardens) for access to St Mary's roof (see page 27). The various staffs of our County Record Office, County Library and Dorset County Museum showed us the professional skills and courtesies they extend to all and also gave permission for photographs of material held. Thanks are extended from Mr Bartlet (see Chapter 8) to Dorchester Reference Library, Dorset Record Office, Somerset Record Office, and Wiltshire and Swindon Record Office for approval to reproduce documents held in their archives.

In the physical production of this book thanks are due first to Joanna Higgs, who patiently processed acres of foul typescript into immaculate wordage sponsored by our Cerne Historical Society. Later, Halsgrove's Community Histories Editor, Miss Naomi Cudmore, tempered efficiency with humanity in assimilating us to the earlier volumes of Halsgrove's exceedingly handsome series. Finally, a salute to the phantasmal population of this book, our precursors: 'Those who made the village, But never made the news' to whom (usually anonymous) photographers have restored form and figure, so that we in turn may the better seek to re-clothe them in their historic identities.

V.V. and P.H.V.
Cerne Abbas AD 2000

Looking south from the field where the Abbey once stood.

An outing with the Durnovarian, 1912.

Long Street, possibly 1870. The Red Lion is on the left but burnt down in 1897 and was subsequently rebuilt.

A NOTE ON SOURCES FOR CHAPTER 11

The 19th century Dorset labourer, it has been dramatically said, was a byword for poverty and degradation. Certainly no part of the county's agrarian history has been described and documented in such detail for the benefit of both government and countrymen at large as this prolonged period of depression. Perhaps we may therefore be excused the doleful duty of replicating here that large body of evidence which met the eye of officialdom, either through parliamentary papers or from reports of close and sympathetic individual observers.

Parliamentary papers, in the form of commissions' findings of evidence given to House of Commons select committees, run through most of the century, from the 1834 report of the Poor Law Commission, through the 1867 parliamentary commission of inquiry into conditions of employment (children, young persons, women) in agriculture, and onward to the House of Commons select committee on criminal convictions of 1879-95. Ignorance could be nobody's excuse. The same information was available to subscribers to the standard periodicals; proceedings of the English Agricultural Society and the *Journal of the Dorset and West of England Agricultural Society.*

To these witnesses must be added a long line of individual observers, some of them testifying before the above-named bodies, such as R. Henry Rew to the select committee in 1895 (p.p.xvii p.9); and other compassionate men through their own varieties of book - Arthur Young: *The Farmer's Calendar* (1805), Sir Frederick Morton Eden's *The State of the Poor* (1797), Rider Haggard's *Rural England* (1903) and Thomas Hardy himself: *The Dorset Farm Labourer* (1883). A survey of these varied modes of reportage, accompanied by an excellent selection of local photographs, is in J.H. Bettey's *Man and the Land 1846-1996* (D.N.H. & A.S., Dorchester 1996). For labour organisation, see S. and B. Webb's *A History of Trade Unionism.*

FOR CHAPTER 13

For 'The Washington Connection' (see page 147), the following sources were used: *Congressional Directory* (1989-1990), Records of the Columbia History Society, *The City of Washington: Junior League of the City of Washington*, and Eustace R. Pearson's *The Notleys of Maryland.*

The 1956 clean-up. Top right is Dave Fox and Frank Cornick is second from the left.

Rebuilding the Giant's nose (or just speculating?), 1992.

Chapter 1
The Giant Himself

Cerne without the Giant is like *Hamlet* without the Prince of Denmark. The village is famous for him, and although there are Iron-Age, Romano-British relics and Celtic fields all around the area, the Giant is all. He was scheduled as an ancient monument in 1924 and is now in the care of the National Trust. But what is known of him? Study and speculation, words spoken and written are endless, but there are no certain answers to any of the questions asked. This comment is, therefore, also a mixture of speculation and fact.

The first known factual reference to the figure occurs, apparently, in the churchwardens' accounts for 1694, when 3 shillings was paid 'for repairing the Giant'. Well before this, however, there appears perhaps to have been another reference.

The Cerne Giant, over 182 feet in length and over 2000 years old.

Julius Caesar seems to have been the first to report giants in Britain - see *De Bello Gallico, Libra VI CXVI.* J.A.Thwaites, who lived in Cerne in the 1930s and carved little wooden giants as souvenirs, translates Caesar thus: 'They [the British] enclose their victims in wickers of osier and burn them at the tops of Giant men'. Could some ancient folk memory account for the fact that the Trendle was locally known as 'the Giant's frying pan'? This of course is speculation, but in the Museum of Arles in France there is a little collection of terracotta statues of our Giant. They were found when the Roman barracks there were excavated. Could there be a connection here?

Returning to the churchwardens' accounts of 1694, one sees a possible link with the death of the young Lord Holles in that year, he being the last of that title to hold the Abbey lands. In 1754 Bishop Pococke reported that the lines of the Giant were scoured every seven or eight years by order of the lord of the manor. After years of wrangling about the lordship the Giant was probably sufficiently neglected in 1694 to require urgent attention. Although this was not the responsibility of the churchwardens it would seem that when those who were responsible failed, the local population was prepared to step in. The Church did not reject the Giant. In 1800 and 1843 the churchwardens added stylised figures of the Giant *(see over)* to the lead panels marking roof repairs to the church beside their own initials.

Throughout the 19th century the hill figure survived various recorded cleanings, interested groups sometimes visiting him and reporting poor maintenance. In 1886 he was professionally cleaned and in 1889 was surrounded by iron railings which would have kept grazing cattle off. In 1905 the *Daily Mail* reported that the Giant was sorely neglected, and barely visible; the cost of cleaning was to be £12. In her diary a teacher newly appointed to the village school in 1908 made the observation that 'it was cleaned out last year by some ladies', but this perhaps insufficiently, as he received a professional clean-up in 1908.

Cerne people who were children during the 1930s remember running about in the Giant's trenches, but in 1977, the iron railings long gone, he was re-fenced. The years 1956 and 1983 saw more professional cleanings, and the National Trust has since packed his trenches with chalk from Shillingstone. And so it goes on. In March 1996 the Bournemouth University School of Conservation Sciences arranged a commission of enquiry (subsequently printed under the title 'The Cerne Giant, an Antiquity on Trial'), in the course of which the age and significance of the Giant was argued by

Above and inset: *The Giant, enclosed by a fence, from a postcard of the 1930s, and a 2-inch-wide figure of the Giant on the church roof.*
Left: *The Giant with his female friend, 1997.*

They gave her a cloak to carry, both to help balance the figure and because it is thought that the Giant himself may once have carried a cloak or animal skin over his left arm. Unlike the Giant, the temporary hillside figure was not given a club; instead her arm was extended in friendly greeting to her fellow. Now the Giant is alone once again.

specialists. It was an interesting day, but as with all previous studies there were no definite answers. Mr Roy Castleden in his book *The Cerne Giant* still cannot reach a definite conclusion.

In 1997, for a bit of fun and as an unusual field archaeology experience, a group of students from Bournemouth gave him a female companion for 24 hours. The group modified a scale drawing of the Giant to create their Giantess, which was laid out with yards of white plastic on innumerable skewers.

Perhaps until some in-depth scientific excavation takes place Harvey Darton (1935) should be allowed the last word. 'For his own folk he is something intimate and natural. His exact age does not concern them. He is just 'old' and was always there'. And who are his own folk? When we moved to Cerne 30 years ago a man living in Duck Street told us 'if the Giant don't like you, you'll be out in six months'. Perhaps he decides who his own folk are!

Chapter 2
The Abbey

If a village's history is in some sense its biography, then Cerne's birth might perhaps be said to have sprung from a sudden death. After the martyrdom of Edmund, King of East Anglia, at the hands of the insurgent Danes in AD870, his brother Edwold (it is later recorded), refusing the succession, retired from the world to a 'silver spring' on a hill about four miles west of Cerne, perhaps at Hermitage or Stockwood *(see over)*. For a professional assessment of the evidence see Laurence Keen in the 'Cerne Abbey Millennium Programme' (1987) pp.7-10.

In Cerne itself there must already in the previous century have existed some kind of religious house, since one of its monks, Ethelwold, was to become Bishop of Winchester and reputed author of the manuscript known as the *Book of Cerne* (c.760). This was a tripartite compilation comprising the prayerbook of a 9th-century bishop, a cartulary (register of charters, deeds, properties, etc.) of the Abbey, and a miscellany in 15th- or 16th-century handwriting including an inventory of relics.

The reign of King Edgar (959-975) was propitious for a revival of Christian learning and of Benedictine monasticism as reformed by Dunstan. Though he himself made only a single grant of land hereabouts (in the Piddle Valley to Abbot John and his successors), Edgar encouraged the establishment, or revival, of abbeys throughout his kingdom through ministers of his household willing to endow them from their own respective estates and those of their families. One such, Aethelmaer, Earl of the West Saxons, in 987 by letter to Archbishop Dunstan and the Bishop of Winchester, donated to God and certain saints the place called Cernel where he and his kin possessed inherited rights of tithe. To this he promised to add upon his death the reversion of the township of Cerne - thus distinguishing between the town itself and the Abbey it would outlast. A 12th-century copy of that letter constitutes the so-called 'Foundation Charter' of the Abbey *(see page 17)*. To this house, dedicated to the Blessed Virgin, St Peter and St Benedict, the bones of Edwold were later removed from their original burial place beside the silver spring, now credited with curative power. They were re-interred in the monastic

The frontispiece of the Gospel of St Luke from the Book of Cerne (c.760)

church at Cerne, the bones having (it was said) themselves frustrated an attempt to transfer them to Sherborne.

To Aethelmaer also belongs the credit for securing the transfer to Cerne of the monk Aelfric from Winchester, the place of his novitiate under Bishop Ethelwold (whose biographer, indeed hagiographer, he was later to become). For 18 years thereafter Aelfric had charge of teaching at the Abbey, and here he wrote, in Latin or in vernacular prose of high quality, most of his books - Bible translations and paraphrases, lives of the saints, Catholic homilies and colloquies *(see page 17)*. It is for his grammar that he remains most famous. But the purpose of his writings transcends pedagogy: and although Aelfric was transferred in 1005 to be Abbot of another of Aethelmaer's foundations, at Eynsham, they continued in use until well after the Norman Conquest.

The tiny church of Stockwood, dedicated to St Edwold.

St Augustine's Well.

CERNE ABBEY FOUNDATION CHARTER

AD987, AEthelmaer, one of the officers of the court of King Ethelred notifies Archbishop Dunstan of Canterbury, AElfaeg, Bishop of Winchester, and all the bishops and wise men of the English that he gave a place called Cerne to God in honour of the Virgin Mary, St Peter the Apostle and St Benedict, for the benefit of King Ethelred, for himself, and for the souls of his ancestors; that he has given the estates of Cerne and Esher after his death; that he has given to the monastery and the monks during his life and after his death for ever 6 cassates of land in the little estate which the people call Minterne, 10 holdings in Winterborne (Abbas), 6 in (Little) Bredy, 12 in Long Bredy, and 3 in Renscombe (in Worth Matravers); that Leofric, the clerk of Poxwell, has augmented these gifts by giving his estate at Poxwell to the monks, which King Ethelred afterwards confirmed before witnesses; that Aelfrith, his kinsman of Bincombe, has given 4 cassates of land at Affpuddle after the death of Leofwine, their kinsman; that Alfwold has given 5 holdings in Bloxworth after the death of his wife; and that he orders in the name of God that there be given to the monks a tenth of all his yearly rents in Cerne and Ceselbourne and tithes of honey, cheese and fat hogs out of his other lands; and that he wishes the monks to keep to the rule of St Benedict; and concludes with a prohibition of selling or dissipating these gifts and a prayer that some faithful person will increase the property of the monastery and that Christ will increase everlasting riches for it many times.

EXAMPLES OF AELFRIC'S TEACHING COLLOQUIES

THE FOWLER
- *How do you say Fowler?*
  How do you catch birds?
- *Give me a hawk... they feed themselves and me in the winter, and in the spring I let them fly away in the woods.*

THE SALTER ★
- *My craft is useful to you all.*
What man enjoys food to the full without the flavour of salt? Who fills his pantry or storeroom... you will lose all butter and cheese without me.

★ *Cerne most probably obtained its salt by panning at its coastal manors, Renscombe and later Kimmeridge and Symondsbury. Salt working at Radipole may be indicated by pig-rearing there recorded at Domesday – salt and pork production were very lucrative. Salt also had religious significance in the Angle-Saxon Church and was used in consecrations and blessings.*

or table. The pool is bounded to the east and north by medieval rubble walls which may have formed the angle between nave and south transept of the Abbey Church: repaired after recent collapse, they are now shored with a breeze-block buttress. Still visible in stone is a representation of St Catherine's wheel, also yet discernible on a much-weathered block behind the New Inn. Saint and wheel appear together on an abbot's oval seal of the 15th century *(see page 25)*.

That this early foundation chose to add St Edwold's name to that of its original dedicatee, St Mary, makes it appear all the more unjust that Cerne's truly patronal saint should have been neglected in favour of dubious ascriptions to St Augustine, who probably never visited so far west. Unfairly or not, it is the latter around whom popular but spurious local myth and anecdote have accreted, and to 'St Austin's Well' that pilgrimages have been made. Right up to the early-20th century it has been St Augustine whom we have celebrated, as witness a local newspaper's report of the proceedings of a May morning in 1918:

All went to St Augustine's well, the parish priest in cassock, surplice, stole and biretta. An improvised processional crucifix was used, and a hand-bell rung through the streets. A little company assembled at the well, including one churchwarden and some visitors to the town. One lady presided at the harmonium, kindly lent for the purpose... The parish priest read prayers, including the collect for St Augustine's Day. Then was sung the hymn beginning 'Apostle of our own dear home'. The Blessing brought to a close the happily revived commemoration at Cerne Abbas of its first Apostle and Evangelist.

From Aelfric's time the oldest physical feature surviving is the well just north of the Parish Church, a rectangular pool with a spring rising from the north west and flowing out to the south east, which may once have been surmounted by a small chantry. Only the bases of 17th- or 18th-century pillars now remain such as could have supported a stone bench

Surely it would be more appropriate instead for local Christians, on every 13 August, to remember St Edwold's birthday, formerly the occasion of an annual fair?

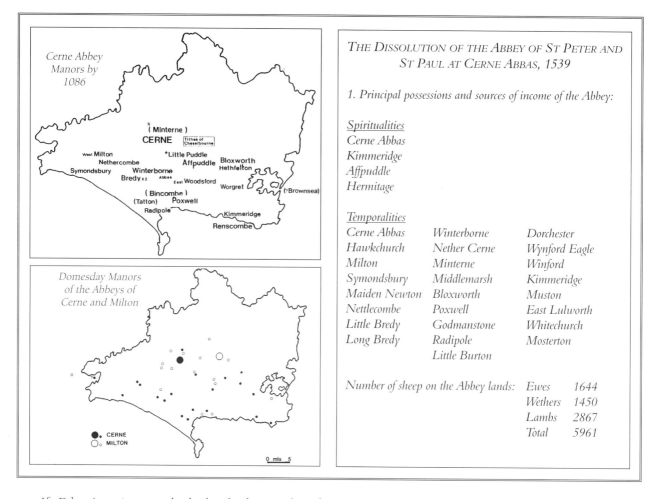

Cerne Abbey
Manors by
1086

Domesday Manors
of the Abbeys of
Cerne and Milton

● CERNE
○ MILTON

0 mls 5

*THE DISSOLUTION OF THE ABBEY OF ST PETER AND
ST PAUL AT CERNE ABBAS, 1539*

1. Principal possessions and sources of income of the Abbey:

<u>*Spiritualities*</u>
Cerne Abbas
Kimmeridge
Affpuddle
Hermitage

<u>*Temporalities*</u>

Cerne Abbas	*Winterborne*	*Dorchester*
Hawkchurch	*Nether Cerne*	*Wynford Eagle*
Milton	*Minterne*	*Winford*
Symondsbury	*Middlemarsh*	*Kimmeridge*
Maiden Newton	*Bloxworth*	*Muston*
Nettlecombe	*Poxwell*	*East Lulworth*
Little Bredy	*Godmanstone*	*Whitechurch*
Long Bredy	*Radipole*	*Mosterton*
	Little Burton	

Number of sheep on the Abbey lands:

Ewes	*1644*
Wethers	*1450*
Lambs	*2867*
Total	*5961*

If Edgar's reign marked the highest tide of monasticism since the golden days of Bede, that of Ethelred II (d.1016) saw an ebbing: first because of factional feuding during the King's minority; then with his coming of age and his capricious favouritism and attempts to reclaim former royal grants to religious foundations – all this in a period when Ethelred lacked any consistent policy of resistance to the Viking invaders. Fortunately, the willingness of their King Cnut (d.1035) to protect (though alien to its traditions) the English Church ensured the latter's continued influence at the seat of secular power. That its name was included in the obits of the Abbey – the monks' year-round commemorative roll of departed souls, principally benefactors or abbots – suggests that Cerne in particular recognised a debt despite the reputation for sacking and plundering during earlier pagan years.

Another benefactor was William the Conqueror. When the Domesday Book was completed in 1086 another nine estates had been added to those of Aethelmaer's Charter, of which two had been given by William, although there had been some losses too. William's practice was to classify ecclesiastical land-holders with his tenants-in-chief and to assess them for knight service. In Cerne's case this service lingered on for centuries in the function of watch and ward in Purbeck and at Corfe Castle for one month of

the year. This apart, the abbots were left alone to manage their estates as they deemed most profitable, supplemented from time to time by feudal dues such as wardship or escheat (in feudal law, the reversion of property to the lord on the owner's dying without legal heirs). Thus in succeeding centuries the Abbey waxed. In 1198 it held 13 estates (confirmed as 'de dono regnum Anglorum' (in the gift of the King of the English) at each king's succession; an assessment of 1291 for the purpose of papal taxation showed the acquisition of another half-dozen, including Brownsea Island, an income assessed at £177.8s., and a grange at Middlemarsh for the abbot's own use. We know that only a small part of these possessions would have been occupied and worked by the Cerne monks themselves: the rest would have been leased out, at fixed annual rates though upon a variety of terms.

Sadly, the records which would have shed most light upon the Abbey's growth and management in these earlier centuries were irrecoverably dispersed at its dissolution in 1539. Perhaps this hiatus justifies the *Victoria County History's* verdict (vol.ii, p.54) on Cerne Abbey's history as 'perhaps the least eventful of any of the Dorset houses' (with one minor exception of a sisterhood).

Nevertheless, surviving judgments of the appropriate courts, ecclesiastical or royal, reveal an ongoing busyness. Cutting into the monastic community's life in the 13th century we discover a variety of suits involving the abbot or his representative, on his behalf or that of his people. In some he confronts the king or his agent, some are against other land-owners, some against one or other of his numerous tenants. At this time, the Abbey routinely had to preserve its cattle and horses against theft, its pasture against overstocking with a tenant's beasts, its woodlands against excessive felling of timber. The deer park (a remnant of which exists today as Cerne Park, to the west of the village) had to be controlled and the abbot's right of droveway through his estates enforced. He had to defend his servants against violence offered by the servants of another abbot. Debts were reclaimed, dues from wardship and marriage exacted, and steps taken against would-be abductors of heirs. The Abbey's right to coastal wreckage granted by Henry II was reasserted upon occasion. Boundaries had to be held against encroachers, trespassers repelled, walls strengthened. There was a watermill and a deer park and rights to hold a fair and a market.

Not all demarcation of boundaries, one may observe, led to legal contention. Thus, in March 1227, the Abbot of Cerne peacefully perambulated with the Abbot of Milton the course of the boundary separating Cerne from Sydling (including the present demarcation with what looks like a boundary stone which may or may not be the 'Bellingstone' referred to by the contemporary scribe of this occasion). Sometimes, however, the litigants were at the opposite extreme of distance, as when in 1219 the Abbot of Cerne commenced proceedings against the Abbot of Croix St Leufroy in Normandy for recovery of a manor allegedly granted to the latter by William the Conqueror.

The new century opened promisingly in a blaze of celebrations; on 14 June 1311 the suffragan (bishop appointed to help a diocesan bishop in his administration) to the Bishop of Salisbury, the Lord Gilbert, visited from Ireland to dedicate an altar of the Abbey and another in its Infirmary Chapel; he may also then have climbed north-eastward to dedicate the site of the future St Catherine's Chapel. Seven years on, another Bishop of Salisbury, Roger de Monteval, dedicated the high altar of the convent. Altars of other, smaller, churches in the vicinity also received dedication. The erection of fine new Abbey buildings (including the Guest House and Tithe Barn) signalled a growing prosperity which the town must equally have enjoyed.

It proved a false dawn; neither civil strife nor natural pestilence spared the secular or the sacred. The Black Death of 1346 left the incumbency of St Mary's vacant. And the Wars of the Roses provoked at least one inglorious episode when in 1471 the doughty Margaret of Anjou (1430-82), Henry VI's queen, lodged at the Abbey en route from Weymouth (with her son Edward, Prince of Wales, and his wife) to the field of Tewkesbury. There on 4 May the last hopes of the Lancastrian cause were crushed and her son slain, her husband also being shortly after murdered. For part of that fatal journey Margaret's escort was a Dorset-born cleric destined to be one of the few great survivors of civil war. John Morton (1420-1500) rose under Henry VII to be honoured successively as Archbishop of Canterbury, Lord Chancellor of England and Cardinal; and to be commemorated in the splendid church roof of his native village, Bere Regis. The century closed sordidly with the tithing of Cerne Abbas fined £15 for its alleged part in the 1497 rebellion of Perkin Warbeck.

After an Act of 1534 had vested sole earthly supremacy over the Church of England in Henry VIII, his chief minister Thomas Cromwell dispatched throughout the land two bodies of commissioners. One was to compile a comprehensive account of the income of all monasteries, cathedrals and churches – the great *Valor Ecclesiasticus*. When all parishes and temporal possessions of Cerne Abbey were listed therein, down to the last sheep, it was seen to enjoy an annual income approaching, in today's equivalent money, half a million pounds. A second body of commissioners investigated the behaviour of monks and nuns. Clearly, the greater the wealth disclosed by the former commission, the greater the incentive for the second to find scandalous abuses.

In seizing monastic assets to the Crown, Cromwell in 1536 moved first against the softest target, those smaller religious houses with an annual income of less than £200. Since that of Cerne approached thrice that figure, its turn awaited the second wave of confiscations. And here Cromwell's path was eased by a direct delation from one Dan Will de Christchurch, formerly (by his own story) a monk of Cerne's Abbot Corton. The monk claimed that he had been several times imprisoned and finally expelled by Corton, and now seized the opportunity to accuse him and his establishment of

Above: *A weathered block of Abbey stone unceremoniously dumped behind the New Inn.*

Above left: *The church which grew from a small chancel to its present size with the Abbey's support.*
Above right: *St Augustine's Well.*

The Tithe Barn.

Above left: *The oriel window of the Guest House.*
Above right: *The Guest House itself.*

Abbey Farm House, Cerne Abbas.

The Abbey Farmhouse, 1904.

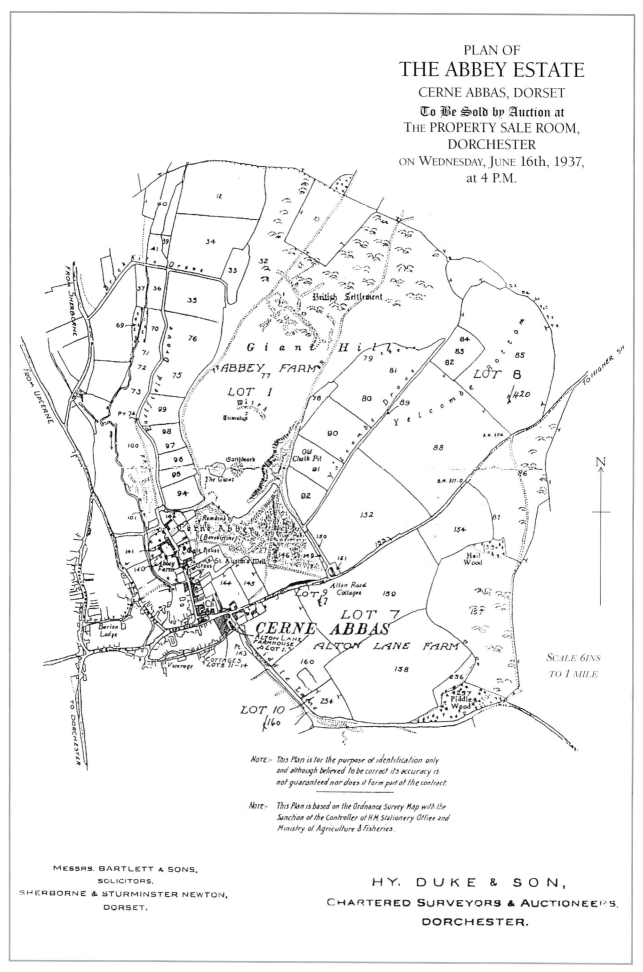

PLAN OF
THE ABBEY ESTATE
CERNE ABBAS, DORSET
To Be Sold by Auction at
THE PROPERTY SALE ROOM,
DORCHESTER
ON WEDNESDAY, JUNE 16th, 1937,
at 4 P.M.

SCALE 6INS
TO 1 MILE

NOTE:- This Plan is for the purpose of identification only
and although believed to be correct its accuracy is
not guaranteed nor does it form part of the contract.

NOTE:- This Plan is based on the Ordnance Survey Map with the
Sanction of the Controller of H.M. Stationery Office and
Ministry of Agriculture & Fisheries.

MESSRS. BARTLETT & SONS,
SOLICITORS,
SHERBORNE & STURMINSTER NEWTON,
DORSET.

HY. DUKE & SON,
CHARTERED SURVEYORS & AUCTIONEERS,
DORCHESTER.

iniquities both carnal and spiritual. The allegations were that in favouring his own family Corton had let church and lands go to ruin; that he was openly soliciting and housing (named) concubines who sat at table with him and on whom he had begotten natural children; that he had allowed such women to consort with the brethren, who played at dice and cards all night and then celebrated mass unconfessed in the morning; that he had abolished some masses, failed to maintain obits and doles (charitable contributions) and permitted some monks to become proprietors in their own right.

What kernel of truth may have lain within all this cannot now be reassessed, but that the whole-hogging nature of the indictment must raise some doubt and reveal an element of personal vindictiveness cannot be ruled out. Suffice to say that to Tregonwell and his colleagues it must have been very welcome. We can say, however, that where documentary evidence survives (e.g. in the observance of obits) it is clear that such routines were, in the 1530s, still being scrupulously performed. But Corton's most favorable witness must be the architectural historian. The Abbey and its artisans had built St Mary's Parish Church. The very large enterprise of adding the clerestory (an upper row of windows above the aisle roofs) is dated to the early decades of the 16th century – in which case building operations must have continued until almost the eve of the Dissolution. The assembling and 'hands-on' supervision of a necessarily considerable and highly skilled workforce, still warm, as it were, from completing the great west gateway and lodging, does not suggest a laxity of dedicated purpose and can have left little time for fleshly preoccupations!

In December 1538 Sir Thos Arundel reported to Cromwell that the Abbot of Cerne was making drastic efforts to obtain the continuance of the house and was prepared to offer to the Crown 50 marks and to Cromwell himself £100. It was not enough and, on 15 March following, Thomas Corton and his 15 monks surrendered their Abbey and all its properties to the Crown in return for pensions ranging from £100 p.a. for its late head down to £2 p.a. for its most junior monk. By a letter of the following September to Cromwell from the Receiver-General, Richard Phelyps, it would seem that the situation at the Abbey was temporarily frozen – its stock to be supervised and the Abbot himself to be allowed 'to ride abroad about the affairs of the monastery' only after payment of a fee of five marks sterling – until the new purchasers or lessees moved in.

By then Cerne's fate was paralleled in a score of other West Country monastic sites; rapid demolition, partly to realise the material value of a fabric of such high quality, partly so as to render physically impossible any future reversal of royal policy. From local

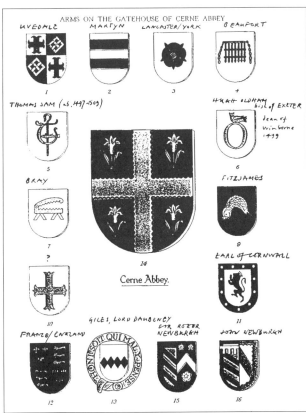

Top and above: *The Abbot's Porch and the arms of benefactors carved beneath the oriel window.*

witnesses in a legal dispute of the 1570s over parishioners' right of access to the former monks' burial ground we learn of the speed and completeness with which almost everything above ground was razed. The Abbey Church was down by 1585, lead was stripped, stone quarried and sold (some of the latter being incorporated in the manor house at UpCerne, built in 1601 on land owned by Sir Walter Raleigh). Of what remained much is today

The Tithe Barn from the air, 1987.

incorporated in village houses; for example, in the first floor at the rear of the Post Office.

One 13th-century Purbeck monument at least is believed to have been transferred via Farnham to the Pitt-Rivers Museum in Oxford. Many other treasures were widely dispersed, including documentation for which historians must now seek among record offices and private collections. Very little was sent where it should have been, to the Court of Augmentations in London: the commissioners were strictly instructed 'incontinently to call for the convent seal, with all writings, charters, evidence and muniments concerning any of the possessions to be delivered to them, and to put the same in safe keeping.'

What remains of the Abbey today? On the south west of the site, surviving probably by its usefulness as a private dwelling, stands the three-storey porch to the Abbot's Hall, built by Abbot Thomas Sam (1497–1509) with its magnificent two-storey oriel window, below which are panels enclosing shields of arms and the rebuses of Abbot Sam and Bishop Hugh Oldham of Exeter. The abbot would drive in through the adjacent north gate, the main entrance from which all 'convenyent high waies' radiated. The south gate, destroyed in the 1550s by rioters, was normally kept locked and portered.

To the south of the Abbot's Porch stands, much altered, a two-storey building with first-floor oriel window, which was probably the Abbey Guest House: but since the initials of Abbot John Vanne (1458–70) appear on a fireplace later removed to the Abbey Farmhouse nearby, it has been suggested that it may have been an earlier abbot's lodging. About 100 metres north-north west of this building stands a barn of seven bays and collar-beam roof, probably 15th century but with modern porches and sympathetically converted to serve as the veterinary clinic.

Part of the Abbey buildings, including a Saxon doorway and what may have been the pintles of the south gate, is still visible where it is incorporated in what served as the Abbey Farmhouse at the top of Abbey Street. This was largely reconstructed after a fire in the mid-18th century and underwent further restoration by the Digby family in the 1950s. About half a mile to the south west of the main site is the Abbey's 14th-century Tithe Barn of knapped flint with great ashlar buttresses and two wagon porches. Originally a single-storey building, it has been considerably truncated at its north end: its south end was converted in the 18th century to a dwelling house and further restored in the century following.

In its effects the magnitude of the 1539 catastrophe can hardly be exaggerated. All of Cerne's subsequent history is in a sense an account of attempts to compensate for loss; in education for loss of the chantries, in poor relief for the demise of the Abbey itself. Moreover, that institution having been for half a millennium Cerne's raison d'être, its closure removed the heart from the village or township, requiring the search ever since for another social purpose, a search conducted for much of that time within a structure of economic insecurity and hence exposure to depression. In a sense, like other victims of the 'Age of Plunder' (as one historian has aptly denominated Henry VIII's reign), Cerne's disaster of 1539 illustrates in miniature the cataclysmic transition, with unnecessary brutality, from medieval to modern England itself.

ABBOTS OF CERNE
(From Mr G.D. Squibb)

Aelfric, appointed AD987, on the re-founding
as a Benedictine monastery.
Alfric Puttoc, occurs 1023
Aithelmus, occurs 1085
Haimo, deposed 1102 for simony (buying or
selling of ecclesiastical privileges, e.g. pardons)
William, occurs 1121
Bernard, became Abbot of Burton 1160
Robert, occurs 1166
Denis (Dionysius), resigned 1220
re-elected 1220
William de Hungerford, el.1232
Richard de Suwell, el.1244, d.1260
Philip de Blokesworth, el.1260
Thomas de Eddlesbury, el.1274
Gilbert de Minterne, el.1296, d.1312
Ralph de Cerne, el.1312, d.1324
Richard de Osmington, el.1324
Stephen Sherrard, el.1356
Thomas Sewale, el.1361, d.1382
Robert Symondsbury, el.1382
John Wede, el.1421, d.1427
John Winteborne, el.1427, d.1436
John Godmanston, el.1436, d.1451
William Cattistoke, el.1451, d.1454
John Helyer, el.1454, resigned 1458
John Vanne, el.1458, d.1471
Roger Bemyster, el.1471, d.1497
Thomas Sam, el.1497, d.1509
Robert Westbury, el.1510, d.1524
Thomas Corton, el.1524,
surrendered his Abbey 1539

The 1640 pulpit and canopy, photo 1960s.

Much-pewed church. The photograph is dated 1930s or earlier showing the stone screen - the image comes from a postcard.

Chapter 3
The Care of a Church

The countrey parson hath a special care of his church that all things there be decent, and befitting His name by which it is called... and all this he doth not as out of necessity, or as putting holiness in the things, but as desiring to keep the middle way between superstition and slovenlinesse.

(George Herbert: A Priest to the Temple, *Ch. XIII*)

It was probably the natural and mutual desire for a parochial, rather than a conventual, place of worship – that is, for one where the ordinary worshippers would no longer be confined to the Abbey nave – which led to the erection of the Church of St Mary the Virgin. The enterprise seems to have been free of the strife which marred some similar undertakings in Dorset, and perhaps to have been facilitated by the benefaction of a nobleman of the preceding generation, Richard Earl of Cornwall (1209-72), second son of King John. Be that as it may, the first vicar, Robert de Muleborn (Milborne) was inducted, albeit conditionally and for a few months only, on 15 April 1317.

His church, of random cracked flints and probably a thatched roof, would have embodied much of the present chancel. On its north wall can now be seen one of his bishop's consecration crosses, a six-pointed black star inside a red circle. When, in the 1920s, the lancet window nearby was reopened, the adjacent work exposed four mural depictions of the life and death of St John Baptist. Four decades later, in the 1960s, the corresponding south window was reopened above the 14th-century piscina, to reveal a depiction of the Annunciation dated by Professor Tristram to AD1350-80 (*see page 144*).

Doubtless the medieval church carried these glorious colours all around its walls. An early dedication of the church to St John, to whom was also devoted a chantry in the Abbey, is suggested by the will, dated 1431, of one Thomas Tanner (a Dorchester merchant?), bequeathing 'to the parish church of St John Baptist 6d.', and 12d. to its priest: the same saint is likewise referred to by one Fowke, whose will of 1502 desires burial in the Abbey of St Peter.

The course of later enlargements is readily traced. In the mid-15th century the greater part of the present nave and aisles was added, intruding so boldly into the old chancel as to break an arch on its south side. Later in the same century the west end was rebuilt in neat and regular alternate courses of Ham Hill stone and chipped flints. At the same time, the tower was also raised, in three stages, its double-panelled arches and quatrefoil friezes resembling, and contemporary with, those at Sherborne Abbey. On either side of the west window are shields, the northern bearing the monogram 'XVAX' of John Vann, Abbot 1458-71. Late-medieval doorways to the north and south probably gave passage to formerly adjoining houses in Abbey Street. Fragments of the fractured holy water stoup at the west entrance were discovered recently in the east wall of the tower. Of the same period as the tower (1450-1500) is the splendid stone screen whose mullions and open tracery separate choir and nave.

The clerestory was raised in the 1530s, probably by Thomas Corton, 34th and last abbot, assuming that they are his initials which appear on the soffit of the two western windows on its south side. The south porch was rebuilt in 1696 and bears the names of the churchwardens at that juncture - Willi. Tulledge and Tho. Dussell. Adjoining it is a grotesque face with a smoke-blackened mouth, an outlet for the fire either of a priest's chamber or of an oven with 'girdle plate' to bake the communion bread or 'wastel loaves'. Contemporary churchwardens have also memorialised themselves with their twinned names, J. Bunter and W. Jacob, on the country-styled screen and doors (1749) separating tower from nave, others in the leads of the north and south aisles where these were re-roofed in 1682, 1793/4, 1843 and 1963/4. Their initials they have cut into the rafters below: yet others are engraved on the 'iron chest' made in 1817 by Josh. Bennets for £4.3s.0d., used to house the parish registers of baptisms and weddings from 1653 to 1843 and which can still be seen in the vestry today. But who made the screen? The carpenter most favoured by the wardens at the time was John Vincent. Among the bills he presented that year was one for the sum of £12.12s. for an unspecified item. Could this have been the screen? Through the pages of their accounts, surviving for St Mary's since 1628, we may watch, sometimes almost overhear, these doorkeepers in the house of their God discharge, with cautious arithmetic but venturesome spelling, their 'dutyes' across three centuries. To the nature of those historic duties we must now turn.

THE CHURCHWARDENS

Until the Reformation the office of churchwarden, known under that title or some other since the 12th century, was essentially and solely ecclesiastical. As the 'proper guardians or helpers of the parish church' those who held it were first and foremost to be regarded as 'wardens of the goods of the church', administering its multiform resources as the support and good order of public worship required.

By the end of the 16th century, Tudor sovereigns had overlaid these purely ecclesiastical functions with a hotch-potch of miscellaneous new duties which bore no direct relationship to the sacred, and indeed sometimes threatened to eclipse the latter in their demands on the parish's time, money and business capacity. From then until parish administration was largely secularised by the Local Government Act of 1894, wardens could not hope to escape some measure of responsibility, in practice if not in form, for almost every aspect of local government as the secular role vied with the sacred. The former of these twin roles we shall consider in a later chapter. For the moment we may extract only the ecclesiastical items from their account as it typically appears in a year of James II's reign:

THE ACCOMPT OF
ROBERT SHEPHARD & THOMAS DUSSELL *
CHURCHWARDENS FOR YE TOWN OF CEARNE ABBAS
AD 1686

*Imprimis Paid Thomas Thorne and
Robert Ford for makeing ye rails and
Ballesters round ye Communion table £6.5s.0d.
It. payd for paviers for ye Chancell 3s.6d.
It. spent at ye Lord Bishop's visitation 7s.10d.
It. Gave for Ringing ye Lord Bishop into
towne 5s.0d.
It. Paid for ye Booke of Articles & entring
ye Register 4s.0d.
It. for Wine & Bread at ye Sacrament at
Whits. 6s.4d.
Pd. for a new Common prayer Booke 12s.0d.
Pd. the penticost mony 3s.0d.
Pd. Benjamin Summers & John Hodges
for mending ye church windows £3.14s.0d.
Gave to ye Ringers on ye 5th November 5s.6d.*

We doe make choice of Stephen Farr & Thomas Hodges Jun: to be Churchwardens for ye next year. We doe nominate John Thorne Cardmaker and John Hodges ye shomaker Waywardens for ye year ensuing.

* Dussell was to serve a second term as warden ten years later. The persistence of the Dussell family in Cerne may be judged by the name – Dussell's Lane – given by the 18th-century mapmakers to the thoroughfare linking the north end of Duck Street to Baker's Cross (the site of the present National Trust look-out).

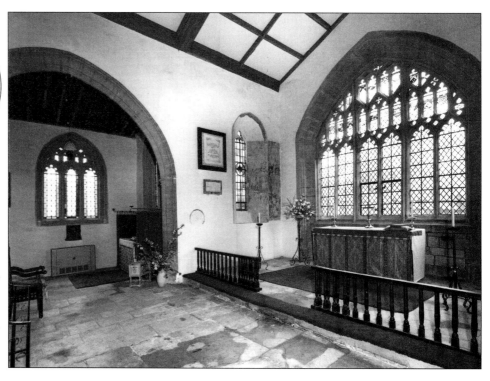

Right: *The east window, the wall painting in the north window embrasure, the bishop's consecration cross (circle) and the altar rail. This photograph was taken after church restoration in the 1960s.* Above: *Detail of the consecration circle.*

The 1638 communion table, now in the south aisle.

These functions the wardens exercised as chief officers of the Vestry. To this body the wardens, acting in pairs, submitted their accounts at the end of their annual term of office during which they had had custody of the greater part of the parish's financial assets. Unsalaried, the warden's lot was sweetened only by the audit or visitation feast 'on the parish', and even that, in Cerne's case, was not lavish:

> *1727 spent with some neighbours when the*
> *old Church warden gave in his Acct. 15s.4½d.*
> *1763 Expences at the Grayhound & oyling*
> *ye [fire] Engon 2s.0d.*
> *1765 May 27 when Oyled the Engin in*
> *Beer 6d.*

We must not cynically regard the latter as a euphemism for oiling the wardenal neck. (For most of our period only a minority of wardens served for more than a second term. The modern long-stay officer is not seen before Frank Clark, who remained at his post for the seven years of the period 1911–18.).

In certain of their ecclesiastical duties the wardens had the help of a few sidesmen - originally 'synodsmen' - being selected to attend synods or visitation courts as witnesses when the wardens made their presentments. Their evolving usefulness as general assistants to the latter was reflected in the canons of 1603 which enjoined on every parish the duty of appointing two or three discreet persons to this office. A more cynical appraisal of both their usefulness and their discretion was offered by an anonymous Lancastrian of the 19th century:

> *To hear and see and say nowt,*
> *To eat and drink and pay nowt,*
> *And when the Wardens drunken roam*
> *Your duty is to see them home.*

By 1880 the recognised practice in Cerne was for the two newly-elected wardens to nominate their respective sidesmen for the year ahead. But in 1914 they numbered five and by 1919 had reached eleven.

INSIDE THE CHURCH

Wardens' obligations here may be briefly listed and then more copiously illustrated. They covered the maintenance (including structural alteration) and cleaning of the fabric of the church, its equipment, utensils, ornaments, service books, fuel and light, and the administration of certain other resources. Financial resources are discussed separately below. In Cerne's case 'equipment' included the parish fire engine, bucket and poles (although not, it seems, the parish armoury or the potentially disastrous powder chest). Innovations or removals of furniture, etc., might require the wardens to petition the bishop for a faculty. Service books and vestments were diversified in accordance with mutable religious dispensations. Special forms of victory prayer, for instance, were observed indifferently for the frustration of Monmouth's rising in 1685 and James II's expulsion three years later:

> *1685 June 3 It. Booke for giving thanks for*
> *ye obtaining a victory against Monmouth's*
> *forces 1s.6d.*
> *1688 Pd. for a boke of Thanksgiving being pre-*
> *served from Popery and arbitrary power 1s.0d.*

Their chief concerns we may follow down the years, interleaving a commentary where explanation seems due:

> *1639 March 16 Paid for a new Communion*
> *table 12s.0d.*
> *1640 It. paid for a new pulpit & canopy &*
> *covering for the font & a little chest with 3*
> *lockes £9.3s.0d.*

Taken together with the installation at the same juncture of the great east window, perhaps from the Abbey, these items suggest that some ripples of Archbishop Laud's beautification of the Anglican Church may have reached Dorset.

> *1650 November 28. Paid William Powell Esq.*
> *elder for pointing the church windows and*
> *for deforming the Kings Armes in ye*
> *church being commanded to do so 18s.0d.*
> *1660 Pd. Mr.Cockeram for florishing the*
> *King's Armes £2.10s.0d.*
> *Latice Sheapeard for beare for the*
> *mean that made the scafold in Church 2s.6d.*
> *1679 Pd. Robert Ford for new drawing the*
> *Kinges Armes and new writing the Lords*
> *Prayer and the Creed & 3 more sentences*
> *& for new making nine the sum of £2.5s.0d.*
> *1682 pd. for a balsam to sweeten the church 2d.*
> *1701 Item paid Robert Fords bill for ye diall*

and drawing ye sentences & ye vaunt £4.15s.0d.
   Item for washing ye surplush two
times and skowring ye plate and flagon   *5s.6d.*
 1706 *paid for binding of ye Church bible*
  & bishop Jewell   *17s.0d.*

The royal arms and ten commandments would have adorned the chancel arch until the Revd Bull's alterations of 1870 (q.v.). The 'sentences' doubtless refers to the black-letter cartouches, their texts from the Geneva (or 'Breeches') Bible of 1560, mostly in the spandrels of the nave arches. Bishop John Jewel's *Defence of the Apology* (1570), i.e., of his latin *Apologia pro Ecclesia Anglicana* (1562), long remained a staple deposit in Anglican churches.

 1714 *Pd. for 4 Matts & Matten about ye*
  Chancell   *5s.6d.*
 1723 *Pd. for 12 butts for people to kneel*
  upon   *4s.0d.*
 1730 *Bread & wine for ye whole year*
  Whitsuntide, Micklmas, Crismas and
  Easter   *£1.11s.4d.*
 1736 *May 8. Pd. for 3 yds broad Cloath*
  for ye Communion Table & Desk with silk
  for ye fringes and Making   *£2.5s.0d.*
 1755 *Paid Mr Cockeram for beasoms for*
  2 years   *1s.0d.*
   for a burchen broom for ye Clark   *4d.*
 1776 *Pd. Jno Roberts for white washing*
  the Church   *£2.11s.6d.*
   for the use of a Tub when ye church
  was white washt   *1s.0d.*
 1783 *for playing the Engine three times*   *7s.6d.*
 1789 *making of Desk & Pulpit Cloths*
  & Cushion   *10s.6d.*
   [plus a total outlay of £16.9s.11d. on Genoa
 velvet, fringe, tassels, ribbon, silk and dowlas]
 1801 *April. Repairing the Oak Doors to the*
  enterance of the Church, and for two New
  Gates &c in the Church yard   *£5.14s.11d.*
 1805 *Two candlesticks for the Pulpit*   *£5.9s.0d.*
 1813 *John Barnwell's Bill repairing*
  Chancel Window broken by the Bishop at
  the Confirmation   *10s.6d.*
 1862 *12 December Mr. Biles undertook*
  to repair the Fire Engine and to trust to the
  next annual Vestry consenting to pay the
  cost thereof
 1893 *East window much out of repair*

Parish fire engines were frequently lodged in churches. The chancel window referred to in the incident of 1813 can only have been the east window. If for 'by the bishop' we read 'nearby the bishop' we are free to draw the more plausible inference that the damage came from some miscreant outside the building.

THE SITTINGS

At least a dozen transactions for sittings (in north, south or middle 'alley') are recorded every year throughout the 17th and 18th centuries, the rental rising steeply from 6d. to 2s.6d. over the turn into the 19th. Interspersed with graveyard receipts, they reflect in the simplest fashion the passing generations:

 1628 *Sold to John Skillen the seat wch. was*
  Robt. Randalls   *4d.*
 1630 *Recd... of John Randall for that seat*
  wch. was Elinor Carews for his Wife   *4d.*
 1677 *Recd. of Geo. Randall for 2 childrens*
  Graves   *13s.4d.*
 1682 *Sold Tho. Randall his Fathers seate*   *4d.*
 1690 *Received for Wm.Tulledge & Miss*
  Randoll's Graves   *13s.4d.*
   Rec. of Tho. Hodges & ye Wid.
  Randell's Graves   *13s.4d.*
   Rec.of Hannah Randoll for her
  mother seat   *4d.*

On 12 April 1819 a meeting was held of 'the Proprietors and Claimants of Pews and Sittings' to debate 'the best method of improving and increasing the sittings for the greater comfort and more general accommodation of the inhabitants'. The particular objectives, expressed in ten resolutions, were to provide the poor of the town with 'free and unappropriated sittings and at the same time reduce the Pews into more regular and convenient forms'. But present proprietors were to be shifted as little as possible and life tenure continued 'according to... custom' with priority for those with families. Every extra pew yielded by the change was to be sold 'to the best advantage, in private or public, preference being given to those who contribute most liberally' towards the cost of the scheme. Any deficit on the whole operation was to be met by a levy on each appropriated sitting.

 The body of the church was to be enclosed from the belfry and two wings added to the existing central gallery, so as to provide free places for which the Sunday School was to have priority. The railed area around the communion table was to be reduced to leave more room for free sittings there 'and also at the corner where the vestry chest now stands'.

 Altogether at least 300 free places would be made for the poor. It is not certain that this target had been reached by 15 March of the following year when a public meeting was held to determine the rights of existing pew-holders, their widows and descendants (matters about which it is clear the wardens would have to be umpires). However, the cost of the operation – £373.1s.8d. 'to Messrs. Northover and Biles' for nothing less than a complete re-pewing of the church had been met.

THE CARE OF A CHURCH

Finance

Pew rents and interments, though far from negligible, constituted of course only part of the church's regular receipts, properly to be considered in the wider financial context. From the point in time from which the Cerne churchwardens' accounts survive, the Elizabethan Church Rate, enforced (with or without adequate statutory basis) by the secular arm, continued to be levied on some 100 parishioners - at a charge of between 2d. and 5d. in the £, realising sums varying between £25 and £65 per levy. This income was regularly supplemented by the pew rents, burial fees and certain other fees ad. hoc. Out of these aggregate proceeds - leaving aside almsgiving and relief - church and parish had to be maintained. Salaries had to be paid to clerk, sexton and so on, and certain other standard disbursements, whether regular or occasional, be provided for.

The compulsory Church Rate having been abolished in 1868, the Cerne Vestry in 1870 resolved that 'an offertory collection be made after every service'. For the year immediately following (1871–72), this reliance on in-church collecting sufficed to yield not only the £45 then minimally necessary to meet church expenses for a twelvemonth, but a further £24 and more for dispensing to charities, broken down as follows:

To parish school	£3.8s.10d.
To Church Missionary Society	£3.10s.0d.
To Church Pastoral Aid Society	£2.0s.5d.
To hospital (harvest thanksgiving)	£3.16s.0d.
Alms for poor	£11.15s.6d.

Over the next decade, however, a shrinking populace began to make some supplementation necessary. At the 1880 Vestry Mr Clark reported the fact that many of the parishioners objected to the present mode of collecting the money for the church expenses (by boxes carried around after each service), and he proposed that as an alternative an attempt be made to raise the necessary amount by voluntary subscription. Though carried unanimously this measure did

The west window and church pews, 1930s.

not avail and the voluntary subscription failed: by 1885 its aggregate yield plus concert-giving left a deficit bridgeable only by resuming the unpopular church collections. On 15 December 1905 was to appear 'the cloud no bigger than a man's hand' - the first recorded jumble sale in the parish.

So uncertainly financed, and facing a decline of population so steep that it would halve itself over 50 years, St Mary's in the second half of the 19th century may be seen to present a marked contrast between private generosity and official parsimony.

On the one hand, for instance, restoration and redecoration in 1860 was the occasion for the Hellyer family, including its branches at Castle Cary and Rochester, to present a pair of stained-glass windows to head the two aisles, at a cost of £25 apiece - which price, as noted in a local report, might have been double that figure had not the windows been designed and constructed by Mr Ford. Yet, on the other hand, at the following Vestry a deficit of up to £40 had to be met by voluntary subscription to supplement the Church Rate. And still by December 1862 the churchwardens' call for a rate of one penny in the pound for coals, re-glazing and a new surplice for the incumbent was opposed by:

... several persons present who thought the parson could wear his surplice for some time longer and that other things might be done without.

So only one half-penny in the pound was voted. Again, as to valuables, an inventory taken by the churchwardens in 1879 lists the following items as being in their care at that time:

*One silver Chalice ***
One flagon (silver) & two Pattens (silver) in
  Oak Chest
*One Pewter Flagon ****
One Pewter Patten
Velvet cloth for Table
One linen cloth
One linen napkin
Two surplices

Table cloth in vestry
Large map of the Parish in box

Note:
* **1767** *August Pd for the chalice* £4.14s.0d.
** **1630** *Itm. pd for a new pewter pott for*
Wine for the Com 10s.0d.

Yet of these the only truly precious items – the silver flagon and paten in their chest – would have been the personal benefaction of the Revd James Hay Waugh and his wife in 1843 (Waugh being the incumbent from 1842-45 and the great-grandfather of the novelist). The couple had already in the previous

Above: *Photograph taken in 1959 by Harold Ruston of the west face of the tower.*
Left: *The tower enjoys a cleaning, 1980s, by the vicar's son.*

year presented 'the Inhabitants of Cerne Abbas' with the following for the chancel:

A pair of Carved Oak chairs, two Altar services, morocco bound. A Crimson Velvet Altar Cloth a pair of Crimson Velvet Cushions. A pair of Crimson Velvet Stools, a Brussels Carpet, Four Circular Kneeling forms.

as well as:

For the Reading Desk by Mr Waugh A Large Bible, morocco bound and gilt a large Common Prayer Book ditto, Two versions of Psalms ditto, a painted box for these books, with partitions, lined with green baize – One damask linen Communion cloth. Two Corporals.

Of these, only the high-backed chairs are likely to meet the visitor's eye today, one or other being brought out from the chancel to seat the visiting bishop.

THE MUSIC

The same antithesis – private generosity as opposed to official parsimony – appears when in 1863 the church's music comes into reconsideration. Hitherto the churchwardens' accounts had merely noted such occasional items as, in 1792, 'Pd. for a book for the Quire singers, 4s.0d.' and, in 1847, 'Mr Woodford's Bill repairing organ, £1.10s.0d.' But the latter instrument was a barrel organ which, in the opinion of those who should know:

... retards rather than aids the musical portion of public worship, for it is well known that it possesses eccentric notions of music and will not be guided by the laws of harmony and concord.

Hence, 'a general desire to get rid of it'. So, after a well-attended public meeting at the New Inn, private subscriptions were readily forthcoming. On 20 October 1864 the new 'finger organ', installed by Messrs J.W. Walker at a cost of £180, was opened with two special services, 'the musical part of which', wrote the local newspaper reporter with two-edged praise, went off:

... very much better than could have been expected from the short period the choir have had for training, and considering that the organ was only completed the evening before.

Yet almost immediately the concomitant question of salaries – £10 p.a. for the organist, Mrs James, plus £2 for her blower – precipitated something of a constitutional crisis when the Vestry found itself divided evenly over the proposal that these be paid 'from the Church Rate next to be collected'. Resort was had to a poll of all ratepayers, taken at the church door between 10a.m. and noon on 20 April 1865. Balloting was 32 for, 30 against. Mrs James had scraped home by two votes. This seems a little hard on one who, with her husband the schoolmaster, regularly raised the wind for village funds with concerts in the schoolroom.

One particular Vestry resolution dated 29 June 1865 remains inexplicable:

> ... that the Churchwardens and the Committee of Management of the Church Choir be earnestly requested to enquire into the causes of the resigning of the choir of singers and to take such steps as may be deemed appropriate.

Several payments to 'singing boys' continue to be noted in the 1870s. Durable successors to Mrs James, however, proved hard to find: rather illogically their salary was reduced in 1888 to £8 p.a., not to climb back to £10 for another 20 years. Nevertheless, the choir steadily sang its way through Caleb Simper's book of *Short Anthems For All Occasions*, and when, in March 1910, Mrs Parry resigned as organist, with a presentation, it was after 25 years in the post.

In 1876, heartened perhaps by the new instrument, St Mary's embarked on its first Harvest Festival, 'not known before' and so 'exciting a lively interest', said the local newspaper, which for years thereafter carried a detailed description of a building lavishly decorated for the annual event. This 1867 venture also inspired Mr Fooks at the Tithe Barn to revive, with the Cerne Band ('which, by the way, we had thought almost defunct') the custom of harvest home. But the greatest single act of private generosity was to come from the next incumbent himself. Early in his ministry (1869) the Revd Augustus Howie Bull projected some radical alterations to the interior of the church. The space above the rood screen, hitherto walled up and bearing the royal arms and the ten commandments was to be opened up and a new chancel arch constructed. The west gallery and its wings on either side would be removed, reducing the total seating from 630 to about 550, but not less than 200 of which would continue to be free. The organ would descend from the gallery to the north-west corner of the ground floor and a vestry be made behind it. The chancel would be re-seated and the nave pews and their doors reduced in height.

To a Vestry already facing the expense of replacing the north-west pinnacle and tower weather vane (felled by a bolt of lightning), this offer must have been very welcome indeed. The architect appointed was the versatile Thomas Henry Wyatt (1807–80), president of the RIBA, already credited with the Liverpool Exchange, the Lombardic Wilton Church, Knightsbridge Barracks, the Guards Chapel at Woolwich, the Adelphi Theatre and various hospitals. In due course, he was also to be held responsible, with Crickmay and Hicks, for the majority of 'Victorianising' enterprises in Dorset churches. The cost to the Revd Bull of his 'very kind and liberal offer', unanimously accepted 'with cordial thanks' by his Vestry, was about £200 — nearly double one year's stipend.

The closing decade of Queen Victoria's reign saw relatively minor embellishments and improvements. In 1890 came improved gas lighting – brass lamps of the new patent 'Rochester central draught' model with ornamental suspenders, each burner nominally of 75 candlepower – the gift of Mrs Derriman of Providence Villa. Three years later, at the expense of her husband (himself an organist), the Walker instrument was cleaned, repaired and moved diagonally from the west end of the north aisle to the east end of the south. In the same year the big east window was repaired. When, in March 1901, the churchwardens entered in their accounts the sum of 19s.3d. to 'Miss Clark for black serge for draping the church on the death of the Queen' we may feel that a historic page is being turned.

Doors separating tower from nave. William Jacob, one of many innholders who became churchwardens, was landlord of the New Inn.

The Congregational Chapel Anniversary, 1911. The elderly gentleman on the right is Mr Whittle, Cerne's last shoemaker.

A production of A Midsummer Night's Dream *at the Tithe Barn, c.1925.
Left to right, back: Betty Mabb, Cecil Fox, Dolly Philpott, Revd Durose (Bottom the donkey),
Ginny Harvey, Elizabeth Hall, Win Warren, Dun Everitt, ? King, Joan Philpott;
front: Betty Birge, Margaret Gibson, Eric Fox, Wilf Gibson.*

Chapter 4
Dissent

The earliest surviving record of dissenters in Cerne has been left by the Society of Friends and is not without drama. It arose out of a general meeting of Dorset Quakers in the village (called by them Broad Cerne, presumably because of their detestation of the word Abbas) in 1659. As it is the sole such incident recorded, we may justifiably quote their own breathless story in full:

A True & Faithfull Record of ye Sufferings of ye Lord's people Belonging to severall meeting in ye County of Dorset... Being written & recorded by ye order & advice of the Lord's people at their General Meeting at Broad Cerne ye 18 day of March 1659.

Upon ye 17 day of ye 3 month 1660 the servants of the Lord being mett together to wait upon him & to worship him in spirit & truth in a town called Broad Cerne in ye county of Dorsett, after a little tyme many rude people of ye baser sort (in ye sayd town) gathered themselves together, ye Cheiffe being Leaders of whom were Goerge Fox alias Roman, William Carydew alias Creade, Edward Fox alias Roman, Phillipp Channell, George White, John Piden, John Durden, George Hodges, Phillipp White & Peter Vowell, wicked men, who with a multitude of their Rude Persons began to rage like ye troubled sea, and beat a drum about ye town to gather more (like themselves) together, who (unanimously) came about ye house, wherein ye Innocent were mett, in prayer to wait upon ye Lord as aforsed with several sorts of weapons (vizdlt) Gunns, Clubbs & Shards, with Stones, Dirt, Dung & other filth of ye streets, shouting of many Gunns under ye window of ye house, whereat ye meeting was; beating a drum greater part of ye Time of their sayd meeting. The meeting being ended & they comeing forth of ye house, to pass away quietly to their severall habitations the ye said rude people being gathered into a Considerable Body, layd in wait in severall parts of the Towne, to sett upon & otherwise abuse ye Innocent (who offered vyolence to none) with their sayd weapons, beating ye Drum near their horses heades, stopping them in the streetes, that there was hardly any passage, beating Divers with great poles, & some with their Guns. One wicked man strook one of them vyolently upon ye Arme, so that with ye
stroak hee break the stock of his Gunn, another received a dangerous blow with a great stone on his Ribbs, whereby he was in great payne many days after, others of them sayde waite, at a great water, where there was a narrow passage, through wch those Innocent people assaying to pass, one wicked Belialist went into ye river, with a flint stone of great bigness in his hand threatning them with death itselfe if they did come any farther, demanding of them if they were for God or ye King; and whyle they stopt their horses in the Water, many more rude people came behind them, & some gott themselves on ye other side of an hedge by ye rivers side, throwing stones at them, very thicke so yt only two of ye people, who are by ye world scornfully called Quakers, got through them. But ye rest were forced back again into ye towne, where they mett with ye like usage as before, & were constrayned to Ryde out of ye towne another way. These lewd people, who are even thristing after Innocent bloude, were also congregated at another narrow passage, & there stopt ye Lord's people, who went to passe that way, striking Divers of them on horseback with their poles wch they brought as it seems for that purpose & doubt less much Innocent Bloude had been there spilt, had not some moderate people prevayled over them, yet many were soe smitten by them, as yt they were scarce able to help themselves, some spitting bloud a long tyme after, their bodys swollen, being black & blew a long tyme after. Thus with much hardshipp, even with ye hazrd of their lives, they at last got through them, out of ye towne.*

Mill Lane, 1930s, once the meeting place of the Methodists and Salvationists.

Unlike (say) Sherborne or Bridport or Hawkchurch, Cerne had no Quaker colony and none of the 19 Friends' names noted as present on that unfortunate day is identifiable as an established village family here. One must infer, nevertheless, that one of them acted as host; and that before dispersing they contrived to transact some business in the form of 14 'Propositions by way of Advice' to Dorset Friends generally, reflecting their 'Sufferings for Conscience Sake' elsewhere in the county. These arose from their refusal to pay what they regarded as the iniquitous exactions of the established Church - tithes, Easter dues and Church Rates 'so called' - and from the retaliation of the local authorities by seizing goods in lieu.

Such seizures, from the mid-18th to the early-19th century, the brethren listed faithfully and systematically for various Dorset locations (but not Cerne Abbas) in minute detail and clerkly hand, registering the name of the claimant Friend, the name of the constable who seized his goods and at which authority's behest, the articles taken - barley, wheat or malt, shoes and clothing, soap and candles, cheese and tea, furniture, trays and pier glasses, or simply money snatched from the till - with an estimate of their value against some indefinite date of restitution.

The modern conscience may be assuaged by reflecting that this is the first and the last recorded religious persecution of its aggressive kind in the parish. Certainly there survived into the 19th century prejudices of a religious nature in Cerne, but these were latent rather than active. For example, in 1847, at a time when every MP (until 1866) was required to take his oath 'on the true faith of a Christian', a Rothschild was returned for the City of London. Consequently, and as noted by the local press at that juncture:

... a petition against the admission of Jews to Parliament has been adopted here, and has already been signed by the Minister, Churchwardens and upwards of 30 of the most influential inhabitants [and it] remains for signature at the Vicarage and at the New Inn.

What public violence survived into the 20th century was associated with political, not religious, controversy, as when in the spring of 1908 a lecturer with an itinerant Conservative van was pelted with eggs and stones in the village square by 'Cerne Radicals'.

From The War Cry, *12 November 1898, page 12.*

METHODISTS AND SALVATIONISTS

Although Wesleyanism in Dorset has been traced back to the 1740s, the first mention of Methodist worship in Cerne is made by an historian of the movement, publishing, in 1870, a reminiscence of the village of more than a generation before:

Once the place was alive with the various sounds which ring out from mail coaches, post carriages, and all the paraphernalia of the road; but the railway has driven all these away, and Cerne is left like Caesar, wounded, dying calmly beneath his mantle. Autumn is the most appropriate time of the year in which to visit the old abbey town – its fortunes are so like its own sere and yellow leaves. On 6 of May, 1834, Mr John Barnett, now of Stickland, took his stand in the open air and proclaimed 'deliverance to the captives, the opening of the prison to them that are bound'. The visits of the Methodists were repeated, and in process of time a carpenter's shop was secured, for which £6 a year had to be paid. The wind and rain used to rush and drive through the rickety shed, but the hours spent there will long be remembered by those who then gathered together in the name of God. One evening some wild fellows in the town, having captured an owl, let it loose among the congregation; the mingling of its sad notes with the voice of the preacher added an air of mournfulness to the service for which those assembled were not prepared. In this building the worship was celebrated for ten years, after which the present chapel was occupied. The society here is small; once it was in a very flourishing state, but the disease of the place has infected it.

Here the 'present chapel' must refer to the building in Mill Lane first occupied by the sect in 1843. This was credited by the '1851 Census of Places of Religious Worship' with seating for 146, standing room for another 48, an average Sunday attendance of 50 in the morning, 120 in the afternoon, and some three dozen children of the Sunday School, all under the eye of the Revd John Stevens. The same census showed seven Wesleyan circuits in the county, of which Cerne was on the Dorchester circuit, within the Bath district, although according to the Methodists' own schedule of accommodation of 1873 it was classified as 'other preaching place', not 'connexionally settled', which may cast some doubt as to whether its Mill Lane base was purpose-built rather than rented.

Be that as it may, in 1883 the Wesleyans moved to a building on the south side of Long Street, leasing their old venue, for three years in the first instance, to the Salvation Army as a barracks. The new abode was renovated in 1906 and regularly cherished thereafter, its preachers itinerant rather than resident. In 1952, however, it was decided to sell as it was too costly for its shrunken residual congregation to maintain. Thenceforth until its demolition in the 1960s it served as the village's reading room, but is now the site of the public lavatories.

As for the Salvationists, who continued for several decades in Mill Lane, although the local press consistently referred to their activities with some condescension, their 'field days' and 'Hosanna Meetings', with instrumentalists on brass or banjos, must have done much to brighten the community. More than one Cerne veteran was to recall in after years the pleasure the band gave in the village square on Sunday evenings.

SOME QUAKER NAMES FROM LOCAL REPORTS

Thomas Bagg
George Bewley
Joseph Coale
Roger Coward (Piddletrenthide)
Samuel Curtis
Edward Cutler
William Ferris (Hawkchurch)
George Harrison
John Grundige
Henry Hutchins
Thomas King
Joseph Melling
Peter Maber
John Scott
Edward Tucker
Francis Williams
Richard Williams
Thomas Woodsone

Left: *Inside the chapel, 1892.*

Below: *Mechanised transport for a Sisterhood outing in the 1930s.*

Above: *Harvest Festival and the chapel decked overall*

Right: *The Congregational chapel in Abbey Street with Elders of the chapel in 1892 - Deacons Derriman and House.*

CONGREGATIONALISTS

That Methodism was overshadowed in Cerne by an alternative strain of nonconformity is not a reflection of the rarity of John Wesley's own visits to Dorset. Rather, it was a matter of chronology, inasmuch as religious independence had already entrenched itself in a different form.

A regularly-funded ministry in the village does not seem to have begun until 1706, and the first meeting house on the site in Abbey Street was not erected until 17 July 1729. For the next 15 years the ministry was supported by both the Presbyterian and the Congregationalist Fund Boards and then by the latter only (about £5 p.a.) until 1800. This funding was supplemented by small bequests from time to time, the Cerne Trustees in 1785 being named as John Hodges, Joseph Bennett, James Homer and Levi Groves junr. By the end of the century, according to Hutchins, 'the meeting was frequented by perhaps 40 of the townspeople, and as many of the neighbourhood'.

The first ministry (of more than 50 years, 1812-63) to have left a distinct impression on the village was that of James Troubridge, once a chorister at Salisbury Cathedral and by this point deploying his mature voice to great rhetorical effect upon his Dorset pastorate of which an account of his jubilee address, harking back to his arrival in 1812, is a good sample:

Darkness covered the place, and gross darkness the people. Vice and immorality abounded on every hand. The Sabbath was universally profaned, being used for pleasure, business and getting drunk. There had been only occasional services in the old chapel, and at the church there was no supply, at one time, for eight weeks. He had seen men and lads playing ball against the walls of the church on a Sunday... The tradesmen spent almost all their leisure time in the public houses: everything holy was scoffed at, and infidelity prevailed to a fearful extent.

As a result of this, not only was a Sunday School of 100 built up, but the chapel required enlargement in 1820, at a cost of £400, all locally subscribed; and Troubridge's preaching duties extended over neighbouring villages. Heads of Cerne households drawn into participation included J. Frampton (solicitor), Thomas Pitman (schoolmaster), John Hodges (tanner), Levi Groves (fellmonger) and members of the Bennett, Thorne, Beer, Cave and Hodder families. Particularly generous benefactors were the Hon. Mrs Digby (widow of Admiral Digby), her companion at Minterne House, Miss Carnegie, and Mr and Mrs Henry Petty of Forston, with whom the pastor lodged until his marriage in 1821. Mr Troubridge's jubilee, shortly before his retirement, was celebrated widely and deservedly.

Under his successor, the Revd John T. Smith, a new schoolroom adjacent to the chapel on the north side was opened in November 1863. It was over the matter of schools, however, that a rift was to open between dissenters and the Church of England's National School. The 40 or so day-school pupils of the former had then recently joined with their Anglican counterparts on the same basis of weekly pence payments. As from May 1864, however, the Revd William Henry Davies, incumbent of St Mary's, took it upon himself to require extra payment from dissenting parents whose offspring attended the daily National School but not his Sunday School.

After a great deal of deliberation among Congregationalist trustees it was resolved to use the improved capacity of their new schoolroom, plus if

Left: *Once The Manse for the Congregational Minister – now a private house, as is the chapel itself.*

need be the chapel galleries, to set up their own school on the British system under their own committee of management. Whether this separate enterprise failed to prosper, or whether amity was shortly restored between Church and Chapel, it is clear that in 1873 nonconformist pupils were reincorporated in the National School, which bought up their last nine desks for £3.10s.

Upon the Revd Smith's Welsh successor in 1869, the Revd David Thomas, was to fall an unexpectedly heavy burden of renewal. Leases on the chapel itself, now increasingly dilapidated, had been renewed with the Pitt-Rivers family at roughly 50-year intervals, in 1729, 1782 and 1825. After a disastrous fire at the schoolroom (insured for £67.12s.6d. but, like the chapel itself, thatched) it was resolved to secure the freehold of the site from General Pitt-Rivers and rebuild completely. The plans were prepared by Jackson of Weymouth, the contract for the work taken out by Messrs. Rendell of Dorchester for £570, and the foundation stone laid on 14 July 1888. In October a declaration of trust was signed between A.H. Fox Pitt-Rivers and trustees of 'the Independents being Paedobaptists' confirming transfer of the premises in the sum of £100 for religious and philanthropic uses; in clarification of which the six basic tenets of the latter's faith were therein set forth. Total expenditure was stated to be £826, most of it raised locally.

The new building, which incorporated a schoolroom to the rear, was opened on 16 April following, tea being served to 250 people at the National School, the hospitable use of which seems to have signified the renewal of good fellowship with the Church. The building along the 54-foot line of frontage on Abbey Street, originally the minister's house but by this point described as 'unsightly cottages', was demolished.

In 1893 a new organ and a choir platform were installed, the gift of Napoleon Bonnett, tailor, of Long Street next to the New Inn, to mark the inaugural ceremony ('recognition') of the Revd George David Davis. Where the ministers were residing at this period is not clear. In 1929, on the death of the occupant Frank Clark (relieving officer and brother of the artist Joseph Benwell Clark), the Dorset Congregational Association bought the handsome house on the north side of Long Street, then known as No. 96 in the Pitt-Rivers catalogue and now as The Old Manse, for the accommodation of the pastor. It was re-sold into private occupation in 1958.

By then Congregationalism in Cerne was suffering a decline which entry, in 1972, into the United Reform Church failed to reverse. (In 1982 chapel and site were sold to an individual purchaser and by his own hands converted into a private residence.). The figures may be allowed to speak for themselves:

Date	Members	Sunday Scholars	Teachers	Lay Preachers
1899	28	75	8	1
1909	16	54	7	1
1919	29	35	4	1
1929	15	26	3	0
1939	19	17	3	3
1949	17	12	1	1
1959	10	5	1	0
1969	6	0	0	0
1979	4	0	0	0
1981	5	0	0	0

(Statistics kindly supplied by Mr John Creasey of Dr Williams' Library, who also compiled the list of ministers following.).

MINISTERS OF THE CONGREGATIONAL CHAPEL

By 1706-15, Robert Sims
1715-20, Richard Orchard
1720-22, Paul Jennys
1722-31, Richard Orchard then Bernard Banger
c.1732-33, John Bushrod or Bulstrode
1733-?, No settled minister, church served by supplies, who were Messrs. Phelps and Daniel in 1735.
?-1756, ? Malden/Maulden
1756, Daniel Varder
1756-74, John Short
c.1776-1801, William Harvey
1801-04, Joseph Lamb
c.1806-09, ? Lloyd (probably John Lloyd, from Lymington, supplying Sydling in 1803)
c.1809-10, William Evans Bishop (probably supply)
1812-63, James Troubridge (1786-1881)
1863-69, John Thomas Smith (1798-1872)
1869-92, David Thomas (1830-92)
1893-97, George David Davies (1865-1950)
1897-1902, James Alfred Balshaw (1842-1915)
1904-08, William Henry Picken (1847-1919)
1908-13, Alfred J.H. Thompson (Evangelist)
1914-15, William Protheroe (1859-1915)
1916-20, A. Maloney (Lay Pastor)
1920-25, Norman B.B. Bevan (Evangelist)
1925-29, Reginald Walter Durose (Lay Pastor)
1930-34, Walter Todman (Lay Pastor)
1935-41, James Graham Whittock (Evangelist)
1942-44, Horace Ernest Joseph Vickery
1945-47, J.G. Whittock (a second time)
1948-49, Walter Seymour Seager (1895-1949, Evangelist)
1949-54, James Percy Tattersfield (1888-1955)
1954-58, Hector David Woodhouse
1958-64, Supplied
1964-81, Kenneth Clare Sawyer (1918-87), Minister at Dorchester, had pastoral oversight. On his retirement in 1981 the church was closed.

Chapter 5
The Care of a Parish

Already we have remarked that by the end of the 16th century Tudor sovereigns had overlaid the purely ecclesiastical functions of the churchwardens with a collection of secular duties. The variety of these may be simply illustrated if we compare the kinds of duties listed in the churchwardens' accounts for the year 1686, inserting, asterisked, the non-sacred items recorded alongside the sacred:

Imprimis Paid Thomas Thorne and Robert Ford
  for makeing ye rails and Ballesters around ye
  Communion table   *£6.5s.0d.*
It. payd for paviers for ye Chancell   *3s.6d.*
It. spent at ye Lord Bishop's visitation   *17s.10d.*
It. Gave for Ringing ye Lord Bishop into
  towne   *5s.0d.*
It. Paid for ye Booke of Articles & entring ye
  Register   *4s.0d.*
* *It. Given Thomas Deere a slave in Turkey*   *6d.*
* *It. Payd for 6 dozen of sparrows heads*   *6d.*
It. For Wine & Bread at ye Sacrament at
  Whits.   *6s.4d.*
* *Gave to Johanna Wall a poor Irishwoman*   *6d.*
pd. For a new Common prayer Booke   *12s.0d.*
Pd. the penticost mony   *3s.0d.*
* *Pd. Robt. Vincents son for a stotes head*   *2d.*

Pd. Benjamin Summers & John Hodges for
  mending ye church windows   *£3.14s.0d.*
* *Pd. for 2 bushells of Lyme*   *1s.4d.*
* *Paid 3 Labourers to mend Aulton & Piddlehill*
  wayes   *5s.0d.*
* *payd William Cocker for mending ye North*
  bridge   *3s.0d.*
Gave to ye Ringers on ye 5th November   *5s.6d.*
paid the Cunstable his bill, as appears   *11s.0d.*
* *Gave to Thomas Thorne for a new Bridge at*
  Southers Foord   *19s.0d.*

To be sure, in discharging these duties the wardens had the assistance of other historically recognised officers – the surveyors of highways, or waywardens, and the salaried constables and watchmen. But in a small parish like Cerne these duties evidently rotated frequently among a small group nominated by the wardens themselves. John Bunter, for instance, whose year of wardenal office (1749) is commemorated over the rustic doors at the west end of St Mary's, had been a 'way-warding' 30 years before; and many other wardens had, so to speak, graduated through such lesser offices. Administrative responsibility, then, was in practice concentrated heavily on a necessarily limited number of available men.

An ancient bridge south of Cerne carrying the drove road.

THE SURVEYORS OF HIGHWAYS

For three centuries the statutory foundation of highway maintenance was the 1555 Act requiring every parishioner with tillage or pasture or draught of horses to provide a cart with two able men, and every other man (not a hired servant) to provide his labour, for four (later six) days a year. Until 1835 supervision rested with surveyors, usually men of substance, appointed at a special 'Highway Sessions' by the Justices, to whom they were responsible until 1832 when control was transferred to the particular vestries themselves. They were to view the roads three times a year and present their condition to the appropriate magistrate. The financial basis of their operations remained an ordinance of 1654 allowing the making of a parish highway rate not exceeding 1s. (later 6d.) in the £.

Being unpaid, though commutable for money, the office of waywarden rotated swiftly. Its unpopularity may explain the (not untypical) dearth of documentation surviving for Cerne's. What mostly remains before the 19th century with regard to the roads is a number of discrete, ad-hoc items such as:

> *1712 Robt. White, mason, for making Pain's bridge and carpenter and other labourers about ye highways* £4.17s.17d.
> *1713 Pd. for carriage of stone from Longburton* £4.16s.8d.
> *quarries [stone blocks]* 14s.6d.
> *1762 a new shovel to work on the turnpike drawing a petition about ye turnpike road* £3.5s.8d.

The same is true of work on bridges, water courses and wells. There are 17th-century records of repairs to Jennings' bridge, Williams' bridge, Lock's bridge and Payn's bridge 'and the whirlegog'; to Allen's well, Bennet's well and Randall's well, and, in 1684–5, to the wells of Acreman Street collectively. Up until 1772 there were regular outlays of a shilling or so 'for cleaning St Austin':

> *1691 August 6. paid Bartholomew Gale for empting [sic] of St Austin's well, changing ye water course and putting in several piles* 1s.6d.

and on 4 November three years later the wardens made the exceptional entry of 3 shillings 'for repairing of ye Giant'. At the other end of the scale is the equally fascinating item of 1635: 'Paid Anth. Thorne & others for taking down ye Maypole & making a Town ladder of it'.

Even for the 19th century, information about Cerne's waywardens is sparse, being mostly a list of

Top and above: *The bridge in Duck Street, formerly Bridge Street, and footbridge over the mill stream.*

works performed under the surveyors during half-a-dozen years of the 1840s. The printed headings are 'day labour and where performed', 'materials got & prepared & from whence', 'work executed by contract', 'team work' and 'where done', with the names of the workers – in those particular years basically nine scarcely varying men. From Alton Lane in the east to Sydling Hill in the west, summit to summit, they carted and laid the stones they had cracked, they hedged and they ditched, at a rate per day varying between 8d. and 1 shilling. Their tools included a donkey cart, donkey harness and pump. Their recorded work and pay, and the tradesmen's bills, certificated by the two waywardens, were annually examined and allowed by six signatories from the Vestry. The account for a typical quarter's work at that period balanced at around £70.

We have no record of the cost of a single extended operation, such as the widening and ditch-filling of the entire length of Alton Lane in 1898. Cerne was then still appointing its waywardens. For the fiscal year 1865–6 the newly created Highway Board reported for a district of 25 parishes containing 122 miles of road and for properties whose rateable value totalled over £53 000. Out of an annual expenditure of nearly £1200, salaries and 'common charges' amounted to over £152. But by then the age of the new turnpikes had begun. By 1884 the salary advertised for the post of 'District Surveyor' was £140 p.a.

THE CONSTABLE (OR TYTHING-MAN)

This historic officer, down the centuries the man most immediately responsible for the maintenance of law and order in the parish, occupied an equivocal position, answerable directly to the magistracy yet the servant of the Vestry which paid him. Of parish officers, the very nature of his duty was likely to render the constable the least popular of local figures, and one exposed to satire. On the other hand, in a community as small as Cerne, we are not surprised to find his functions sometimes blurred or diffused by being executed by another officer – surveyor, warden or overseer.

The role of constable was many-sided. His power of arrest symbolised by his staff, he could intervene, apprehend, detain and bring the suspect before the Justices at Quarter Sessions. Had James Birt, labourer, absconded leaving wife and family chargeable to the parish? Had Jacob Hodder, carpenter, failed to maintain Sarah Wareham's female bastard? Did John Matthews refuse to pay 6 shillings of poor rate? In such cases (these from the 1800s) the constable would be armed with the printed order from the Justices' clerk for their apprehension and summons, himself if necessary collecting the fines:

5 July 1823   Received by the Tything man of Cerne Abbas the sum of four shillings the conviction money of Robert Mabry Billett, Taylor, and William Northover, cordwainer, for profane swearing, and distributed to the poor of the parish as under...

It was the constable who saw to the keeping of watch and ward, maintained the stocks and oversaw whippings. For local defence he had charge of the parish butts. He regulated the muster: at the height of the Napoleonic scare in 1798 a special arrangement was made for assembling a 'Posse Comitatus' (body of law enforcers) in case of invasion or insurrection. He kept an eye on the alehouses and reported thereon to magistrates' special licensing sessions. He it probably was who tended the parish bull: the village map of 1768 shows a bull pit some few hundred yards north west of St Catherine's Farm.

But most evident of the constable's duties in the surviving Cerne records is that of apprehending vagrants and organising their removal by handing them on to other constables from parish to parish, throughout (if necessary) the length of the kingdom until returned to their original place of settlement. Thus was a great principle of 17th-century Poor Law implemented. The workless not of the parish might, if actually chargeable thereto, be removed to their place of origin. Transitory relief could be given to certain categories of vagrants travelling with passes: but settlement certificates were issued only reluctantly and conditionally. The county archives contain 'a registered book (1661) of all rogues and vagabonds as have been punished accordingly at Cerne Abbas in Dorsetshire'. From time to time, as in 1697, orders were issued to constables against indiscriminate and fraudulent relief. From time to time, too, the constable benefited from the assistance of watchmen:

1814   June By money paid the Watchman in Arrears due to Him   £1.13s.4d.
1853   Paid Man for keeping watch in the Churchyard at Whitsuntide   2s.6d.

In the 1720s one Thomas White received 2 shillings a year 'for towling the bell' and in the 1760s a bellman was paid an annual 3 shillings. Overseers were also responsible for paying the parish clerk's salary – 5 shillings a year in the 1800s, plus 1 shilling for parchment. It was possibly also the parish clerk who in 1822 received 3s.6d. 'for taking the population'.

The stocks now secured outside the church.

Above: *The rookery. Catherine Granville the school teacher was given
Rook Pie in 1909 and found it 'not unpalatable'!*
Inset: *Foxes we still have. This one found a home at the New Inn 60 years ago.*

VERMIN CONTROL

An Act of 1532 laid down that in consequence of the 'innumerable number' of rooks, crows and choughs, every parish was to provide and use a net for their destruction. Twopence a dozen was to be paid by the owner or occupier of the lands concerned. Re-enactment in 1566 added magpies and young owls to the list of 'Noyfull Fowls and Vermyn', the heads or unbroken eggs of which were to be shown to the wardens who, with six other parishioners, would assess holders of land on tithe proportionately. Thereafter the black list continued to be extended and up to the early-19th century supplied one of the most numerous classes of entry in the churchwardens' accounts. Indeed, so prodigious an annual rate of destruction as these accounts reveal might, if applied to our shrunken wildlife population today, seriously upset the balance of nature:

*1753 85 doz. Sparrows heads, 37 Hedghogs,
9 Polecatts, 9 Stoats, 4 Foxes
1762 May 9. Att a Vestry this day held wee the
Churchwardens Overseers & principal
Inhabitants of Cerne Abbas doth agree that from
this day to pay one half-penny each or Six pence
per Dozn. for Rats heads agreet and Signed by us
[2 churchwardens, 4 overseers and 4 others].
1806 Sparrows heads 84 dozen at 2d
doz   14s.0d.*

Several hundred rats were paid for during 1763. Even into the 19th century such entries crop up most unexpectedly:

*1847 The Archdeacon's fees for the Incumbent of
the Living of Cerne Abbas Rectory   7s.11d.
Do. for the Incumbent of the Living of Cerne
Vicinia   2s.11d.
Churchwardens' Expences attending visitation at
Dorchester   7s.6d.
79 Dozn. sparrows' heads   13s.2d.*

BASTARDY

One small but persistent category of persons whose chargeability to the parish was to be guarded against was bastard children and their mothers. Of these the churchwardens' accounts provide a specimen or two:

*1740 Bonds & Indentures wch. are put into ye
Church box – Wm. Mullett's bond for a Bastard
Child on Ann Terell... to pay 50s. & 9d. a week for
the maintenance of Ann Terell's Bastard.*

Most such cases were, however, left for the overseers to handle, and their number seems to have increased at much the same rate as the general and inexplicable rise of such throughout the country after 1750. The file of bastardy papers in Dorset's County Record Office lists 20 such mothers and reputed fathers between 1758 and 1801, but this tally must be far from complete since the overseers' accounts for the year 1820 alone record five village bastards; in the year 1835 there were seven.

To ensure that the cost of 'sustentation' of mother and child did not fall on the parish, steps were taken against the reputed father for their upkeep. In cases where he was from another parish, deportation thereto of the entire family might very occasionally occur. But usually he would be required either to enter into a bond to maintain the parties directly himself, or perhaps undertake to make them regular weekly payments through the parish officers – usually of 1s.6d. or 2 shillings, hence the term 'eighteen-penny child'. It was cynically observed that for men at the bottom of the economic heap, women receiving support for bastard children made very eligible wives.

Poor Relief

But the issue on which parish administrators spent as much time as on all other matters of local concern put together was poor relief. At the Dissolution the tithes of (it was estimated by the Webbs) about one-third of clerical livings, hitherto regarded as a source of relief for poor parishioners, passed to the Crown and thence to private persons. The suppression of the Abbey, and the seizure of other charitable sources, must have added abruptly and heavily to the massive burden of poverty in Cerne, with the prospect of an entire community of needy folk in search of another source of alms.

In the first instance the churchwardens inherited the moral and practical responsibility for taking up the network of relief, in which capacity they were to remain enmeshed for another 300 years. An Act of 1536 had charged them and the parish clergy 'to gather and procure voluntary alms with boxes every Sunday and holiday' for the benefit of the impotent poor. They were not, however, to carry the sole burden for long. Late in Elizabeth's reign the State acknowledged and organised, with the parish as the unit, the duty towards the poor which it had taken over from the Church.

By the great Poor Law of 1601 the wardens were to be joined by two, three or four substantial householders in each parish appointed annually by the Justices and nominated overseers of the poor. These were to maintain the needy and set them to work (the old distinction between able-bodied and impotent being preserved), the money for this by a Poor Rate levied on specific, but comprehensively defined, classes of parishioner. Overseers met monthly in the church after divine service on a Sunday afternoon to consider the needs of the poor and at the end of the year render their accounts to the Vestry.

A later Act ordered that houses of correction be built, whereto rogues and vagabonds, absconding parents and 'lewd women' with bastards would be committed. To clarify the matter of eligibility for parish support more generally, an Act of 1662, extended by much subsequent legislation, defined the condition of settlement for a newcomer and provided for the removal therefrom of uncertificated strangers and vagrants. This corpus of legislation governed the administration of relief until 1834.

The overseers' accounts for Cerne Abbas survive from 1632 to 1825. Unfortunately, two volumes covering the period 1779 to 1814 are missing. Laying the remaining five volumes side by side with the churchwardens' accounts for the same years we note some division of operations but much overlapping – again, what one would expect in a small community. The categories of particularly needy types, to be supplied by the wardens, included such folk as those 'having lost all by fire' or 'totally ruined by the inundation of water', but many more displaced personages, such as discharged sailors, poor 'decayed' soldiers, castaways, ex-prisoners of war or simply itinerants with or without a lawful pass:

1682 *July 29. It. Gave a Traveller whose Tongue*
was cutt out of his mouth   *6d.*
1686 *Gave to an Itallion who was cast away* *6d.*
         Gave Thomas Willis & Henry Blacke Turky
slaves   *6d.*
1733 *15 October. Gave a poor man for to Git*
him out of town   *3d.*
1758 *19 June. Gave a Soldier's wife with sick*
children   *6d.*
1761 *25 March. Gave 13 sailors come out of*
french prison   *3s.0d.*

Two pages of the 1695-7 accounts list 76 such cases at a total outlay of nearly £2. For villages on a main road the burden cannot have been negligible.

For the overseers, by contrast, the basic concerns were to do with in-relief – the Almshouse or workhouse (of which more later) – and the personal needs of its inhabitants. Over and above this category, however, were the 'extraordinary' disbursements which show on the whole a greater scope and variety than encountered in the churchwardens' accounts. Here for instance are some of the extraordinaries for the parish's fiscal year April 1745 to March 1746:

Paid for stretching out and Diging the grave
  for Emy Gillingham   *2s.0d.*
Gave Sarah in sickness and her Coffen &
  Shourds & Stretching out & Beer   *15s.0d.*
Paid for 20 Badges att 3d. a piece   *5s.0d.*
Gave ye Taylor for soing on ye Badges   *6d.*
Paid Mary Gifford for looking after

Sarah Goff   *1s.6d.*
For Horse hire & Expenses going to ye justice
  with Jno. Dark Paid for a warrant   *3s.3d.*
paid Mr Voys Bill for curing Moll King's
  legs   *15s.0d.*

and from 1748-9:

Paid for taking Thos. Morris & Marrying
  him   *£7.16s.0d.*
Gave Mary Warren a Shift   *2s.7d.*
Gave Robt. Green's wife in her lying in   *1s.0d.*
Paid Mr Jacob for Liquor for poor Roger   *1s.0d.*
For mending ye Belman's lantern   *9d.*
Paid ye Waywardens bill   *6.17s.4d.*

and from 1771-2:

Pd. Thomas Crook for sweeping Thos.
  Harben's Chimney   *6d.*
Sa. Gale a neck of veal & other necessaries   *4s.6d.*
Pd. Mr Hassell for the prosecution of
  Ann Morrish   *£3.1s.0d.*
Lous. Bennett for taking care of Sa. Gale
  & Thos. Harben   *5s.4d.*
Sope and Candles for the above   *10d.*

Indeed, the overseers' items are abundant in their variety and contain such diverse items as 'for filling a bed', for 'dowlas' (coarse linen/cloth), for mending a kettle, for furze and other firing, for an iron pot, for shoes, buttons and a pair of stays. They include mention of payment for people's house rent, for sweeping their chimneys, delivering their babies, curing their itches and meeting the apothecary's bill. They list also the hiring of horses to convey somebody to gaol, and for paying the coroner at inquests – for all the necessities of life and death, in short, from lyings-in to layings-out. This last may make melancholy reading on occasions, as when, during a few weeks of the winter of 1702-3, 15 children died of the smallpox, and at its recurrence in 1722 and 1756. By Acts of 1666 and 1678 the overseers were to ensure, under heavy penalties, that the corpses of all save plague victims were to be buried in sheep's wool only. Such a register exists for Cerne Abbas.

Only in one or two small fields did overseers have the chance to act more constructively. They might, for instance, provide testimonials for servants seeking employment in other parishes. More significantly they were given the power, under 17th-century legislation, to bind poor children of 15 years or over as apprentices – boys until the age of 24, girls until 21 years or marriage. The Record Office's file of Cerne Abbas indentures between 1745 and 1835 lists 27 such apprenticeships. Of these, six are women, indentured respectively to silk throwers and button

makers in Sherborne, to a labourer in Cheselbourne and a shepherd in the village. The remaining 21 men are severally apprenticed into the trades of cordwaining, carpentry, fellmongering and coopering, mostly local but two as far afield as Cranborne and Melcombe Regis. Cerne does not, however, appear to have followed the practice, noted elsewhere by the Webbs, of formally leasing out or auctioning its penniless young to a round of local farmers.

An Act of 1819 allowed the appointment of salaried assistant overseers, and in 1828 one such was designated in Cerne, 'the same as if he had been actually appointed as Overseer', at £20 p.a. plus travelling expenses. Otherwise, a regular quartet of officers, annually chosen and accountable to the Vestry, made their basic and their (separately listed) extraordinary disbursements either fortnightly or monthly according to the chronological period. Normally dispensed at the church – although in April 1776, for instance, paid out at the Nag's Head 'on account of the cold weather' – both categories show a fairly stable proportionality to the rateable population at any given time. To take a cross-section in 1717, £100.19s.7d. was disbursed against a rate collection of £106.12s.6d., the latter raised from a list of 90 parishioners headed by George Pitt at the Abbey Farm (£2.8s.5d.), succeeding Thomas Freke as the biggest contributor, down to those assessed at one penny, the majority paying less than 2 shillings. By the mid-18th century total annual disbursements were still kept below £150. But the incidence of the Napoleonic Wars was reflected when a century later (1818) the ratepayers list had risen to 156 names realising £650.6s.0d. with monthly disbursements below £50 but rising in one case to nearly £78. The following year a record number of 145 paupers were recorded as having been relieved. This heavy rise seems consistent with the overall rise in poor rates for the United Kingdom as a whole, estimated by historians as five-fold between 1785 (£2m) and 1817-19 (£10m).

Over and above the proceeds of the Poor Rate, overseers could count on very few extraordinary assets to set against expenditures. Some 'conviction moneys' levied at Petty Sessions were earmarked for charitable purposes:

Received February 3rd. 1779 of Daniel Sherry forty shillings a fine being levied by Sir John Smith for taking hay out of the Rack for the Draggoons Horses & Distributed to the poor as follows...

Received 16th July 1822 of Robert Mabry Bilett the sum of Five shillings (as a Fine) convicted of being drunk at Cerne Abbas on the twenty seventh day of May last and distributed to the Poor of the Parish of Cerne Abbas as under...

Received 24 Janry 1823 of James Old, labourer the sum of Five Shillings for a fine of convicted of stealing and carrying away a Quantity of Furze, the property of Thomas Cockeram, and distributed to the Poor of the said Parish of Cerne Abbas as under...

During the 1760s and '70s the accounts note some income from rent of 'the Silk House' - at that period a cottage in Duck Street - made every Lady Day in the sum of £1.10s. by the Cerne representative of Messrs. Willmott, silk manufacturers of Sherborne. Very occasionally the death of a pauper brought the overseers the benefit of sale of his or her household furniture and effects, of which they would doubtless have made a prior inventory.

Were there any guidelines which overseers might consult in their attempt to rationalise these expenditures? One such at least is famous, or notorious, in the history books. In the autumn of 1792, perhaps in apprehension of local unrest, the Dorchester Justices in Quarter Sessions accepted, and voted to publicise county-wide, a resolution prepared at a general meeting of county magistrates:

That having taken into consideration the difficulties the poor labour under from the present high price of corn and other necessaries, the Justices within their respective Division will make an order on the parish officers, on the complaint of any industrious and peaceable poor person, which shall appear to be well founded, to relieve him or her with such sum as shall make up, together with the weekly earnings of him, her and their family, a comfortable support for them: and that the Justices, having thus provided for the necessary subsistence of the industrious and peaceable poor, declare their determination to enforce the laws against such as shall meet together for any unlawful purpose.

Here was the germ of the 'Speenhamland system' whereby (to simplify a locally variable process) magistrates were to calculate, and overseers to supply, such a sum to an applicant for poor relief as would make up a deficiency in wages below a notionally acceptable standard of living for himself and his family, taking into account the fluctuating price of bread. Parliament being unwilling to legislate nationally, this 'Justices' Scale' of 'Rate in Aid of Wages' became in Dorset, even earlier than in other English counties, for 40 years from 1792 onward, the official yardstick of out-relief. Its impact upon rural poverty here we can assess only within the context of Cerne's communal development over those years. For the moment we must look at the other branch of the overseers' charitable duties, the administration of 'in-relief' through a sequence of appropriate institutions.

ALMSHOUSE

That an almshouse existed in Cerne in the late-16th century is implied in the will, dated 11 September 1592, of one William Cardoe, mercer of Dorchester, bequeathing each of its inmates 'five shillings and a black gowne of cotten, the money to be paid and the gownes to be worn at my burial'. Not until May 1664, however, do we find a more specific entry in the churchwardens' accounts detailing payments of £12.13s.6d. to John and Andy Thorne, respectively mason and carpenter, for building (or perhaps rebuilding?) 'an habitation' for some of the said poor: with a further £1.15s.9d. divided between Nicholas Cropbury for providing the reeds, John Farr for carrying four loads of straw, John Petty for thatching and John Carpenter for use of his reed shears. Thereafter the parish regularly maintained it - rethatching, glazing, making good the approaches, etc. - up to at least 1683.

By that date the general legal situation had long remained unaltered, overseers being empowered, with the consent of the majority of the villagers, to buy or hire a suitable building, contract with anyone for maintaining it, and employ such of its inhabitants as were able-bodied. Persons refusing to enter would forfeit their entitlement to relief. The next stage, however, in Cerne's accommodating of its poor was stimulated by a special Act of 1722 which encouraged overseers, with the consent of the Vestry and in conjunction if desired with other parishes, themselves to build workhouses. Within ten years, it reckoned, 60 such houses had been raised countrywide. In November 1734, accordingly, Cerne Abbas Vestry resolved to build a parish house 'on the waste in the lane leading to Broadfield Gate or thereabout'. Over £105 was quickly raised and spent on what was thereafter referred to as the Almshouse or poorhouse. Broadfield Gate is now untraceable. But when in the 1840s the overseers and churchwardens came to offer the house and site for sale to the Pitt-Rivers family, it was described as being at the bottom of Lime Kiln Lane or Burnt Lane (i.e., at its junction with Alton Lane) and measuring (the adjoining fuel house included) 100ft north-south by 18ft east-west, with a front courtyard 75ft by 50ft and a garden 84ft by 36ft.

Routine maintenance of these premises, year in, year out, is regularly entered in the overseers' accounts up to the lacuna after 1778 - the rethatching, sweeping of chimneys, digging of the well, repairing doors, windows and locks. In December 1740 a contract is recorded with one Wm. Farr, who had just rebuilt the south end, to keep the house in repair for the term of 20 years. It is not clear whether this included the pump, which 12 years out of 20 required mending until its deadweight of 3st.3qr. was sold to Mr Foord for £2.12s.6d., presumably as scrap iron, in 1772.

By the time that the surviving accounts resume in 1815 the picture has changed again. Whether or not the Almshouse of 1734 was still in use as such, the focus of attention and expenditure had become the workhouse, or poorhouse 'in Duck Street'. As to its precise location, all we know is that it included a fenced garden; but for knowledge of its operation - repairs, provisioning, insurance - we have a surviving account book for the ten years after 1808, with copious detail down to the 7s.6d. paid to Wm. Cottle in February 1817 for 'emptying the privy vault.' The number of inmates from 1808-12 varied between 18 and 10, but then dipped into single figures to rise again by 1817 to 17 - 9 women, 5 men and 3 'childers'. Of these only a small minority were at any time able to undertake paid work to set against the cost of their keep. In attendance was a maidservant or manservant paid 4 shillings or 2 shillings a month according to the number of inmates. Monthly outgoings for provisions and fuel fluctuated around £20. Insurance ran at 7s.6d. a year and the constable was paid £1 at rare intervals. The very occasional funeral cost is noted at 3 shillings, with 15 shillings for a coffin. There is one mishap listed:

September 21st 1816. Ruth Maynard delivered of a bastard child Jno Sartin of Sydling to pay £3.14s.6d. expenses & 2s. a week and if Ruth Maynard doth not nurse & take care of the said bastard child she is to pay 1s. per week.

This account book closes in the year 1818. In less than another 20 years the housing of the country's destitute was to be placed on a uniform footing which (it was hoped) would greatly reduce, if not eliminate, the relieving of the needy in their own separate dwellings. In 1832 a non-party Royal Commission was appointed to inquire into the whole problem of Poor Law reform. Its report of 1834 envisaged a radically reshaped system, and in that Cerne Abbas was to play a significant local part.

*Mary Jones, who wrote a book about Cerne,
outside her cottage in Back Lane in 1931 complete with the then water supply.*

Chapter 6
The Union Workhouse

by Jean Turner

By the second quarter of the 19th century, enclosure, industrialisation, and the ending of the Napoleonic Wars had led to a massive increase in the numbers of able-bodied poor relying partly on help from the parish rates. In Dorset, most would have been farm labourers displaced by machinery or paid so little that their wages had to be supplemented by 'outdoor relief'. Many involved in cottage industries such as spinning, weaving and rope-making were similarly affected. In 1830 the government was alarmed by the 'Swing Riots', an outbreak of rick-burning and machine-breaking throughout southern England in protest against the introduction of steam-driven threshing machines (*above*) which reduced the labour force required.

In an attempt to address the problem the newly-reformed House of Commons passed the Poor Law Amendment Act of 1834, empowering parishes to form 'unions' and to set up workhouses. The principles at the root of the system were to cut down on outdoor relief and to reduce the number of paupers applying for relief by making workhouse life for the able-bodied pauper such that 'his situation shall not be made... so eligible as the situation of the independent labourer of the lowest class'.

This principle came to be applied to all types of pauper, both deserving and undeserving. Contrary to the original suggestions made by the Poor Law commissioners, each of the the dozen Dorset unions set up general mixed workhouses in which sick, aged, feeble-minded and orphaned individuals were housed in the same conditions as able-bodied adults and vagrants.

Cerne Union was formed by the amalgamation of 20 parishes, comprising a total population by 1870 of over 6700, each of which sent an elected guardian to represent its interest, except for Cerne Abbas which sent two. Voting was plural, each ratepayer having one to three votes according to the rateable value of his property.

The Board of Guardians of the Cerne Union held their first meeting at the New Inn (rental 4 shillings) on 29 December 1835. John File Hart and Henry Hodges were the guardians for Cerne Abbas. It was resolved that John James Smith be Chairman and John Samson Relieving Officer at a salary of £90 p.a. A committee was appointed:

... to consider what steps to take towards providing workhouse accommodation for 130 paupers, to cause plans and estimates to be prepared... and to report thereon to the Board.

John Frampton, Parish Clerk, was charged to require the churchwardens and overseers of the several parishes to pay one-eighth of the amount of their underwritten average expenditure by the following February. For Cerne this was recorded thus: population 1209; poor expenditure: 1833, £564.6s.4d.; 1834, £571.3s.6d.; 1835, £476.5s.8d.; average £537.5s.2d.

By 12 February 1836 most of the parishes, though not Cerne Abbas, had paid their contributions, and the Building Committee reported that they would be able to lay before the next board meeting plans and estimates for the workhouse. A fortnight later the Board authorised the employment of Charles Wallis, surveyor, to view a ³⁄₄-acre field called Baker's Cross Paddock as a possible site, and to prepare a plan 'with specifications and estimates for a workhouse calculated for the reception of 130 paupers'. His plan was laid before the Board on 15 March, tenders for the work were sought, and on 27 April the tender of Messrs. Northover and Biles was accepted in the sum of £2050. The Board further resolved to apply to the Poor Law commissioners for permission to sell the old Poor House of 1734: this must have been granted, for on 25 May we find the Board deciding that the building, its fuel house, courtyard and garden should be offered to Lord Rivers for £110. This transaction was signed and sealed in March 1844.

It had not proved possible to buy Baker's Cross Paddock. Instead the guardians consented to the purchase of a 1¹⁄₄-acre site called Weam for £150, and

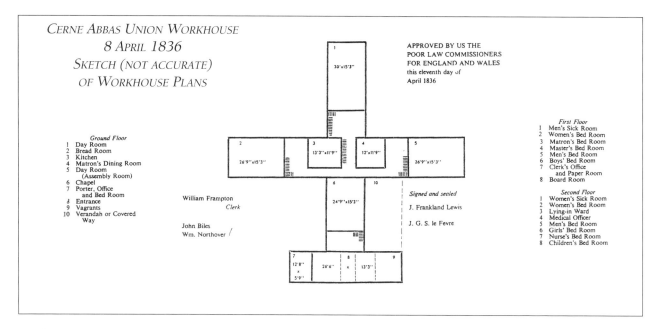

CERNE ABBAS UNION WORKHOUSE
8 APRIL 1836
SKETCH (NOT ACCURATE)
OF WORKHOUSE PLANS

APPROVED BY US THE
POOR LAW COMMISSIONERS
FOR ENGLAND AND WALES
this eleventh day of
April 1836

Ground Floor
1 Day Room
2 Bread Room
3 Kitchen
4 Matron's Dining Room
5 Day Room
  (Assembly Room)
6 Chapel
7 Porter, Office
  and Bed Room
8 Entrance
9 Vagrants
10 Verandah or Covered
   Way

William Frampton
Clerk

John Biles
Wm. Northover

Signed and sealed
J. Frankland Lewis
J. G. S. le Fevre

First Floor
1 Men's Sick Room
2 Women's Bed Room
3 Matron's Bed Room
4 Master's Bed Room
5 Men's Bed Room
6 Boys' Bed Room
7 Clerk's Office
  and Paper Room
8 Board Room

Second Floor
1 Women's Sick Room
2 Women's Bed Room
3 Lying-in Ward
4 Medical Officer
5 Men's Bed Room
6 Girls' Bed Room
7 Nurse's Bed Room
8 Children's Bed Room

to the construction of the workhouse at a cost not exceeding £2550. They also gave authority for the money to be borrowed and secured by a charge on the poor rates of the several parishes constituting the Union. In June the guardians applied to the commissioners for the issue of Exchequer bills for the sum of £2700, to be repaid in ten equal annual instalments. The formal deed was executed in September and the bills issued in October. These bills were sold as the work progressed, and a building account was opened from which Northover and Biles were paid.

Courts were paved and drains and a well dug. By 18 October building was so far advanced that the Board were authorising the installation of 'water shoots and pipes', and in December the building committee was told to secure estimates for the fitting-up of the workhouse. In January 1837 it was agreed to purchase coal for airing the building and the Board also authorised the purchase of fittings and furnishings, and insured the new building for £1500. From March onwards, a dietary table having been approved, tenders were sought for supplies of food, clothing, bedding, coals, etc., and for medical relief to paupers in and out of the workhouse. Samuel Burrough's tender for 'best second bread' at 5½d. per 4lb loaf was accepted.

Meanwhile staff were being recruited by local advertisements. First, tenders were invited for the post of 'Medical Officer', his work to include:

... all cases of Sickness, Surgery, Midwifery and Vaccination and also Medicines which may be necessary for all paupers within the District, whether belonging to the same or otherwise.. [and] to make a weekly return of sickness and mortality to the Board of Guardians.

Two Cerne Abbas surgeons – Alfred Davis of Long Street and John Fox of Abbey Street – were to divide the whole area between them, their remuneration before long being transmuted into salaries and fees.

Second, for the post of 'Relieving Officer' the successful applicant would be required:

... to reside in Cerne Abbas and devote his whole time to the employment, not following any other Trade or Profession whatsoever; he must write a good hand, and be capable of keeping accounts... (He) will be required to enter into a Bond, with sufficient sureties, in £100, for the due discharge of the duties, and to take charge of the Union immediately.

The £90-p.a. salary of the first appointee (John Samson, soon to be displaced by William Cave) reflected the scope of his duties. These were to compile and present his records of out-relief expenditure for examination and authorisation by the Board and to administer money or bread (up to 600 loaves a week at first, costed at 6d. a loaf).

Next, they sought a man and wife 'without encumbrance' to fill the offices of 'Master' and 'Matron', the man to be able-bodied, not over 50, and a good accountant. The salary would be no more than £40 p.a., plus 'coal, candles, and such provisions as the House will afford'. The following April another couple were sought, he to be 'Porter' and she to be 'Nurse/Schoolmistress', at a joint salary of 8 shillings a week, plus the usual residential allowances. He was to keep a book wherein 'all persons visiting the workhouse shall enter their names with such observations as they shall think fit to make', especially with respect to the discipline and management of the place. A Mr and Mrs Baker were selected and were promoted to Master and Matron as the original appointees resigned the following June. The Board thereupon advertised for a schoolmistress who, it was stipulated:

... must be a Member of the Established Church... capable of Instructing the Boys and Girls in Reading, Writing and the Principles of the Christian Religion, and of imparting to them such other instructions, as are calculated to train them to habits of usefulness, industry and virtue.

The applicant must produce 'Testimonials of Character as to sobriety, honesty and morality... with Specimens of Handwriting.'

Anne Sealey was appointed at a salary of £15 p.a. plus allowances. As in the cases of the other workhouse officers, these latter were later commuted to money payments, the master receiving 6 shillings a week in lieu, the matron and schoolmistress 5 shillings per week apiece. The vicar of St Mary's, the Revd John Davis, was invited to accept the non-resident position of Chaplain at a salary of £25 p.a., raised in 1839 to £40 p.a. A treasurer and auditor were also designated. Local JPs (Justices of the Peace) were to be members of the Board ex officio.

Meanwhile the relief lists of the several parishes of the Union were revised and orders signed for the admission of paupers. A visiting committee was appointed and the medical officers of the various

Above: *A sunny upstairs ward.*

Right: *One of the metal baths; not very comfortable but few villagers would have had better than this in 1836.*

Union districts were directed to attend to examine the paupers to be admitted. On 26 May 1837 it was resolved that:

The relief now afforded by this Union to non-resident paupers shall, from the 3rd day of June next, cease, unless the Board shall... be satisfied of the necessity of such relief being continued.

The amount given in outdoor relief was immediately halved, as was the bread order, but help continued to be given, especially with funeral expenses, the binding of apprentices, and food for women and children left to fend for themselves. Other miscellaneous decisions were taken. In September it was decided that persons dying in the workhouse should be interred on the fourth day after their decease unless the surgeons ordered otherwise. Mr William Henry Clarke's offer of a pall at the price of 30 shillings was accepted. On the same day the medical officers were ordered to vaccinate all the children in the workhouse forthwith.

The workhouse had been built in ten months, but it was not all plain sailing. On 9 August 1837 the treasurer was directed to sell the last £200 worth of Exchequer bills, and it was decided shortly afterwards that the Lords of the Treasury be asked to extend the time for repayment from 10 to 20 years and to reduce the interest rate from 5 per cent to 4 per cent. This must have been agreed, for on 11 September the Board ordered the treasurer to pay into the Bank of England the first instalment of one-twentieth part of the loan, i.e. £135, and also one year's interest (£108). But expenditure on fitting

The inner courtyard.

THE PARISH BOOK OF CERNE ABBAS

out the premises, feeding and clothing the inmates and paying the salaries of its officers had mounted so alarmingly that by November the Board resolved that a committee of three be appointed to inquire into management and expenditure with a view to economising but at the same time 'having especial regard to the comfort of the paupers'. This committee recommended that new standard dietaries be adopted from 26 December, as set out in tables I and II below.

As to operations, although the transition from obsolete overseers to new guardians is not a clear-cut one, yet certain responsibilities of the former were immediately assumed by the Board. It was they who, in the early-19th century, through the Relieving Officer, sought the filial orders from the Justices against the reputed fathers of bastards, they who prosecuted delinquent sons who failed to maintain their elders, they who dealt with cases of desertion, scrutinised settlement certificates and applied for removal orders against pauper families not properly chargeable to the parish. Through his control of the outdoor relief account the Relieving Officer paid (although rarely) for the binding of apprentices and for pauper funerals. He also disbursed small discretionary loans to the needy and

TABLE 1: DIETARY FOR AGED AND INFIRM PAUPERS

		Breakfast Bread	Cooked Meat	Dinner Potatoes	Soup	Sweet or Rice Pudding	Supper Bread	Cheese
		oz.	oz.	oz.	pt	oz.	oz.	oz.
SUN	Men	6	4	24		5		
	Women	5	4	24		4		
MON	Men	6		6	1½		5	1½
	Women	5		6	1½		4	1½
TUES	Men	6	4	24			5	
	Women	5	4	24			4	
WED	Men	6		6	1½		5	1½
	Women	5		6	1½		4	1½
THUR	Men	6	4	24			5	
	Women	5	4	24			4	
FRI	Men	6		12	1½	10	5	1½
	Women	5		12	1½	8	4	1½
SAT	Men	6		6	1½		5	1½
	Women	5		6	1½		4	1½

People of 60 years of age to be allowed 1 oz. tea, 4 oz. butter, 5 oz. sugar per week. The sick to be dieted as directed by Medical Officers.

TABLE 2: DIETARY FOR ABLE-BODIED MEN AND WOMEN

		Breakfast Bread	Gruel	Cooked Meat	Dinner Potatoes	Soup	Sweet or Rice Pudding	Supper Bread	Cheese	Broth
		oz.	pt	oz.	oz.	pt	oz.	oz.	oz.	pt
SUN	Men	6	1½	4	24			6		1½
	Women	5	1½	4	24			5		1½
MON	Men	6	1½		6	1½		6	2	
	Women	5	1½		6	1½		5	2	
TUES	Men	6	1½	4	24			6		1½
	Women	5	1½	4	24			5		1½
WED	Men	6	1½		6	1½		6	2	
	Women	5	1½		6	1½		5	2	
THUR	Men	6	1½	4	24			6		1½
	Women	5	1½	4	24			5		1½
FRI	Men	6	1½		16		10	6	2	
	Women	5	1½		16		8	5	2	
SAT	Men	6	1½		6	1½		6	2	
	Women	5	1½		6	1½		5	2	

indemnified the traditional parish officers against loss in cases where, for example, the latter had maintained paupers at the Forston lunatic asylum.

When on 1 November 1860 a Poor Law inspector paid an unexpected visit to the Cerne Union, he reported (according to the *Dorset County Chronicle*) thus: 'I have found everything in exemplary order... The state of the establishment reflects credit on all concerned in its management.' The institution had by then been operative for a quarter of a century and already internal changes had been effected. Some were small, as when the Board ceased to advertise for a schoolmistresses, since by 1867 the children's schooling had been transferred to the National School in Duck Street. But some alterations were so considerable as to necessitate modification in the use and even the structure of the building itself. As early as February 1838 the Board resolved that accommodation be provided for the reception of vagrants and other 'casual poor', and two rooms on the north side of the entrance hall were fitted up for that purpose, each with a chimney and fireplace.

After an outbreak of typhus three years later the Union attracted criticism because its infirmary section of 20 beds lacked ventilation and sanitation and there was no isolation ward. As a result, a detached block was built, with a new maternity ward as well as isolation wards. Many such alterations in 1895 enabled the older infirm to be almost completely segregated from the able-bodied and allowed for the first time married couples to live together. Additional bathrooms were made in 1898 in 'the Boys' yard' – but after 1915 the Union ceased to accommodate children altogether.

Regarding the general picture of the Union's inmates, one basic planning miscalculation must be recognised. The original scheme of the 1834 planners was to make the Union the sole legitimate channel for community care:

... that except as to medical attention... all relief whatever to able-bodied persons or to their families otherwise than in well-regulated workhouses shall be declared unlawful.

But this stipulation necessarily required guesswork as to the relative proportions of 'permanent' residents, transitory residents and non-resident applicants for casual relief. The 'House' was designed for 130 inmates, but, although an unbroken line of statistics has not survived, we see that for the remainder of the century the decennial census figures of resident paupers ran as follows:

1841: 65	1871: 51
1851: 69	1881: 30
1861: 54	1891: 31

Small wonder, then, that a strong tide of local opinion, voiced by Capt. Mount Batten of UpCerne, was for dissolving the Cerne Union and redistributing its inmates among the 'half empty' unions of Sherborne, Sturminster Newton and Blandford at a saving of between £300 and £400 per annum. Come the 1920s, furthermore, some of the onus of short-term relief was to be shouldered by the Franciscan friary at Hillfield. One must also bear in mind that, looked at from the local authority's viewpoint, the pauperism problem was dwarfed by that of insanity. According to the census source quoted above, the resident population of the County Lunatic Asylum at Herrison Hospital had by 1881 risen to 484 inmates.

A possible reason for this marked reduction suggests itself in the fact that the standard hard labour required of the able-bodied applicant for relief, over and above gardening and bone pulverising, was the cracking of flints, carted under contract from Sydling Hill to the Piddle Valley in loads of 300 cubic yards. In March 1890 the purchase of new flint-pounding equipment, less laborious to operate, may have removed one pretext used by casual vagrants for refusing to work. But this of course is mere speculation.

More concrete is the evidence that office-holding under the new system acquired esteem and hence a measure of continuity. When a vacancy arose for a Cerne guardian in 1863 there was competition to fill it, voting papers being distributed to every ratepayer on Saturday and collected (in this case from 78 respondents) on the Monday. When James Hellyer died on a Sunday in October 1878 he had been a guardian for 17 years: the church flag was flown at half-mast and the 'Dead March' played after morning and evening services. Again, as 'Clerk to the Guardians' the long service of William Beach is noted elsewhere (see page 95). When one of his successors, A.E.A. Cole, resigned in 1915 it was after 25 years in the post.

As to the mastership itself, we have insufficient information to deduce an average length of tenure. On the one hand, when Robert Curme died in harness in February 1870 he had filled the office for 23 consecutive years – the younger of two brothers who had actually worked the lime for mortar in the building of the House itself. On the other hand, there were several incumbents in the 1890s who reigned for less than three years. For the post of Curme's successor-but-one in 1874 there were eight applicants. Moreover, there seems quite early on to have evolved something like a career structure for the 'Master' (and his wife) of a Union workhouse, so that it became a common practice for an incumbent couple at Cerne to have come from a similar post in another place such as Weymouth and, in due course, to move on to the equivalent one elsewhere.

The Union workhouse, 1940s.

Inset and main picture: *The overhaul in progress in 1990 and ready for occupation in 1991.*

If the Master's duties remained fairly static, yet his Board of Guardians, without changing its designation, gradually and insensibly over the years enlarged its sphere of operation. Though not themselves primarily charged with rate-setting or with the compiling of jury lists, the requirements of the Parochial Assessment Act of 1862 necessitated a new committee of the Board. The following year liaison with the new Highway Board became a regular necessity. The Prevention of Diseases Act and Sanitary Act of 1866 required unions to form sanitary committees, inspect all nuisances, and report to the local authority: the first 'Inspector of Nuisances' was appointed in 1873. Again, one practical consequence of the Education Act of 1870 was that certain members of the Board acted as a de-facto school attendance committee. A survey of the Board's composition in 1879 showed an overlapping of its personnel between, for example, an assessment committee of ten (including school attendance officer), a sanitary committee of the same number, and a financial committee of four.

Just how far the scope of the Board's surveillance had widened by the eve of the Local Government Act of 1894 is illustrated in the report to the Board in April 1893 by its medical officer, Dr E.E. Dalton, which went far beyond the Union's own premises in its general recommendation that ordinary dwelling houses in the village should be more frequently cleaned and limewashed and their rubble removed. Overcrowded, damp and insanitary, 'many cottages and other dwellings':

... become void, and some, in a dilapidated condition, were often re-let to the aged and other poor persons at a very low rental, which would not allow the owner to incur any expense to put them in a tenantable condition.

It was decided that there should be proper disinfecting of the catch-pits in the roadways, which often received drainage from houses, etc. Though cholera, of course, was no respecter of workhouse walls, in scope of agenda the Board had come a long way since 1837.

The Act of 1894 indeed endowed the area with a Rural District Council, whose legal responsibility for the workhouse superseded that of the Guardians. But for a few years at least thereafter any change detectable in practice can only have been slight. The new Council shared with the Guardians the same venue – the Union boardroom on Mondays fortnightly – with some overlapping of personnel. As Clerk, the above-mentioned Mr Cole simply changed his official designation. The same officials – Sanitary Officer, for example, and Inspector of Nuisances – reported to both bodies. In their first year the RDC

was already discussing jointly with the Guardians certain defects in the village's water supply, the decayed state of the Long Street drain to be replaced with a brick-barrelled arch, and the need to repair the millbank. In October 1896 both agreed to accept Mr Fox's tender for cleaning out the village pond. And so on. Only their financial accountings are kept strictly separate. A single surviving report in a local newspaper states that during the fiscal year ending April 1904 the Board of Guardians spent £1329 of which £653 was re-imbursed from 'government and other official sources' and sustained by a local rate of $5^{1}/_{4}$d. and a county rate of 5d. in the £. Auditing took place twice a year.

The new century, however, brought in the final stage of decline. By 1930 the population of the Union's catchment area had dropped by one-third from its original size to about 4400 and the Board saw no alternative to closure. As Chairman, the Revd Brandeth of Manor Farm, Buckland Newton, explained (himself a servant of both the Board and the RDC for some 30 years), no public body could be found with an interest in taking over the premises. After valuation the workhouse was offered for private sale and bought for £300 by Thomas Harvey, a retired police serjeant, who moved his numerous family into partial occupation. Part of the main building he ran for a time as a boys' remand home. During the Second World War the village school found it a convenient site for a number of extra-curricular operations, from laundry and carpentry to the provision of hot lunches. From 1961 it served for a few years as a youth hostel. A final transformation remains to be recorded. On 26 July 1989 the entire building and site was put on the market at an asking price – £300 000 – 1000 times what Serjeant Harvey had paid for it 60 years before! The purchaser was Mr Colin Bailey and a new era for the old institution began with considerable reshaping inside and out.

We conclude with a retrospect. In the light of the present day it is pleasant to reflect that in some essential ways the 150-year-old institution's original purpose has been sustained by the new and present owners of what is now Davidson House. At most times in its history the Union has been the object of attention and concern by villagers high and low. Now and then, indeed, a note of local pride has been struck and parochial tribute paid, as by the *Dorset County Chronicle* of 27 March 1902:

CERNE ABBAS. REMARKABLE LONGEVITY. Between the 10th and 19th instant, four aged people passed away at Cerne whose united ages totalled 346 years. They were John Rolls 85; Henry Rolls 83; Emma Christopher 89; and Jane Northover 89. The three first mentioned died at the workhouse – evidence alike of the sturdiness of Cerne people and the congenial and hygienic influences at the institution mentioned.

Ceremonial village processions, such as those of clubs and societies, saluted and serenaded the Union in their perambulations. The annual horticultural was one occasion, as in 1878, for members of the Digby family to entertain all the inmates to dinner in the show field, with plenty of tobacco, snuff and 'John Barleycorn'. Invariably recorded was the hospitality contrived by many friends by way of the annual Christmas and New-Year treats:

On Christmas Day 1867 the inmates of the work-house had their usual feast of roast beef and plum pudding, with a pint of beer given to each adult, and after dinner a treat of nuts and oranges as a

dessert... In the afternoon the men were allowed an unlimited indulgence with pipes and tobacco, and they thoroughly enjoyed their 'weed'. On New Year's Day, by the kind liberality of Lady Digby and the Hon. Mrs Marker, the old people and children were again remembered by being sumptuously entertained with tea and cake... The principal apartments of the workhouse had been previously decorated with evergreens for the occasion, and presented a cheerful and attractive appearance.

Today this establishment, with its slogan 'serving with love the very dependent elderly' may be said to be fulfiling, within a greatly altered contemporary context, a purpose which has never altogether been lost sight of.

MEMORIES FROM MRS IDA FOX, BACK LANE

Mrs Ida Victoria Fox (1992), who as a young Miss Martin was Assistant Matron at the Workhouse in the 1920s.

I was nursing at the Workhouse for several years and I was kept very busy. There were quite a lot of patients - upstairs and down-stairs, as well as a Tramp Ward - and I had to look after the whole place. I actually met my husband through working there. He used to come up to see some-one he knew in there and as it was my job to show visitors to the wards we got talking...

When I first went there the Matron was someone called Howell who came from Tisbury near Gillingham. Then she and her husband left and we had a temporary Master and Matron who were really retired and were quite elderly.

One night - it was very late - the front door bell rang and I went and opened the door and found a huge man standing there. He wanted a bed of course and I let him in but I don't know how he got on; I didn't give him any blankets; I was just pleased to get him out of the way and lock the door again. I wouldn't do it now though. They were very cross with me and said 'Never do that again; always call the porter'. Too dangerous you see; it could have been anyone.'

We had a little old man there who used to come down to Marsh's Farm to get milk in a huge can. One morning he started to ring the large bell out-side one of the doors and it fell on him and killed him. I was upstairs working on the wards at the time and didn't know anything about it, but the Master and Matron put him in the mortuary and arranged everything. I said 'You didn't call me' and they said 'We knew you were busy'.

One of the jobs the inmates had to do was to break stones with a hammer and if any of them broke a hammer handle he had to go out into the woods to find material for another one.

I had a deaf and dumb person to help me make beds; there were such a lot of them to make. She was very nice and I think she came from Buckland Newton. She taught me sign language and I even-tually became quite good at talking with my hands.

That workhouse was quite a landmark! It was there that I saw my first baby born. A girl came in - she was quite young but not very intelligent and she had nowhere else to go. She wasn't married of course and I had to help Matron with the delivery. The girl was making rather a lot of fuss and Matron said 'You didn't think about that when things were happening!'

The Master's room before re-development.

MEMORIES FROM MR AND MRS ELLIOTT OF TUCKING MILL

I was a schoolgirl in 1910 and tramps were still coming to the Workhouse to get accommodation, but they weren't allowed to stay more than one night; they had to move on.

We children would be walking to school in the morning at the time when the tramps were turned out. There were sometimes five or six of them but they never walked all together, only in ones or twos but mostly in ones. They always seemed to walk with their heads down, not looking to the right or left. We weren't frightened of them; they never even looked at us. Sometimes if they had acquired a copper or two by some means before they arrived at the workhouse they would hide it in the hedge and recover it again in the morning. We would go and look for it but we never ever thought of taking it; we just covered it up again.

At Christmas the Master and Matron gave a party for the inmates when many people in the village - grown-ups and children - would take part in the entertainment: I and my sisters would help by playing the piano and singing.

When we were at school we went to an old lady in the village for our lunch as it was too far to walk back to Tucking Mill and of course there were no school dinners then. She fed us well but eventually she became very frail and was put in the workhouse. We visited her there but, although they were kind to her, she wasn't very happy there as she hated losing her independence. Her name was, in fact, Mrs Old!

During the 1914-18 war they sent boys from remand homes to the old workhouse, to give them a holiday. Little devils most of them were. They were sent to work on the farm but they weren't worth it. They did terrible things, such as putting water in the petrol tanks of the tractors and draining the oil from the sump. They were always stealing and one boy actually told me that he had once stolen a car from Portsmouth, driven it to Bristol and, before the police could catch up on him, had stolen another one and driven it back to Portsmouth. One of them pricked a horse's hoof with a hay fork and the horse was lame for several days afterwards, so none of them were ever allowed to use a hay fork again. Later the workhouse was used as a Youth Hostel and those boys were much more help on the farm, though they all wanted to drive the tractors!

Before there was a village hall, the W.I. held their meetings at the old workhouse and used the kitchen for making jam and other preserves.

Right: *The South courtyard, where the bell fell on one unfortunate inmate's head.*

Left: *The copper which was used for heating water for baths.*

Then the village was sold - Mr Broadhead of UpCerne, who wanted to knock down every building within sight of his own residence, tried to buy the workhouse so that he could demolish it.

MEMORIES FROM MRS SHEILA LAKE (NÉE HARVEY)

My Grandfather, who had been a Police Sergeant, bought the Union workhouse in 1930. He had ten children so needed large premises!

I was born in 1940, when it was a Youth Hostel and Grandfather was the warden. We children all had to help. We peeled buckets and buckets of potatoes for feeding the dozens and dozens of walkers and cyclists who used the Youth Hostel and mother washed dozens and dozens of sleeping bags each day. Each boy and girl was provided with a cotton sleeping bag, a pillow and blankets and each dormitory contained 15 or 16 beds. The only lighting then was by lanterns which had to be taken up to the dormitories each night.

We also had a thriving market garden and we sold produce all around the village.

The Ancient Order of Foresters marching through the village in 1912.

The Abbey Farmhouse, once the home of Sir Thomas Freke.
It was rebuilt in the 18th century after a fire.

Chapter 7
Charity and Self-Help

Though limited in scope, and small in relation to the total resources available to its poor population, charitable enterprises in Cerne nevertheless exhibited a great variety. Some were earmarked for a specific purpose or institution, others for a general category of 'the needy'; some one-off, as well as one or two which have survived on a more permanent footing; some administered via Church authorities entrusted by statute with the control of such benefactions, others by secular trustees.

A single historical example, albeit a rare one, of wholly church-administered charity was the phenomenon of 'briefs' – royal, originally papal, mandates to collect money towards some supposedly worthy if distant causes, addressed to parson and churchwardens and duly proclaimed from the pulpit. Proceeds, usually in Cerne's case small, would be handed over at the bishop's visitation:

1686 *collected for White Chapell & Stepney*

5s.0d.

collected for ye French Protestants *8s.0d.*

Also administered by Church officers, but targeted locally, were certain types of occasional benefaction noted summarily:

Jany. 7th, 1798 *distributed late Mrs Sarah Eveleighs charity [£5 between 52 named persons, and again in 1799]*
Feb. 18. 1800 *Executrix of Mr. Saml. Davis £10 charity*

Rather more durable was the charity of Philip White, yeoman, resident at the Market House, whose will of 1810 bequeathed the interest or annual produce of £400 in government securities to the minister and churchwardens for:

... the education or tuition in reading, writing and arithmetic of as many poor boys natives and inhabitants of the parish of Cerne Abbas aforesaid.

These were chosen in the first instance by White's executor during the latter's lifetime. A similar boon,

though under secular control, was Betton's Charity from the Ironmongers' Company, which succoured the village school to the tune of £5 per annum through the 19th century.

All this of course takes no account of the tide of general compassion which in the hardest of times was ready to bring relief in a particular situation. In January 1861, for instance, a meeting was held in the Red Lion:

... to consider the best means of providing relief for the poor of the town who have suffered many privations in consequence of the weather, etc. It was unanimously determined to have a soup kitchen and provide soup at a cheap rate, and a committee was at once appointed. Above £15 was subscribed for the purpose, and the poor people now obtain good soup twice a week, at one penny per quart, being, we understand, about one-third the cost price.

The Market House, on the right c.1898, once the home of Philip White.

Top and above: *Holly Bank (once the Glove Inn) and Tucking Mill – both of which were demolished in 1964 by order of Mr Broadhead.*

Two views of UpCerne in 1892. The village was demolished in 1964.

Late in 1848 the Clothing Fund for the Industrious Poor established itself at a meeting in the school-room, and in January 1859 its 72 members voted to subscribe £36 between them to which was added £8 from other well-wishers. There was a reading of prayers and the vicar addressed them from the 45th Psalm: 'She shall be brought unto the King in raiment of needlework'. In the 1880s, indeed, a Dorset Needlework Guild flourished to provide, under the direction of Mrs Mount Batten of UpCerne, for perceived cases of need. Shading into self-help, from 1846 until nearly the end of the century, the Dorchester, Weymouth and Cerne Abbas District Association for the Improvement of the Labouring Classes met annually in the Town Hall of the county town to exhibit produce and award prizes, occasionally carried off by Cerne natives. 'Mutual improvement' societies, though short-lived, appeared locally in 1872 and 1898: but by the latter date much of the reforming spirit had been channelled into the booming Temperance Movement - 'Temperance and Thrift' - preached in the Wesleyan and Congregational chapels, and to the children in the Band of Hope.

MELLOR'S CHARITY

From the contingent and the particular we now move to the other extreme of charitable provision - Cerne's only source of regular subsidy of its poor to endure throughout more than three centuries. In 1621 the royalist Sir Robert Mellor, or Meller (1564-1624), builder of the first house at Bridehead and the manor at UpCerne, set up, with his wife Dame Margaret, a charitable trust out of the tithes and rents of his estates at Up Loders and Upton 'being desirous to dispose and impart some part of that which God hath mercifully and plenteously bestowed upon them'. (For more about Mellor see Hutchins' *History of Dorset*, 3rd. edition of 1873, under 'Little Bredy').

The yearly sum of £40 was to be distributed for the succour of the poor and needy of certain parishes in those parts of Dorset and for 'the binding forth to be apprentices' of some of their children. Half of this sum was to be shared between the parishes of Cerne Abbas and UpCerne and paid out in equal quarterly amounts at the feasts of the Nativity, the Annunciation, St John Baptist and St Michael.

UpCerne Manor in 1892.

Distribution was to be made by the ministers and 'some substantial householders' (in practice, four overseers) who would nominate deserving recipients without prejudice to any other relief they might be entitled to. Initially the scheme was to be supervised, and all documentation to be kept under lock and key, by Sir Thomas Freke of Cerne Abbas (whose family was linked to Mellor through the latter's second wife) and assistants resident within a 20-mile radius of the Abbey.

A register of disbursements was to be kept and two volumes survive – one covering Cerne Abbas from 1758, and the other UpCerne from 1877, to the present day. At the outset these disbursements were made directly in cash, but from 1762 to 1798 were diversified with the costs of apprenticeship – articles, indentures, clothing – at between £7 and £10 for each lad. For a few years, too, it appears that some doubtfully legal use was made of the Mellor fund as an educational charity, e.g.

1766 8 May to apply to use of 6 poor boys schooling for a twelve-month at Candlemas to Mr Abbott £7.14.4 and to Mr Thos. Andrews a year's house rent at same time £4.

There were similar entries made up until 1774, after which this irregularity ceased.

For the next 50 years or so the entries showed the yearly £20 paid out in quarterly sums among 50 to 70 beneficiaries, but by 1830 the distribution had become a single annual one (made in January or February), in that year made to 86 persons. Two apprentices were bound in 1830, at £5 apiece, but effectually the practice ceased after 1834 – a defeat, surely, for Sir Robert's intentions.

From 1841 his bounty took the form of loaves, coals and blankets in varying combinations. In 1867 a change of administration yielded fewer but larger doles of the two latter commodities, blankets for a while obtained from Messrs Heal or from the Alexandra Hall of Commerce in London's Soho Square, but eventually reverting to local suppliers of a declining population. By 1938 only 16 blankets were distributed; in the following year 300 cwt of coal was shared among 24 recipients, five of whom also got 7s.6d. worth of groceries. The problem of wartime and post-war distribution necessitated for some years the substitution of vouchers presentable at any shop in Cerne. From 1965, back on cash, recipients in Cerne and UpCerne were lumped together, but even so by 1969 the £20 was disbursed among only eight persons deemed truly needy.

The UpCerne ledger starting at 1877 shows distributions made at Easter, 21 recipients that year getting sums of between 2 and 25 shillings. Within ten years their number had dropped to eight and by 1898 to five, not to reach double figures again until the First World War added temporarily to the number of needy dependents. For a few post-war years the money was placed in a 5-per-cent war loan and war bonds, but by 1937 had been changed to half in cash, half in coal and groceries. Distribution problems during the Second World War necessitated full payment in cash, on a scale which favoured old-age pensioners and those with children of school age (2s.6d. per child), this persisting until 1953. The vicar's final entry in the UpCerne volume makes sad reading:

During 1964 the estate was sold by Mr Ferdinando to Mr Broadhead, who gave notice to all the employees. Mr Harry Drew, who lived in a cottage owned by Miss Batten, alone survived.

So while the new owner embarked on his programme of wholesale demolition of the village, together with the old Glove Inn and the Tucking Mill, Harry Drew alone kept the 300-year-old charity alive in those parts.

NORTH'S CHARITY

In 1943 the late Charles North of Cerne Abbas, and for 57 years its vet, left shares in Lloyd's bank whose annual interest (about £20) the vicar and Parish Council were to distribute among the poor who had resided for at least seven years in the parish of Cerne Abbas.

At first this took the form of gifts of coal, 200–400 cwt, to some dozen needy at Christmas. Post-war difficulties of distribution led to an early commutation to cash benefits which by 1969 amounted to £20 divided among eight persons. The North and Meller charities occupy opposite pages of the ledger, the recipients being by the late 1960s almost identical, and the two were formally consolidated in December of 1996.

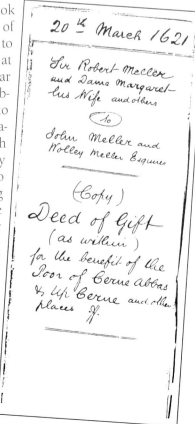

MUTUAL AID

In 1859, in the Victorian heyday, Samuel Smiles was to proclaim 'the spirit of Self-Help' (the title of his celebrated book) to be:

... the root of all genuine growth in the individual. Exhibited in the lives of many, it constitutes the true source of national vigour and strength... whatever is done for men and classes to a certain extent takes way the stimulus and necessity of doing for themselves.

True perhaps of a burgeoning industrial society, but a poor agricultural community had long found that the only sustainable form of self-help entailed some element of mutuality.

This official approval, reiterated by legislation of 1829, 1834 and 1850, and signified by the appointment of a Registrar of Friendly Societies, was grounded in the hope of thereby reducing demands on poor relief and, where local gentry and magistracy were involved, imparting some measure of stability and control. Side by side with mutual support in facing medical and funeral costs, moreover, went the ancient and convivial rituals of good fellowship - the 'Whitsun walkings' (which went around the village - see below), to cite one instance - events which were preservative of both tradition and morals.

Generally speaking, such associations developed much later down in Dorset than in the North, where social patterns had been more disturbed by the Industrial Revolution. An 1818 abstract of answers from Poor Law overseers of the United Kingdom showed Dorset with 6209 Friendly Society members, as against, for example, Lancashire's 147 029. The census of 1821 estimated that 5 per cent of Dorset's population belonged to one or other such mutual association (compared with Lancashire's 17 per cent). And thereafter Dorset's population was to increase at a markedly slower rate (from 144 499 that year to 195 537 in 1871) than the northern county's.

Of these early associations only one tangible class of Cerne relic survives. In our County Museum are a few copper and brass medallions, just over an inch in diameter, inscribed 'Cerne Society' and dated 1805 or 1817 - evidence, presumably, of some mutual traffic within a provident or friendly association; although not to be confused with John Randall's trading tokens of an earlier period, also in the Museum. Rather, it is through their Whitsun walks, chronicled in detail by the local press, that we first glimpse Cerne societies in action. In 1824, for example, the 'Old Established Club' is recorded as processing round the village, then into divine service, before adjourning to the Nag's Head - in the Barnwells' time spacious enough to accommodate 150 diners and their entertainments. On Tuesday it was the ladies' turn, with tea substituted for alcohol; on Wednesday the turn of the young men. Such locally-based societies, however, tended to dissolve and re-form, vulnerable as they were to fluctuating economic conditions. In November 1827 the Cerne Friendly Society, established in 1785, was wound up insolvent - 'another decided proof', commented the press, 'of the fallacious principles upon which benefit societies have heretofore been formed'.

Yet only three years later the same newspaper announced a resumption of the full Whitsuntide celebrations and in June 1843 devoted several columns to a newly-formed Cerne Friendly Aid Society which, 106 strong, followed the old Monday parade route before settling into 'the club room' at the Nag's Head. Its ceremonies remained intact until at least 1858.

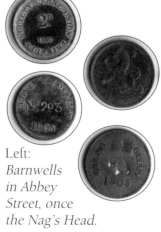

Left: *Barnwells in Abbey Street, once the Nag's Head.*

Above: *Cerne Tokens, preserved in the Dorset County Museum in Dorchester.*

THE FORESTERS

By then the organisation of mutual help had entered a new phase, and one in which the old, locally-based societies were to be superseded by branches of one or other large, nationwide 'affiliated order' of voluntary welfare. The Ancient Order of Foresters, pushing southwards into Dorset, had in a single month of 1860 established 'courts' at Blandford, Shaftesbury and Weymouth. On 24 September that year it met at the Elephant & Castle in Cerne Abbas to open the 'Court of St Augustine' (No 3432) – a compliment to the legendary well-maker.

At this juncture, the order, founded in the North in 1845, boasted a national membership well on its way towards the 200 000 mark, having spread with special rapidity among agricultural labourers to whom it offered considerable flexibility as to terms of association and scale of contributions. At the same time its aspirations were high. Whereas, it was claimed, the old local societies were:

... adapted to the labouring classes, the Forestry aims at higher objects and is especially suited to the middle classes of society, and is calculated to benefit its members both socially and morally.

Each court, for instance, was required to have its own chaplain and professionally-qualified doctor, the latter appointed at an agreed annual set fee per person after competitive local tendering.

Henceforward, until the First World War, the Foresters' 'grand gala and demonstration' provided the biggest annual spectacle, utterly possessing the little town for a day every July or August and faithfully covered by the press, from whose reports, beginning with that of 1861, we have much detail:

At an early hour in the morning the inhabitants were aroused from their slumbers by a feu de joie being fired from the tower of St Mary's church, this being followed shortly after by the ringing of merry bells by the Bellringing Guild... All the main streets were planted with rows of trees on either side... Impromptu avenues had been improvised...Triumphal arches, tastefully composed of evergreens and floral devices were erected... one displaying mottoes inviting the 'Sons of the Greenwood' to come... Another arch called upon them to 'Protect the Orphan' and 'Succour the Widow', while a third exhibited the most appropriate motto of the Order, 'Unitas, benevolentia et concordia'.

Right: *Catherine Granville's account of the Forester's Fête in 1909.*

At mid-morning a procession formed up at the Elephant & Castle consisting of 'the brethren on horseback and foot, in full plumage, bearing the properties [a pair of axes and two giant's clubs] of the Order glittering in the sunshine'; Robin Hood and his merry men, mounted and flanked by beadles and woodwards; and representatives of other Dorset courts. To the church then, where the vicar preached from Galations: 'Bear ye one another's burdens, and so fulfil the law of Christ'. From there, after several calls on the way, to a tent in a local field for a mid-afternoon dinner for a hundred or so, followed by the Chief Ranger's report on the growth of the Order, the toasts and the diversions.

These last in 1867 featured horse racing for ponies and Galloways over half-mile heats with three stakes to the amount of £10 apiece, Mr North the vet being the judge. The company then returned to the tent for an entertainment by the 'Snowdrop Niggers' from Southampton, 'the whole concluding with the well-known shaving and tooth-drawing extravaganza', and rounded off the night with dancing, climbing the greasy pole for a leg of mutton, jumping in the sacks, hurdle racing and 'the bucket race'. By 1913 – the last such ceremony to be recorded in detail – proceedings had been enlarged:

In the Scouts' races the competitors had to capture an escaped prisoner, a role that was ably filled by Mr G. Wellman, master of the workhouse. Attired in a blue skirt and coalskuttle bonnet he impersonated Mrs Pankhurst in one race, and in another he appeared as a diamond thief.

Afternoon teas were provided by Messrs Dubbin,

The Foresters proceed through the village in 1906.

confectioners, and 'Townsend's steam circus was on the ground and came in for much patronage.'

Hardly an orgiastic scene, was it really open to charges of licentiousness? The Revd T.J. Brown, gala preacher in 1870, was reassured that 'from all he could hear, a good Forester must be a good Christian... for the principles of Forestry were based upon Christianity'. Preaching at the event six years later, however, the Revd John Hosegood chose from Genesis his text 'See that ye fall not by the way' in order to dwell on the unstable condition of the drunkard. Drunkenness was 'the curse of the country' and he 'had spoken thus plainly' because employers had said they dreaded the Foresters' Fête – 'it made their men useless for days afterwards'. Yet the proceedings by 1913, the last full-blown such occasion, display a touching sense of innocence on the eve of European catastrophe and slaughter:

Fourteen little girls, daintily dressed in white and carrying baskets of flowers tastefully arranged with greenery, tripped on the field and with clock-work precision performed the pretty spectacle of plaiting the maypole... then twelve elder boys and girls, the former wearing top hats with bells strapped to their knees, and the latter gaily berib-boned and having bells at their ankles, gave a clever display of figure dancing.

They had sound reason to celebrate. Over the 50 years since its foundation St Augustine's Court had known a steady rise in prosperity and self-confidence. After only a decade it had been able to afford to help a much publicised gesture by the National Order, presenting the RNLI with two lifeboats – *The Forester* in Cardigan Bay and *The Foresters' Pride* at Hartlepool – and the means to maintain them. A few statistics may chart its local progress thereafter. By 1878 the Court boasted 140 members and over £400 in the bank; ten years later the treasurer could report over £1000 invested at 4 per cent, the interest from which had met one-third of the sick claims that year. An attempt in 1886 to open a superannuation fund failed, since not enough subscribers could afford a total of 12 shillings a week. But by the end of the century its 223 members (from an 1897 peak of 232) averaged 33 years of age, the court's sick and general fund showed a balance of nearly £1800, plus small balances in its management and subsidiary benefits fund, and the claim for funerals in the preceding twelvemonth had been £49.

THE ODDFELLOWS

Though contemporary with the Foresters, the Independent Order of Oddfellows was slower to put down roots in the agricultural South; perhaps because they were more stringent, or less flexible, in their requirements of new lodges and exercised tighter control from a fixed centre. Nevertheless, the Order claimed 31 Dorset lodges by 1875, in which year they, together with the Foresters, boasted more members nationwide – about 1.9 million – than trade unions and co-operative societies combined.

In Cerne, at the Royal Oak – recently refurbished by Devenish and destined to become the scene of many of its 'smoking concerts' – on 19 May 1892, the 'Self-Help' Lodge (No. 7108) was instituted. To its first annual dinner 28 subscribers turned up, around which number its membership was to remain for the next few years. By 1897, however, there was £65 in the kitty and its future in Cerne seemed assured. Less ostentatious than the rival order, with whom they joined annually on public occasions such as the charitable 'Hospital Sunday' perambulations, the Oddfellows have left fewer local traces – although the lodge's minute book and declaration book up to 1913, together with their illuminated certificate (*below*), have survived in private hands in the village.

Survival, indeed, at the outbreak of war, was suddenly to become the preoccupation of all local branches of both major friendly societies alike. It is easy to perceive how the arrival of the conflict could have disrupted their sociable functions, drawing away the village's younger men, some never to return, and chilling the spirit of conviviality among the remainder in a community then very nearly at its lowest ever population. It is less easy to calculate the impact upon the friendly societies' financially supportive function made by that revolution in social welfare signified by Lloyd George's great National Insurance Act of 1911.

The effect of parliamentary provision – carried further in due course by National Health Acts following the Second World War – was therefore first to supplement and eventually to supersede the supportive function of the great voluntary bodies which had previously penetrated every corner of the nation. Today their London headquarters survive, as does a Dorset outpost of the Oddfellows. But for everyday local reminders of their former significance we have only The Foresters or The Oddfellows Arms.

Thorne the carrier, c.1913.

The Police House, solidly built of stone and flint, c.1892.
The building in the centre of the picture with the children standing outside is the
village stores – still going strong and invaluable to the people of Cerne.

Chapter 8
Services and Sociability

The Age of Reform, the Age of gaslight, the Age of Victoria, as from time to time the 19th century has more or less aptly been called – is most commonly studied in relation to the rapidly industrialising large towns and cities, with a bias towards the North of England. Yet, scale for scale, the smaller townships and the villages, even if sited in predominantly rural areas to which the newly-increased wealth of England did not fully trickle down, have their own tales of 'improvement' to tell. Let us see how Cerne Abbas fared.

FIRE

After pestilence the most feared destroyer, as endemic in the thatched village as in the overcrowded town, was fire. Some notoriously disastrous conflagrations punctuate the history of Dorset, striking Dorchester in 1613, Blandford in 1731 and Wareham in 1762. The fire of Blandford was the most catastrophic for the historian, consuming as it did a large corpus of diocesan record.

In primitive living conditions anything might start an uncontrollable blaze: ignition by burning coals instead of by tinder box, abrupt clearing of a chimney by firing a gun up, nightly dependence on unwatched candles (nowadays beware the thatch fumigator and the blowlamp!). In Cerne in May 1868 Levi Clarke's lad was playing with lucifer matches and destroyed four cottages on Mr Fooks' estate at a cost of £120.

From time to time Parliament made pathetic attempts to minimise risk. Thus, leather buckets were to be kept in church aisles under the warden's eye. Parish ladders were 'not to be loaned out', and the fire engine (also probably stationed in the church) was to be 'kept in good repair' and tested four times a year. Nevertheless, a correspondent to the *Dorset County Chronicle* in June 1882 averred that Cerne's two appliances had not seen daylight for three years. One might as well have relied on traditional charms, conjurations and prayers to St Agatha, for fire-fighting techniques had not changed between the Norman Conquest and the death of Elizabeth I! Until the mid-17th century no fire engine could

From top of page: *The butcher's shop in Duck Street being re-thatched in 1984; it burnt down just two years later in 1986 after closing as a shop; a very different looking building after the repairs.*

project water (even if available) to the height necessary for fighting fires. Under legislation of 1630 the blacksmith was to use nothing but charcoal for his fire, and that only for necessary business; some felt the restriction should be extended to cover dyers, brewers and soap boilers too. Although stone-wall fire breaks were not unknown to builders (in Abbey Street, for example), attempts to isolate a blaze

One cottage still bears its old fire insurance number.

by blowing up adjacent properties simply created mayhem under which cover looting and pilfering could freely proceed. In 1828 an outbreak at the junction of Long Street and Duck Street opposite the New Inn was prevented from spreading as far as Mill Lane only because rooftop 'spotters' were diligent in wetting the thatch. Vigilance was sometimes reimbursed. An entry in parish accounts for 1708 reads: 'Paid 27 men for watching the night the fire happened £1.18s.6d; the men that laboured about the fire 14s.', and celebratory occasions like Guy Fawkes were watchfully patrolled by the constable.

Moreover, operations were often delayed until pre-payment was assured. In July 1868 it was laid down that for every use of engines outside the appropriate rating boundary the charge should be 30 shillings plus damage to the apparatus. At a Cerne Vestry meeting of September 1892 the fire captain reported that in the recent fire at Alton Pancras he had been unable to obtain the expenses of horse hiring: a servant of Mr Elworthy had indeed been sent out to telegraph for the Dorchester engine, but Dorchester had been unable or unwilling to procure the steeds. In future an order in writing would be required. All of which of course assumed water to be within reach. At a fire in October 1842, however, at the Lodge just outside the village to the east, it was not, and between 9p.m. and 11.30p.m. Mr Thomas Cockeram's residence was completely destroyed. Fire insurance being generally unobtainable before the 18th century, a victim poorer than the Cockeram family, reliant solely on briefs (see page 59) or other ex-gratia help would have been driven to destitution, desperation and perhaps suicide.

Organising the convergence of a number of engines, such as were needed to tackle the school blaze of 1911, involved no small effort of planning.

Above: *Abbey Street, probably 1892 or earlier, with the street lighting in place.*

Left: *Thatch was always in danger - cottages in Long Street were destroyed in 1932 by fire.*

STREET LIGHTING

The Lighting and Watching Act of 1833 allowed a ratepayer to convene a public meeting to adopt the Act and appoint 'inspectors' from the occupants of houses rated at £15 a year or more; inspectors were to employ watchmen, provide them with clothing, arms and ammunition, assign them to beats and pay them from the rate.

First, it was resolved to take advantage of this legislation in relation to lighting; in September 1858 'a large and influential meeting' at the New Inn appointed a committee for management. The following summer Henry Hodges affixed a notice to the doors of both church and chapel summoning a meeting in the Vestry room of St Mary's for 26 July. Of the dozen persons attending, nine were in favour of raising £40 for the project by this new rating, rather than continue to levy the annual subscription as heretofore. So a secretary, treasurer and five inspectors were elected, to whose care would be confided all needful apparatus – lamps, posts, irons, brushes, etc., and who should render their accounts and vouchers at annual meetings in July or August. Suppliers were to be selected for lamps and burners, wicks and finest French colza oil (the profit for which stood at 3d. a gallon). Provision was made for painting the metal brackets and a strongbox constructed for storage. A subsequent meeting in October raised the number of lamps to be installed to 27 (later increased again) and designated their positions (later readjusted), advertised for tenders for a lamplighter to provide his own clothings and eventually accepted a tender of 7 shillings a week. Lamps would be lit from the first week in October to the first week in April at 11.30p.m. In summer they would be taken down and stored in Mr Hellyer's malthouse. (Today, a number of the original lamp brackets survive, some of which have been photographed by the Cerne Historical Society.).

Subsequently meetings were not free from controversy, mostly over exemptions claimed by residents in outlying properties. At first these looked to be clear-cut cases: the Giant's Head Inn, the Glove Inn, the Tucking Mill – all buildings in Alton Lane above Dr Beach's at the Lodge. The two isolated cottages under the south brow of Giant Hill collectively known at Filcherton * and all beyond Pudding Knap Gate except Mr Fooks' at the farm also claimed exemption. The Police Station was to be rated at 10 shillings a year: but who was going to pay the Union rate – the Master or the Guardians? The decision was for the latter. Still some opposition remained: the 1862 meeting of ratepayers carried the sum of £35 into the coming winter; that of 1864 actually defeated a proposal of £40, and recourse was necessary to a poll of villagers, on written demand, which reinstated the expenditure by only 39 votes to 33. 'Both parties', noted the local press, 'were very diligent in canvassing and beating up votes and the contest was a sharp one... albeit carried on with good humour on both sides'.

Nevertheless, at the next Petty Sessions three malcontent men were fined 20 shillings each for breaking four lamps. Again, in 1867, there was bitter controversy when the two churchwardens refused to convene the meeting because warden Chick objected to his own cottage being rated. Not before 1868 was the new procedure accepted as a matter of course and at least one lamplighter, Billy Puff (see Jones, M.D., *Cerne Abbas*, 1952), became enshrined in local legend.

* A peculiar name for which there is no obvious derivation. Does its tone seem to imply that the site was somehow regarded as being filched from the common land? Hutchins, Dorset's great 18th-century historian, is of little help here.

Another view of Abbey Street, probably 1892 or earlier, with the street lighting in place.

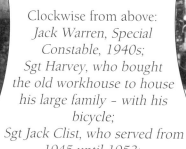

Clockwise from above:
Jack Warren, Special Constable, 1940s;
Sgt Harvey, who bought the old workhouse to house his large family – with his bicycle;
Sgt Jack Clist, who served from 1945 until 1953;
graduation to a car;
Sgt Clist outside the Police Station, c.1953.

POLICE

In the area of policing the key legislation was the County and Boroughs Act of 1856 which made obligatory, after prolonged parliamentary debate, the establishment of a police force under a chief constable in each county or recognised part of a county. Hitherto such legislation had been merely permissive and the response patchy. At one time, for example, Dorset was maintaining a separate force for each of three Petty Sessions divisions and for eight different towns. Now (1858) the new order was signified by the erection of a new county police headquarters, its title still discernible today along the frieze of its chequered façade in Long Street. It comprised cells for malefactors (shared with those from Sydling St Nicholas), a serjeant's house and a courthouse to which Petty Sessions migrated in May 1860 from the New Inn – a complex which remained occupied until its conversion to private dwellings in the 1960s. Occupation reached its height in 1895 with six constables and a serjeant. Recruits were to be aged 22 to 35, not less than 5ft 8ins in height, literate and with no more than two dependent children. They were to attend church once per Sunday.

The records of Quarter Sessions and the Dorset gaol calendar teem with a monotonous series of poachers, coney-catchers, vandalisers of fences, thievers of turnips from allotments and sometimes of horses from grazing, the drunk and disorderly, the utterers of profanity within earshot of the public way, the late tipplers, and the innkeepers open during forbidden hours. Police also checked shopkeepers' weights and measures – their only popular function.

With the increase in road traffic came new types of offence; obstruction, riding on the shafts, failure to display a vehicle's lights or owners' markings. The coming of the railways, moreover, offering a new and joyous mobility to felons, made a new type of supervision necessary. The diaries of two parish constables (P.C. 36 Hebditch and P.C. 89 Searley) survive in the County Record Office. They log not only the distances these men walked (the first safety bicycles were not issued until 1894) escorting prisoners (over 100 miles in a seven-day week) but the hours spent on watch in plain clothes at railway stations.

Not all police action proceeded formally through the courts; some off-the-cuff dealings preserved the spontaneity of an earlier age. At the monthly Cerne Abbas Petty Sessions of June 1861, for example:

Charlotte Churchill of Piddletrenthide (of a persistently obstreperous family) was charged by Isaac Andrews, the parish constable, with having assaulted him by throwing a large stone at him on the 18th of June and breaking his head. The defendant had been 'washing' at the complainant's and was on the evening in question very abusive to his wife. He interfered and endeavoured to get her away from the house, but she refused to go, and eventually the constable, having procured the assistance of another man, put the woman into a

The Dorset Constabulary in Long Street (centre, furthest from camera), a solid, flint building. The left end was the Courthouse, the centre the reception room for prisoners with three cells at the back and the upper storey a constable's flat. At the right was the serjeant's house.

Officer Thought Man Had Weapon
Cerne Police Station Scene
Given Chance to Take Work

"HE came at me in a crouch with his hand reaching into his pocket as if seeking a weapon," declared Police Sergeant Clist. of Cerne Abbas, at Dorchester County Petty Sessions on Saturday, when Charles Ellis, aged 49, of no fixed abode, was charged with being drunk and disorderly at Cerne on Good Friday night

The Sergeant said Ellis called at the police station at Cerne at 11.15 on Good Friday night, seeking accommodation. When told there was none, he became abusive and threatening, and witness had to remove him from the premises. Once outside he became disorderly and insulting. "I took him into the station, but he had no weapon on him," added the Sergeant.

COULD NOT GET LODGINGS

Ellis told the magistrates he was stranded on Friday. He had just come out of Durham Prison and came to Dorset because he had a job to come to at Swanage He was a bricklayer—had been for 20 years—and his employer-to-be knew he had been in prison. He spent Thursday night at the Home of St. Francis and came into Dorchester on Friday with a note from the Home to the Roman Catholic priest in Dorchester. "The priest could do nothing for me, but gave me 2s." went on Ellis. "He said there were plenty of people in Dorchester who could not get homes or lodgings I thought the only thing I could do was try to get back to the Home of St. Francis. as my job does not start until next Wednesday.

"A gentleman gave me a lift and treated me to a nice few drinks. I had about eight pints and, not being used to it, it took effect on me. I went to the police station for safety and to get a night's lodgings.

wheelbarrow, and with this conveyance wheeled her to the policeman's house. The policeman not being home, they wheeled her home and liberated her. It was then she threw the stone that struck the complainant. In reply to the magistrates he stated that the distance the woman was wheeled was upwards of a mile. The bench fined the defendant 1 shilling and reprimanded the constable for his treatment of the woman.

The constable was fortunate. Another night of that same year P.C. Hann was found at 9.30p.m. dancing at the Nag's Head (now 'Barnwells', see page 64) while on duty. He was degraded to constable 3rd class and transferred to Winterbourne Whitechurch at his own expense. Under the new discipline there were to be no more cases of inebriated policemen being handcuffed by revellers while they slept.

THE MILITIA

Between the Jacobite Rebellion of 1745 and Waterloo, localised defence of the realm was entrusted to amateur, though not voluntary, forces. An Act of 1757 required every constable to draw up a list of able-bodied men in his parish or township between the ages of 18 and 50 (later 45) from which men drawn by ballot were to serve in the militia or pay for substitutes. This was sent to the Lord Lieutenant of the county, who supervised the ballot. Certain categories were excepted and an Act of 1902 clarified the terms 'poor' and 'infirm'. If men in the latter classifications were mustered, their wives and children would have to be provided for out of the Poor Rate.

For the common abuse to which this system was vulnerable, we need only recall Falstaff's 'pricking' of Mouldy, Wart, Shadow and Bullcalf (Shakespeare, *Henry IV, II*). Though these militias were never to see active service, the sensation of public alarm prevailing at times, especially along the south coast, is well (if humorously) conveyed by John Whiting's play, *A Penny for a Song*. Moreover, the surviving muster lists are sometimes useful to the historian as revealing local distribution of surnames and occupations.

Between 1796 and 1799, years of the greatest expected peril from Napoleon, two such muster lists survive for Cerne Abbas, showing names, occupations, families and heights ('sizes') for an annual average of between 70-80 men. Only a few of those compiled by the 'Tithyngman' are described as 'labourer' or 'servant' and fewer still as 'yeoman', most being artisans, craftsmen or professionals. Where exemption is granted, it is usually for men having served previously or elsewhere ('seaman', 'yeoman cavalry'); only rarely is infirmity recognised ('stiff knee', 'hard of hearing'). There is but one case of 'serving by substitute': doubtless few could afford one.

Road traffic in Cerne, 1870.
The ditch on the left and the stony road surface would have needed constant attention.

TRANSPORT AND COMMUNICATIONS

By the early-18th century road traffic had so greatly increased that parishes could no longer cope with the old statutory responsibility of maintaining their own highways. By the mid 1700s most through routes in England – though not yet in parts of the West Country – had, in response to local petitions, been brought by private Acts of Parliament under the control of turnpike trusts, empowered to levy tolls for the upkeep and improvement of specifically defined stretches of highway demarcated by toll gates. The trustees in turn customarily auctioned out this function each year to undertakers who hoped to make a profit. After a slow start it is estimated that by 1820 some 27 000 miles of major British roads (local roads remained the parishes' responsibility), were controlled by over 1000 trusts, most set up by private Acts of Parliament upon petition of local land-owners or tradesmen.

The earliest surviving records of a development of this kind in the Cerne Abbas area would appear to be an indenture dated 18 December 1778 for 'amending, turning, altering and keeping in repair' a stretch of road from Sydling St Nicholas, made between the trustees and one John Bragge and his descendants for

21 years (the normal period for which such statutory powers were granted or re-granted); for the tolls Bragge paid £100.

The first such Act of Parliament relating to this district was a statute of 1824, prescribing the route to be turnpiked – from a junction in Charminster colloquially known as Sodom to a point just south of Sherborne, via Godmanstone, Nether Cerne, Pudding Knap and Blackwater to the New Inn, then up through Duck Street to Minterne, Lyons Gate, Totnell Corner and Burton Elm. To help them fulfil their duties of 'amending, widening, improving, maintaining and keeping in repair', the trustees were given the standard powers to erect as many toll gates, toll bars or weighing machines (each with its lamp) as they thought necessary, to apply (with certain exceptions) tolls or tariffs on vehicles and beasts, and to fence, ditch, drain and make bridges, water courses, etc. Tolls were leased locally at Pudding Knap and Dogbury Gate and sold at first for about £200 and £160 respectively. Along roughly the course of the future A352, and 'formed under the superintendence of Mr McAdam', the opening of the new and improved route was celebrated with great réclame on 12 May 1827, as an eyewitness reported:

Acreman Street in 1892. Here the thatch is in good condition, but early in the 1900s Cerne declined. Cob cottages, including the group in the centre of this picture, crumbled in the 1930s. Those on the right, complete with their pump, are long gone.

Acreman Street in 1892. These cottages have now also gone.

Right: *An extract from the diary of the school teacher, Catherine Granville, in which she relates her experience of the roads to 'Dorchester' on a sunny Thursday in 1909.*

Thursday a beautiful bright warm day though breezy. We (Miss Clarke, Miss H & myself) started for Dorchester by Thorne the carrier as the church clock struck 10. Two passengers were already inside & by the end of the journey we numbered 10. I have heard of 24 finding accommodation but how I can't imagine. We passed through a part of Dorchester but I only saw one building of notice – an ancient Grammar School. The three of us then took train at 1.0; (the carrier's cart took 1½ hrs.) M. left us at Poole & I left Miss H to continue her journey to London at Bournemouth. The wind had gone down by now but rose again as the afternoon advanced & with it clouds of dust. My next change was Southampton West and here one of my old College chums,

Last Wednesday afternoon the sound of the bugle horn announced the near approach of the long and well established Duke of Wellington Bath coach, newly fitted up and the horses richly caparisoned, being the first time of travelling this new line of road, so highly approved and preferred to the old one, not only for its ease in passing it, but for its rural scenery and more general accommodation. It being the day of our Justices' meeting the town was crowded and an immense concourse of spectators greeted the arrival of the coach with loud cheers. The attendant guard, in royal attire, performed the national air of 'God save the King' on the key bugle in admirable style. On this occasion the bells rang a merry peal for several hours, and in the evening the ringers were plentifully regaled with strong beer.

The night's stabling, it seems, was just above Buckland Newton, at Revel's Inn, whose proprietor Mr Toms was credited with organising the occasion.

Over the new road came the new mail service – the first daily penny post between Dorchester and Cerne and, intermediately, the messenger leaving the county town at 10a.m., arriving in Cerne at 12.30p.m., and one hour later returning hence in time to catch the east-bound London mail in Dorchester. The new service being dependent on the revenue it could attract, locals were urged 'to second the efforts of the Post Office Department by not conveying their letters, &c., otherwise than through the Receiving Houses which are regularly established at the above places' – an early version of 'Use It or Lose It'.

The first 'receiver' in Cerne was Robert Bennett, succeeded in 1859 by William H. Davis (by then entitled Sub-Postmaster), then in turn by his wife and in 1867 by Robert Childs, cabinet maker. Could it be a descendant of the last, that R.B. Childs who, Postmaster here in the 1890s, was honoured by the Postmaster General with a good conduct stripe and 1 shilling a week extra pay? By then a simultaneous two-way transit of mail had been in operation for some years. Telegraphic communication with Dorchester and Maiden Newton had been opened in 1871. Mail carriers under contract included Thomas Devenish in the 1880s, Stephen Adams in the 1890s and 1900s and Albert Short who, alas, went bankrupt in 1915.

In that decade too the Red Rover, described as a light, four-inside post coach, provided a direct service to Bristol 'avoiding the long and tedious route through Bath', passing Cerne Abbas at about 10a.m. on Tuesdays, Thursdays and Saturdays and returning on intermediate weekdays to Weymouth in time to meet 'His Majesty's Steam Packets to the Islands of Guernsey and Jersey'. Mid-19th century directories mention also 'Dodimead's vans' traversing the same route, and the road-wagon of Richard Baulch of Clifton, common carrier for Gloucestershire, Somerset and Dorset.

From 1858, however, coach services disappeared from the county directory (with a few exceptions, such as Messrs Seager & Crabb's service, which continued into the 1920s). With the coming of the railways, tolls dwindled and turnpike trusts were dissolved as unprofitable. Long-distance carriage was transferred to rail and short-haul carting remained with the carriers. Cerne turnpikes were wound up in 1874, and we are told that the last of the old post-boys, Robert Hides, retired to become Boots at the New Inn. In 1888 responsibility for all main roads passed to the newly-created county councils.

WHAT IF?

Above and right: *What might have been; Back Lane as it is and with the proposed railway line superimposed.*

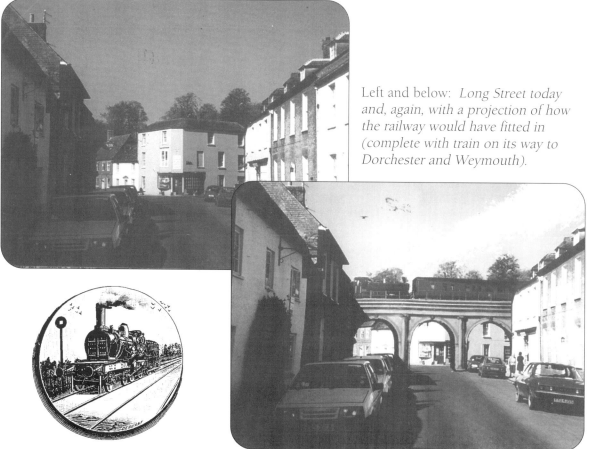

Left and below: *Long Street today and, again, with a projection of how the railway would have fitted in (complete with train on its way to Dorchester and Weymouth).*

WHEN THE RAILWAY NEARLY CAME TO CERNE ABBAS
by Gordon Bartlet

The decline of Cerne Abbas in size and importance during the latter part of the 19th century has sometimes been attributed to the absence of a rail link. A railway was, in fact, proposed down the Cerne Valley in the 1830s from the Great Western Railway near Bath southwards to Weymouth. At this time the national rail network was just beginning to take shape, in fact the Great Western itself was still under construction and not opened in full until 1841. The Cerne Valley line was, then, a relatively early proposal at the dawn of the railway age. But why was it not built?

Having no significant industry, nor a city within easy reach providing a market for agricultural products, there was little incentive for West Dorset to feature in the earlier canal age. The Somerset Coal Canal, which comes into the story later on, served the area further north. In 1793 there was an ambitious proposal entitled 'The Dorset and Somerset Canal' to link the Bristol Channel with Poole Harbour. Alternative routes were investigated; an eastern one through the Stour Valley via Sturminster Newton and Blandford, and a western one through the Piddle Valley. A further variation on the western route would have taken the canal down the Cerne Valley to Dorchester, entering Poole Harbour at Wareham.

A meeting was held in the New Inn, Cerne Abbas, on 5 February 1793 to promote either the Piddle or Cerne Valley routes, but eventually the eastern Stour Valley route was chosen. Initial work involved a branch serving the southern part of the Somerset coalfield. Much effort was put into a novel but technically flawed boat lift as an alternative to a flight of locks. The project foundered and the money ran out before any work could be started on the main north–south canal.

Would a railway be more successful? The line in question was called the Bath and Weymouth Great Western Union Railway. An announcement appeared in the *Dorset County Chronicle* in February 1836 with a glowing prospectus claiming a net revenue more than 10 per cent of the estimated capital cost. A closer inspection reveals this prospectus as having been seriously flawed. Around 30 per cent of the annual income (£45 000) was predicted from passenger receipts. This would require around 150 passengers per day over the full length of 100 miles (including two branches) at the proposed fare of 2d. per mile. Compare this with the single stage-coach, the Red Rover, plying between Weymouth and Bath, passing through Cerne Abbas and calling at the New Inn. This carried no more than 15 passengers.

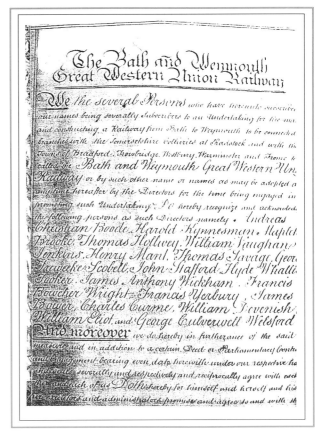

Initial page of the document incorporating the Bath and Weymouth Great Western Union Railway.

It ran on Tuesdays, Thursdays and Saturdays, returning on the intervening weekdays with Sunday spent on maintenance and a well-earned rest for the horses. The prospectus extolled all manner of unlikely journeys that would be made possible by the new railway, including a convenient route from the south of Ireland to the Channel Islands! Such predicted benefits hardly give grounds for a tenfold increase in passengers.

Projected freight income looked equally optimistic. Some 180 000 tonnes of coal per annum was anticipated from the Somerset collieries for shipment to London, with an additional 60 000 tonnes destined for Bath. The Bath traffic, involving only a short distance, generally went by road. The Somerset Coal Canal already handled quite efficiently the coal destined for London, but only to the tune of 120 000 tonnes. Did the promoters really expect to capture all this traffic, plus a 50 per cent increase?

Furthermore, an estimated capital cost of £1m, averaging around £10 000 per mile, looks suspiciously small, even for a line of mainly single track. The double track Liverpool and Manchester Railway, opened in 1830, was estimated at £13 000 per mile, but actually cost £26 500. The Great Western itself (also double track) had been estimated the year before at £17 000 per mile, but finished up at more than £50 000. To justify this discrepancy it was

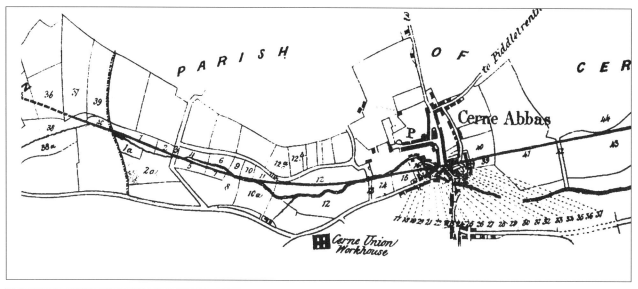

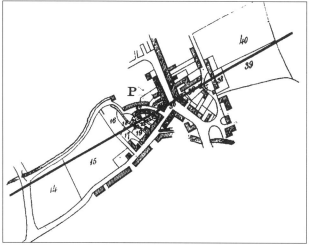

Above and left: The route of the proposed railway through Cerne Abbas and a detail of the same. Numbers refer to sections of land to be affected by the scheme.

Extremely vocal opposition came from the major land-owners who called a public meeting in the White Hart at Bath on 2 February 1837. Colonel Houlton was in the chair. As landowners they were at one in expressing their 'most unqualified disapprobation' of the project 'as involving a needless, wanton and uncalled-for invasion of private property not in the remotest necessary for any commercial purpose', and offering them 'no prospect of any return for their money'.

What exactly was being proposed to cause such consternation? We may learn details from the documents prepared for the Act of Parliament necessary to secure a variety of powers, in particular the compulsory purchase of land. These documents record the names of directors and prospective shareholders. A detailed plan shows the route and a longitudinal section shows earthworks and gradients. Architectural drawings show almost all of the bridges.

Directors included such Weymouth worthies as William Devenish and Charles Curme and, despite the previous failure of the Dorset and Somerset Canal, there was no shortage of investors - in fact the issue was over subscribed. Out of the 10 000 shares of £100 each being offered it was announced on 5 May 1836 that 18 244 had been applied for - 1836 was a boom year for the economy and railways were much in vogue. Most of the money came from Bath, with some investors seemingly falling over themselves to apply. Mr George Northmore, a saddler, applied for 60. Mr Walter Beames, tea dealer, applied for 65, whereupon Mr Northmore topped this with a further application for 70! There were four modest investors from Cerne Abbas. Mr William Roberts, innkeeper, applied for two shares, and Charlotte

claimed that the country between Bath and Weymouth was 'exceeding favourable for a railway'. This statement was manifestly untrue. It neglected the need for several tunnels (one a mile long just north of Cerne Abbas) and the steep descent into Weymouth which would have taxed the locomotives and particularly the rudimentary brakes of the period.

With annual running costs arbitrarily estimated at one third of the revenue, the whole financial basis was distinctly suspect. This situation did not escape the management of the Somerset Coal Canal who clearly wished to kill off this potential competitor. In December 1836 they put a notice in the *Dorset County Chronicle* warning prospective investors that:

Under these circumstances, and in the face of the great competition that must, of necessity, arise from the Somerset Coal Canal, the Projectors of this new Scheme cannot... realise the expectations they have held out from the conveyance of Coals... and that the cost of the projected Works, and the probable amount of annual expenses, have been greatly under-rated; and... a large proportion of the anticipated profits can never be realised.

Dunning, spinster, William Clark, draper, and James Dunning, miller, applied for one share each. This contrast between the scale of investment from Bath and from Cerne Abbas emphasises the difference in wealth between the two communities.

It is clear from the route chosen and from the title itself of the proposed line that its main purpose was to link the infant Great Western Railway with the English Channel. Like the Great Western it was to be built to Brunel's broad gauge. At the northern end there were branches to Warminster and Radstock to serve the Somerset coalfield. Further south, towns such as Sherborne and Yeovil were ignored and the line was to pass some half a mile west of Dorchester.

Oddly enough there seems to have been a perverse desire to pass through the heart of any site of archeological interest. Tunnels are shown through Poundbury Hill Fort (almost at right angles to the present railway tunnel) and through Maiden Castle. Similarly, Cerne Abbas, being in the centre of a narrow valley, receives a direct hit which would have divided the village in two. After emerging from a tunnel under the hills to the north the route enters the village just west of Kettle Bridge. It runs through the present school playing fields and crosses over Long Street by a bridge, involving the demolition of some buildings along the east of Duck Street. It crosses over Back Lane by a smaller bridge just east of the present Vicarage. The plans do not show where the station would have been, but as the route lies on the opposite side of the river to the Tithe Barn, the station would not have displaced that building itself, as is sometimes claimed.

The names of land-owners, lessees and occupiers of all land affected are recorded in the 'Book of Reference'. This provides a comprehensive record of land use, ownership and occupation of land affected by the railway. It is a pity that it only covers a small strip of the village, running roughly north–south to the east of Duck Street and crossing Long Street and Back Lane.

The vast majority of land is recorded as belonging to Lord Rivers, Lord of the Manor, as might be expected. The main road down the valley was in the hands of the Cerne Abbas Turnpike Trust with the waywardens of the parish responsible for minor roads. To the north of the village above Kettle Bridge, where the land was either pasture or arable, land leasing and occupation were quite fragmented and complicated. The major lessees were Henry Hodges (Parish Clerk), James Bonring (who was the Independent minister), Simon Groves, Thomas Durdent and Thomas Coward. Henry Hodges was farming much of this himself, but Edward Bennett was farming James Bonring's and some of Thomas Coward's land; Simon Scard was farming Thomas Durdent's land; and John Fell Hart (who as a yeoman

farmer was mainly occupied with land south of the village) farmed substantial portions of Thomas Coward's land.

There was to be a level crossing at the lane leading to Kettle Bridge. Below this and between the river and Duck Street the land was leased by James Dunning and either farmed by himself or by Thomas Bragg. Towards the village itself, north of Mill Lane, the land was divided into small garden plots leased by James Sherry, John Fell Hart, Elizabeth Willshire, John Hurlston, and Adam and Thomas Beer. It seems that these plots were mainly operated as small allotments with one small plot leased by John Fell Hart having no less than six occupiers; William Young, James Beer, Philip Green, Robert Morris, Charles Gillingham (shoemaker) and William Patey. Thomas Beer himself was a carrier, with stables included within his plot. At Mill Lane we start to enter the village proper with houses to the east of Duck Street leased and occupied by Mary Thorne, William Beach and Thomas Sherry, shoemaker, with William Clark as his apprentice. There was also John Coward who ran the smithy which was on the corner south of Mill Lane (and not north of Mill Lane as at the time of writing).

West of Duck Street, towards the corner now occupied by the saddlery, were houses and shops leased by George Sherry and James Bragg and occupied by Catharine Matthews, Job Bausey and James Bragg. Catharine Matthews was the wife of John Matthews, tailor. South of Long Street in the area now occupied by the New Inn car park, was a house, a shop garden and outbuildings leased by Ann Willshire and Thomas Cockeram and occupied by Ann Willshire and Alfred Davis, surgeon – one wonders whether this arrangement was as socially interesting as might be inferred. The present New Inn garden was also leased by Elizabeth Willshire, and occupied by William Roberts, victualler!

South of Back Lane the house east of the present Vicarage was occupied by David Davis. It backed on to pasture leased by Ann Willshire and Ann Farr and occupied by John Davis and John Farr. Proceeding south, to the limit of the parish, land ownership was much more simple, being pasture and an osier bed leased and farmed by John Fell Hart.

Credit must go to the railway surveyors who were forced to work to an extremely tight timescale. Accuracy was essential, as significant errors in ownership and occupation could lead to schemes being rejected on a technicality. The surveyors must have had a hard time unpicking details of the small garden plots within the village.

Parliament required batches of proposals to be submitted by 30 November each year so that rival and conflicting schemes could be evaluated. Preference would then be given to those which appeared to be the most soundly based and beneficial to the community at large. Entry to agricultural land was only feasible after the harvest, which gave precious little time for all field work to be completed and translated in the drawing office into multiple copies before this strict deadline expired.

Although this 30 November 1836 deadline was met, the national optimism of 1836 was not carried forward into 1837. King William IV died, a general election was to be held, and there was a sudden financial slump. In this unfavourable climate, and faced with the strength of opposition from the land-owners and the Somerset Coal Canal, the promoters must have had a bad attack of cold feet and the Bill was withdrawn from Parliament. The investors would have lost their deposit, amounting to £2.10s. per share, representing the survey costs plus solicitor's fees and other charges.

It was another eight years before a similar north–south line across West Dorset was proposed, and this, the Wilts, Somerset and Weymouth Railway (the present Dorchester West-Yeovil Pen Mill line), took a more westerly route down the Frome Valley avoiding Cerne Abbas. Timing was unfortunate as the euphoria of the railway mania of the 1840s collapsed before it could be completed. It was not until 1857 that trains from Bath reached Dorchester and joined up with the existing line from Southampton to run into Weymouth.

What was the overall effect of the transport revolution brought about by the railways? As well as providing cheaper and faster transportation, the early railways supplied a catalyst for a whole variety of improvements to the well-being of the communities served. Individual wealth was enhanced by the ability of village labourers and tradesmen to obtain employment in nearby towns. This released the stranglehold exercised on local wages by the country land-owners. Journeys formerly involving an overnight stay in lodgings of dubious character were now feasible within a single day. Annual holidays could be enjoyed by an increasing number of people. Trade representatives could travel the country with samples of their wares. Diet was improved by the swift transport of perishable food. Local income was enhanced by a railway's sizeable contribution to the rates. Official communications were transformed by government telegraph lines laid alongside the tracks and troops could be sent rapidly to areas of civil unrest. Last, but certainly not least, postal services were revolutionised, with the penny post only becoming feasible when mail could be conveyed swiftly by a national rail network.

It is difficult to assess the effect that factors such as these would have had on Cerne Abbas. Clearly the community would not have enjoyed to the full the benefits outlined above. Specifically, the New Inn

lost its coaching trade and the village's prosperity must have suffered. Some lessons may be learnt if population figures are compared with similar villages served by the Wilts, Somerset and Weymouth Railway. A rapid decline in Cerne's population occurred after 1850 whereas Maiden Newton, Frampton and Yetminster show a much more gradual decline. Around 1905 Maiden Newton's population actually overtook Cerne's, whereas 60 years earlier it had been less than half.

It is certain that with a railway through the centre of the village and carried over Long Street on a stone bridge, Cerne Abbas' quiet character would have been totally changed. It is fascinating to speculate. Maybe Cerne's famous beer would have found a wider market, with a major brewery established. Maybe the lime works would have continued in production and, just imagine, Giant Hill might have been quarried away! Perhaps such thoughts are a bit extreme, but things could have been so very different had the promoters of the Bath and Weymouth Great Western Union Railway had their way. Some of us think that a rural railway adds life and interest to a scene. Certainly it is a relatively environmentally-friendly form of transport which is only belatedly being appreciated. There are others, of course, who are glad that the railway age bypassed Cerne Abbas. They owe a belated vote of thanks to Colonel Houlton and the Somerset Coal Canal.

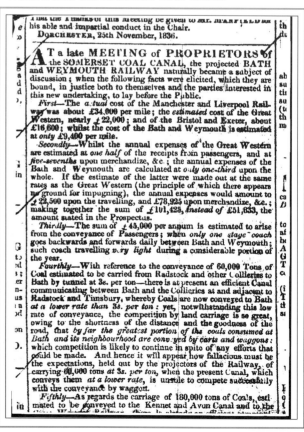

Report on the objections of the Somerset Coal Co. to the railway in the Dorset Chronicle.

THE VILLAGE CARRIER

With the departure of the long-distance coaches and the diversion of the railway elsewhere, village horizons contracted and the scope of transport again became localised. One consequence of this was the heyday of the village carrier.

Though carriers flourished, as we have noted, in earlier periods, it was in the 20th century that the service was to become concentrated in the hands of one particular family, the Thornes. In 1911 Edwin Jacob Thorne handed over the business to his son Frank to collect, convey and deliver goods between Cerne and the localities. His front room, conveniently adjoining the Red Lion, was filled with goods in a personal shopping service whereby notes handed in en route were delivered to Dorchester shops, and goods, many 'on approval', brought back. Sometime oral instructions sufficed, as from a lady wanting a new hat for a wedding ('Ask for Mrs Gould at their bottom shop – she knows the kind I like'). Occasionally pets were carried to the vet. Goods included coal, cattle cake, corn, maize, paraffin, building materials and, on market days, eggs, live poultry, rabbits and calves. For such a mixed cargo, an all-purpose vehicle, such as that illustrated below was essential.

In April 1913 the horse-drawn van was superseded by a two-tonne Albion of 16 horsepower, with a two-cylinder petrol-driven engine on solid back tyres. To take both passengers and goods, seats were arranged along each side which could be folded back.

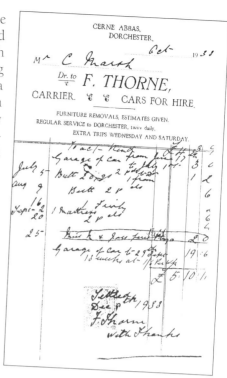

Goods were loaded through side-opening doors or a drop-down tailboard, by an additional tailboard chained to the rear, or even by a vertical ladder leading on to the roof. The result was something large enough to take an upright piano.

By 1917 a more sophisticated model was in use. Within a few years this in turn was displaced by a three-tonner with 32-horsepower, four-cylinder engine, still with solid tyres from Tilley's of Dorchester. Though a double-decker, its top deck could not be brought into use until the overhanging trees on the Cerne-Dorchester road were trimmed as they impeded progress.

Thorne's all-purpose double-decker vehicle.

Main picture: *Acreman Street, c.1910 - the 'slums of Cerne' according to the school teacher.*
Inset: *Acreman Street today. It used to curl away to the left, but the cottages on the right have now gone.*

Men digging a trench for water in Duck Street (looking north), 1938.

From horse-drawn transport before 1913...

*... to petrol. When this vehicle came into service the villagers were given a
free introductory ride around the village.*

Village outings in The Durnovarian (here 1912). The coach was hired from Charminster. When they came to a hill – a common occurrence in Dorset – the passengers had to get off and walk while the horses pulled the vehicle up. Despite this, a happy time is clearly being had by all.

The comfy car for special occasions.

*Pamela Lady Digby opening the bus shelter in the Square, a coronation memorial,
in 1953. In 2000 this is no longer a bus stop as the bus can no longer turn around here.*

Dr Dalton with Farmer Top of Piddletrenthide in 1907 - doing his rounds on a bicycle - although Catherine Granville noted that the roads were so full of ruts and stones that bicycles had to be pushed most of the time!

The village midwife (Mrs Paddick) outside her home, the Folly, 1912.
Left to right: Bill Amey with his wife Mary, sons Tom and Stan, and Nellie the dog,
Mrs Old with daughters Elsie and Annie (sisters of Tom and George),
and Mrs Paddick with her husband and Serjeant Paddick, a veteran of the Crimean War.

MEDICAL

While the 1858 Act set up a General Council of Medical Education representing various learned bodies and made it a civil offence wilfully to pretend to be a medical practitioner, in practice the circumstances of village life required the doctor, in whatever branch his formal qualification lay, to be prepared to engage illness on a broad front. What the village required above all else was capacity for improvisation and versatility. In those days, medicines, if available, reached the village only once a week, via the butcher, and were collected from the village store. At the other end of this scale of professional skill we have a few but rather startling episodes to record, including one extraordinary home visit. The local press of June 1864 records it thus:

SURGICAL OPERATIONS - On Monday a poor fellow named Kingdom... who had been for some time under treatment at the Dorchester Hospital and discharged from there incurable, had his left thigh amputated by Dr D.P. Glover, of this place assisted by Mr Good of Dorchester and three other surgeons. The same, we understand, had been pressed whilst in the hospital, to undergo the operation there, but the fact was, the poor man had a strong wish that the operation should be performed in his own home. We believe that such an operation has not been performed in Cerne for a great number of years. The man is doing well and there is at present every prospect of ultimate recovery.

The earliest private practitioner in continuous residence in Cerne of whom we have record (from 1757) was one Mr Henry Meech, 'surgeon and apothecary', who occupied, as became his status, the house with the shell porch at the south-west corner

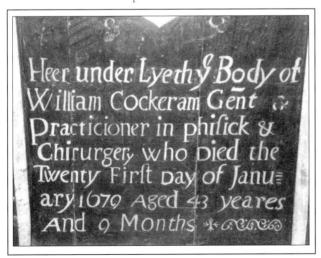

A church memorial to an early practitioner in 'phisick and chirurgery'.

Dr Dalton's bill for attending to the late Mr Wrightman, also of Piddletrenthide.

of Abbey Street. For part of his sojourn in Cerne he also served the parish of Yetminster under a contract of five guineas per year for 'physic and surgery except lying-in women and compound fractures', being followed in his profession by at least one of his descendants, for by his will of November 1784 he left to his grandson Wm. Henry Meech 'all [his] books in physick and surgery with all the utensils and instruments and other things relating to the business, drugs excluded.'

During a smallpox outbreak of 1771-2 Meech was employed by the overseers to inoculate the poor at the parish's expense; and indeed it is usually through their contractual work for the parish - school, friendly societies or Union workhouse - that the names of most of the village's medical men have come down to us. We have noted how workhouse practice was at first divided between Drs Troubridge and Fox: their successors in that capacity included Drs Dowling, McEnery and Dalton. McEnery appears as a man of some substance, a frequent traveller abroad who bought Senington House in Sherborne for his retirement. But it is for his faintly raffish personality that Dr Dalton is remembered here. Riding over from Up Sydling on horseback, he customarily (it is said) opened his home visits, while rolling a cigarette, with an enquiry as to what won the 2.30 and concluded his surgery in a cottage with cherry brandy and a cheroot. By 1909 he had superseded his bicycle with the first motor car in the village. During his 50 years of practice in Cerne Dr Dalton became not merely a well-known figure but a pillar of society through the many and varied chairmanships he occupied.

VILLAGE EVENTS

Yet a mere catalogue of administrative services such as this tells us too little, and that coldly, of a community humming with spontaneous activity. It displays at best a frame without a canvas, a structure lacking intrinsic vitality, inadequate because undetailed by the animation and rhythm characteristic of a community pursuing its regular activities. We need therefore to supplement it with some account of the life of an integrated society as expressed through its numerous voluntary associations.

Historically, the occasions which found the whole village in celebratory mood were the thrice-yearly fairs: but the present writer has been unable to find any reference to their survival or revival later than Michaelmas 1859, when one was held 'in a convenient field situated in Back Lane'. The importance of these events had been fading for the preceding half-century, and their jubilatory function was soon thereafter to be usurped by the annual Foresters' gala. These apart, the only village-wide rejoicings were those marking some national, often royal, occasion, such as celebrated at the defeat of Napoleon when on a June day in 1814:

About Four Hundred Poor Men, Women and Children of this Town were regaled with a plentiful Dinner of Beef, Plum-pudding, and other warm provisions, served up upon a range of Tables in length 255 Feet, in the centre of Abbey Street, terminated at each extremity by a triumphal Arch, decorated with Flowers and Laurels and a Hogshead of good Strong Beer. To commemorate the happy and glorious re-establishment of Peace between Great Britain and France (after thirteen years War) the whole provided by voluntary Contribution, amounting to Fifty Pounds, and conducted by the undermentioned Persons appointed as a Committee for that purpose.

Alas, this was but a mere breathing space for the allies before the Emperor made his escape from Elba. By the war's real end the wardens' funds were exhausted, and no provision could be made to celebrate Waterloo. Not until Victoria's jubilee in June 1887 was there another pretext for universal rejoicing, and that on a scale to eclipse all previous ones. Let a local press observer report it in his own ripsnorting style:

On Tuesday, with glorious 'Queen's' weather, the loyal inhabitants of Cerne Abbas celebrated the Jubilee year of the reign of Her Gracious Majesty Victoria the First. The streets of the town were profusely decorated with boughs and arches. Amongst the best of the latter must be classed

those erected by Messrs. Way, Young, Cornick, Clark, J. Derriman, and Scard.

CERNE ABBAS
JUBILEE CELEBRATION
June 21st, 1887.
GOD SAVE THE QUEEN.

Banners with loyal and patriotic legends were numerous. Those displayed by Messrs. J. Bile, Fox, Childs and Clark were excellent, while one out of the ordinary run by Mr. W. Sherry, bearing the inscription 'Hurrah!' A glorious innings, fifty years and not out', attracted some attention. Praise must be awarded to Mr. G.W. Cornick for his plucky feat in climbing the flag pole on the church tower and attaching the flag. This he successfully accomplished, after several failures by other aspirants for the honour. The demonstrations commenced with a 'Royal salute' of 21 guns, fired from the top of the tower, a splendid peal being simultaneously rung on the church bells, which were temporarily repaired for the day.

This was immediately followed by a general 'uprising' of the natives, who at once applied themselves to the pleasures of the day with a zeal worthy of the occasion. At ten o'clock a procession of the inhabitants, headed by the Cerne Brass Band and the Cerne Foresters in regalia, with the schoolchildren carrying flags, etc., marched through the main streets to the church, where a special sermon was preached by the Revd H.D. Gundry, a large number attending. A dinner consisting of bread, meat, pudding, etc., was, by the kind permission of Mr Pile, served on tables fixed in 'Beaver', fully 650 persons evidently thoroughly enjoying a 'Jubilee' meal under the refreshing shade of the trees, one old man, over 90 years old (James Scard), partaking for a second time during his life of a meal in honour of the jubilee of his sovereign. The people were seated in alphabetical order, and all those who were unable to attend were supplied at home.

Liquors of different kinds were also provided free on a liberal scale during the afternoon and evening, and we are pleased to state that there were no visible cases of drunkenness the whole day. All the arrangements for the cooking and dinner were carried out by a committee of the tradesmen of Cerne and reflected great credit on their management. After dinner there was an adjournment to another part of the field and a varied programme of sports and amusements was carried out in a very efficient manner by the Sports Committee. After dark a beacon was lit on Giant Hill, in visible conformity with many other such (they numbered eleven) throughout the region.

CERNE ABBAS W.I
invites YOU
(Men. Women & Children)

to a COFFEE MORNING
on Tuesday, 11th September
at the Village Hall - 10·30 AM

To celebrate the
75th ANNIVERSARY
of the Women's Institute

FREE Coffee
Doughnuts.
Biscuits, Raffle
(for Adults)

FREE Cold Drinks
Doughnuts.
Lucky Dip
(for Children)

PLEASE COME ONE AND ALL

Lesser occasions were marked appropriately. Upon the Prince Consort's death in 1861, trading was suspended and the whole village closed down. But the bells were rung the following year for the future Edward VII's wedding (was this the pretext for renaming the Calcraft Arms in Duck St 'The Prince of Wales'?), for the end of the Crimean and Boer Wars, and to welcome home returning veterans. In between there had been public rejoicings for Her Majesty's coronation and for the end of the Crimean War; subsequently for King Edward's coronation and marriage (whist drive and dance in the Scout Hall in Duck Street).

Supplementing the annual extravaganza of the big national friendly societies we must record those minor events which followed the rhythm of the circling year; skating at Minterne, the January tradesmen's dinner at the New Inn and the August harvest home in Mr Fooks' Abbey Barn, of which the local newspaper opined:

... these old-fashioned meetings between masters and their labourers ought not to be departed from – they show a healthy feeling and are looked forward to with much pleasure by all well-meaning dependents and employees.

For one half of the populace a Women's Institute branch was opened and was to avail for 75 years. At its inaugural meeting on 8 August 1918, on the Vicarage lawn, the guest of honour was the distinguished daughter of Col John Mount Batten of UpCerne Manor, a lady who after the late World War had been awarded the MM for directing a convoy, herself driving an ambulance under enemy fire to ensure the prompt removal of wounded into hospital.

Of popular outdoor associations the most continuous was the cricket club, 'newly established' in the summer of 1864. Matches were played on the level top of Black Hill, denuded of its former ash grove, to which was transported the necessary apparatus in the saddle bags of Blackbird, the donkey whose normal task was to carry casks of water up to the Totcombe community there. Scoreboards were always reproduced in detail by the local press. Less securely established, surprisingly, was football, the 'Cerne Giants' being mooted in December 1887 but initially disappointing their promoters by an unenthusiastic first meeting. 'If this fairly indicates', read a report, 'the interest taken, a club that shall do anything like honour to the town looms very faintly in the dim vistas of a distant future'. Eloquence indeed! However, a reduction in the entrance fee and a new name, 'Cerne Rangers', seem to have done the trick.

A ladies' badminton club was formed in 1888. Then in 1902, when Joseph Mears, a quoits enthusiast, took over the New Inn, a quoits bed was laid down and matches regularly played against visiting clubs. In 1910 the brewsters' licensing meeting of Petty Sessions noted that a shed was in the course of being erected in the Red Lion's ground without their consent. In 1928 this was solidified into bricks and concrete to form the present and very popular skittle alley.

Of gentler indoor pursuits the nature, scale and variety were necessarily determined by the size and type of accommodation available before the present Village Hall was built by private generosity in the 1930s. One of Cerne's earliest recorded public entertainments was noted 200 years ago by the

Above and right: *Village cricket flourishing in Cerne today.*

predecessor of the *Western Gazette* and is something of a surprise as hailing:

The determination of the select party of comedians from Poole to open a theatre for a short time in Cerne [which] it is imagined will be productive of very superior amusement to that town and neighbourhood. It is said that Mr. Hughes has permitted them the use of his elegant scenes and machinery.

But where did they perform? The only venue large enough would have been the old pre-1844 National School building in Duck Street, much in demand for such other 'superior amusements' as dances, whist drives and for concerts, each item of which, down to the traditional encores, was listed and reviewed by the local press. This venue was to serve also as the first site for a cultural project when in the autumn of 1875 a small committee met and resolved to establish a Reading Room. Raising the necessary funds, it opened in December with four subscribers (the parson and three MPs) and the same number of honorary members and several gentlemen of the neighbourhood who made their aspirations plain:

Intended more especially for the young men of the village, we hope the institution will be liberally supported as it supplies a long felt want and removes the reproach from Cerne of being almost

the only place of any size lacking a competitor with the public house. The daily and weekly papers will be provided and various games and recreations permitted and encouraged.

By 1895 it was occupying its own premises with space sufficient for suppers and dances, and by 1911 was reported as 'going as strong as ever with team contests in billiards, cribbage, draughts and rifle shooting'.

All too soon it was to provide Cerne's young men with Army drilling and its young women with Red Cross work. As the relatively tranquil 19th century drew to a close, however, the arts of peace were to be assembled here in all their variety and enjoyed by a peaceable society. The occasion has been thus recorded and affords a precious glimpse of the old order from a forgotten world:

FROM THE *DORSET COUNTY CHRONICLE* 19 MAY 1898

CERNE ABBAS, MUTUAL IMPROVEMENT SOCIETY. - The concluding meeting of the session of the above society was held in the Congregational Schoolroom on Wednesday evening and proved a splendid success. The gathering took the form of a conversazione. Several small tables were placed around the room, on which were arranged curios from all parts of the world. Among them we noticed a musket with bayonet taken at the battle

Football in the 1950s.
Left to right, back: Len Dubben, Jack Puckett, Charlie Fox, Les Greeming, Tom Brown, Harold Grant, Tip Rowlands, P.C. Arkell, Bunny Nother, Bill House;
front: Brian Lofthouse, Eric Fox, Fred House, ?, Brian Moxham.

of Inkerman, pelican's head and foot, saw fish, lyre-bird's tail from Queensland, gold quartz and nuggets from Victoria, shells from the Sea of Galilee, early editions of the Bible in Latin and English, some of the first copies of the Dorset newspapers, ancient tinder box with flint and steel, a fine collection of British and Roman coins, portions of tesselated pavement dug up at Cerne Abbey, ostrich, emu and other rare birds' eggs, Indian needlework, miniature mummies from the Great Pyramid, scoria from the crater of Mount Tarawera, New Zealand, several family heirlooms with many other interesting relics. There was also a large selection of stereoscopic views of English and Continental scenery, and some good specimens of the new colour photography, and of photos taken by the X-rays. Messrs. Cornick kindly provided a model telegraph, and the two operators were kept busily engaged the whole evening in transmitting and receiving messages. Several selections of vocal and instrumental music were contributed by members of the society. At nine o'clock light refreshments were handed round, and after a vote of thanks to the President (the Rev. J.A. Balshaw) the meeting terminated.

It is tempting and easy to scoff at a period cliché like 'mutual improvement' with its faint aura of pomposity. Yet here, before the cruel 20th century engulfed it, we view a polite and industrious society, properly deferential towards both a half-understood science and an already fragile Empire. It is an irony of history that this cultural superstructure rested on an economic foundation so close to collapse. The next glimpse we have of Cerne's condition is bleak indeed. The opening of the new century, it is generally agreed, displayed the village's fortunes at their lowest. Of visitors during that first decade, the most distinguished to have left an account is probably Sir Frederick Treves, Hunterian professor of anatomy at the Royal College and abdominal surgeon to royalty. He certainly recognised a corpse when he saw one:

Sad to tell, Cerne Abbas is dying, and has already fallen into a state of hebetude... empty and decaying and strangely silent. Grass is growing in the streets; many houses have been long deserted, many have their windows boarded up, or are falling into listless ruin. Here are empty barns, gates falling off their hinges, and doorways grown up with weeds. There are quaint old shops with bow windows, but the windows are empty of everything but a faded red curtain, while over the door, in very dim paint, are traces of a name. One feels compelled to walk very quietly through the echoing streets and to talk in whispers, for fear that the sleep of Cerne should be broken.

More to the same effect was registered a little earlier by Arthur Thomson (see 'Cerne Abbas' in *Art Journal*, August 1902), a friend of Thomas Hardy, who brought to the scene his sketch book and his own brand of whimsy:

I remember my first visit to Cerne. It was on a late autumn day and all the land was telling of the coming of winter, and the air seemed full of the sentiment of farewells and of the ending of many things – of good things and disastrous things. Suddenly, without knowing at all what manner of place I was coming to, I was presented with a view of the town. The road – one deeply set in the chalk hill – took then a sudden turn, and a few minutes after I was in the main street of Cerne. Once there the spirit of the place laid its grip upon me; there was no escaping from it. Neither from the tavern, nor from anywhere in the grey streets came any sound or sight of human beings. Some sheep were feeding on the grey down that made a background to the town, but among them there was no shepherd. After a time a dog came through an entrance to a courtyard and looked at me, and went away down another courtyard and fetched another dog. Afterwards many dogs were brought; together, but none of them brought with them their owners; and when they had looked at me they mostly went home with the air of beings who had great things to attend to. I decided to escape from the somewhat enervating atmosphere of the place with as little delay as possible. Now in the days of its decline, Cerne shows its want of prosperity with equal wholeheartedness – in all Britain there can hardly be a town from which the vitality has so completely fled. There are even shop-fronts from which the names of almost forgotten tawers and parchment makers, followers of the dead industries of Cerne, have not yet been removed. When next I visited Cerne there was a suggestion of spring in the air, and far more life in the sky, and also in Cerne itself. Yet neither on that occasion, nor on the occasion of many subsequent visits to Cerne, have I ever discovered it in a festal mood, or in any moment of commercial activity, nor excited over an election, or wedding, or a birth, or a death, or in any of the paroxysms that are peculiar to any normal town.

There is certainly unanimity here: but also a puzzle. Did these witnesses visit only at weekends? For on a normal weekday they could never find themselves more than a couple of hundred yards distant from the strident sound of up to 160 schoolchildren. In their clamour and activity lay Cerne's hope for the future, and the only direction they could take out of these depths was upward.

Main picture: *The thatched house on the left of the picture is the original Beach's Academy.*
Left: *A school for young ladies was probably run in the building to the left of the picture beyond the street light.*

The present village school of banded flint and stone.
The headmaster's house is next door, but was sold off some years ago.

Chapter 9
Poor Scholars

We begin with the private sector. On 15 December 1802, the death was recorded of 'Mr John Abbot, upwards of 38 years schoolmaster at Cerne'. Since April 1790 Abbot (or Abbots), then aged 45, had enjoyed the sole tenure of his school's premises at the north corner of the junction of Mill Lane with Duck Street. This comprised '2 messuages or cottages with gardens and appurtenances', in all 20 perches but enlarged six years later by addition of a brewhouse and yard hitherto leased by Charles Davis of Cerne Mills. On Abbot's death the lease passed to his eldest child Mary and in 1807, through her kinsfolk by marriage, to William Guy of Alton Pancras, yeoman.

We next hear mention of the school in 1825 as Mr Thomas Pittman's Academy advertising for a plain cook. In December 1827 the institution was bought by William Beach, a newcomer to Cerne, who, it was noted:

... [hopes] from his experience in the instruction of youth, and a strict attention to the duties of his profession, to obtain the confidence of those persons who may be induced to place young gentlemen under his care. Their domestic comfort, morals, health and general mental improvement [to] be objects of his unceasing solicitude.

Mr Pittman, having crossed the Somerset boundary, was then advertising a 'mathematical and commercial school' for boarders only at Gully House, Horsington, near Wincanton.

In William Beach we hail one of the pillars of 19th-century Cerne, where he lived for 50 years, 30 of them as both schoolmaster and Clerk to the Board of Guardians at the Union workhouse, and for much of that time as registrar of marriages as well. At his

School teacher Catherine Granville with her sisters.

death aged 77 in 1880 it was said of him. 'Friend and adviser of the erring and unfortunate, a comforter at the bedside of the dying, few men labour so earnestly for good as he has done'.

In 1858 he moved his academy, boarding with some dayboys, to 'that commodious and healthy residence called the Lodge at the east end of the village', where in July 1864 he celebrated three decades of teaching with a fulsome advertisement for his 'classical, mathematical and commercial school', at which 'young gentlemen are trained not only for Business Pursuits, but for Situations in the several Departments of Government as well as the Legal and Medical Professions'.

If this was pride, it was followed by a swift and terrible fall. The following September Beach appeared in the Exeter Court of Bankruptcy at the suit of his Dorchester bankers. His total debts, exclusive of second creditors, were stated to be £1796.18s., his total assets £1261. Concurrently the representatives of Mrs Jane Cockeram, widow of Thomas Cockeram from whom Beach had been renting the Lodge for the previous ten years, claimed nearly £100 in dilapidations on the grounds that the premises had been 'shamefully neglected' and were now 'in a wretched state'. The commissioner allowed this and the bankers' suit, but rejected the charges that Beach had been guilty of 'rash speculation in entering on a large farming business of which he knew nothing' and of 'unjustifiable extravagance in sending his sons to college and grammar schools and giving his daughter a large marriage portion'. It was perhaps of some consolation to William that his three sons all graduated from their respective universities and followed him into the profession – Henry assisting him in Cerne, John at Bridport Grammar School and the eldest, Thomas, as headmaster (1864–90) of Wolverhampton Grammar School, a post for which, it was said, 'there were 90 candidates most of them clergymen'.

The equivalent boarding school for young ladies was conducted in Abbey Street for the 50 years from 1840 to 1890 by Sarah Elizabeth and (until about 1870) Emma Norman, sisters of Henry Norman, the last of Cerne's master tanners. A probably similar, but short-lived, enterprise was advertised in the early 1850s by the Misses Jerard and Dominy of Long Street. But such academies were only marginal to the needs of the village as a whole. A more relevant and durable system of education required the basis of a stable institution – in this case, the Church of England; and that in turn needed to be able to rely on a modicum of steady financial support from the national government.

If the Church of England did not educate the illiterate, already a young Quaker, Joseph Lancaster, was sowing the seeds of the British and Foreign School Society whose schools, such as that in Greyhound Yard, Dorchester, which Thomas Hardy was to attend from 1850 to 1853, provided instruction of the simple and literal kind congenial to independent religious sects with as little doctrinal content as possible. This new concern of the Establishment was to be taken up and amplified by the Evangelical movement which reached its peak in the 1840s.

Yet the national government's entry into the field of popular education, being by no means whole-heartedly supported by the politically influential, needed to be a cautious and indirect one. Hence the convenience of an intermediate corporation between the government and Church of England such as was provided by Dr Bell's 'National Society for Promoting the Education of the Poor in the Principles of the Established Church throughout England and Wales', incorporated in 1817. The Revd Dr Andrew Bell, of St Andrew's University, had organised in Madras an 'asylum' for the half-caste sons of the British Army in India, whereby some pupils taught others under the general supervision of a single teacher – a method wholesale and economical. Presented to the living of Swanage in 1801, Bell advocated a national scheme for 'Training up the Children of the Poor in the Principles of our Holy Religion and in Habits of Useful Industry', under the control of the parish clergy and through the medium of pupil-monitors supervised by one master in each school.

Organisation was originally upon a county, not diocesan, basis. On 2 April 1812 a meeting in Dorchester resolved that Dorset should bring in a uniform system 'according to Dr Bell's plan, as far as the same may be adapted to the local circumstances of each respective place'. A committee of local VIPs and clergy was set up, in touch with the National Society's London headquarters, which divided the county into nine local areas of which Cerne was one. Central Bell (or Madras) type schools were set up in Dorchester; in the following July for boys and in March 1813 for girls. Rules and an inspectorate were established. Dr Bell himself visited the town to admire and encourage 'these seminaries of virtue and industry'. A list of subscribers appeared and by 1815 it was claimed that 434 children were, in day or Sunday schools countywide, under Bell-type instruction. But some 3000 Dorset children were still to be gathered in.

The situation in Cerne Abbas, the population of which was then approaching 1000, was thus described by the 1819 'Digest of Parochial Returns' made to the House of Commons Select Committee inquiring into the education of the poor: 'A school supported by subscription, open on Sundays and evenings, frequented by about 100 children, one-third of whom attend the evening school'. There was also a smaller school (almost certainly behind the first Congregational chapel in Abbey Street) for dissenters.

The next glimpse we have of the village, population now 1200 plus, is from the 'Abstract of the Answers and Returns to an Educational Inquiry of Parliament' in 1833, which records:

One Infant and Daily School, united, containing 42 males and 40 females; this school was commenced in 1833 at the expense of the clergyman; the children pay 2d. per week if of one family and 1d. each if two or more. Nine Daily Schools; eight collectively containing 76 males and 92 females; the other (commenced 1828), 42 males and 6 females; these are all instructed at the expense of their parents. Two Sunday Schools, one of which, a National School, is attended by 51 males and 42 females, and has a lending Library attached; the other appertains to Independents and consists of 18 males and 37 females; both are supported by subscription.

The Lodge, once Beach's Academy.

It is likely that the first-mentioned of the above had fully amalgamated by the time that the greater part of the present village school, together with the master's house, was built early in 1844. Of this originally simple edifice no plans survive: but it is very probable that the builders were Northover and Biles and that much of the cost was met by Lord Rivers, patron of the living, who in June 1844 inspected it for the first time. A generous figure, Rivers also contributed, in site or money, to school-building efforts at Cheselbourne, Okeford Fitzpaine, Thornford, Southpaine and Burton Bradstock.

The National Society's own inquiry into Church schools, undertaken two or three years later, described Cerne (with UpCerne) as educating 144 scholars in Sunday and/or weekday school at a total estimated cost of £42.12s. per annum and noted:

... from the extreme poverty of some of the people it was found necessary to make this school free. The amount of subscriptions, £42.9s.6d., being insufficient to meet the expenses, a small annual grant of money and a grant of books is required.

Since 1811 the Society had been donating £5 p.a., school premises being 'virtually secured' to the Church thanks to Lord Rivers. But, apart from the patronage of such local notables, the founding of National schools until the 1830s was largely through the efforts of the clergy themselves. Occasionally a school benefited from a local charity, as did Cerne Abbas for much of the 19th century from Bettons' charity of the Ironmongers Company. 'School pence' was charged on a regular basis varying locally from 1d. to 6d. a week. The National Society's first building grant in Dorset went to Buckland Newton in 1816. Although by 1881 it appeared that it had aided some 270 of its schools nationwide with sums of £50 to £200, its resources were limited and any grant had to be subject to certain stringent, though reasonable, conditions. From 1863 each school was required by law to keep a log. Cerne's survives in two volumes covering the years 1867–1925.

By the time Cerne's log commences the National School had absorbed the ragged school of the Union workhouse, and in 1873 it incorporated the remnant of the British School of the nonconformists in Abbey Street (from which it bought the last nine desks for £3.10s.). Management of the school was conducted by a committee of half-a-dozen local notables with the vicar as chairman and, in dealings with the National Society, 'correspondent'. The head (until the First World War usually a man) would be a registered teacher (therefore of 35 years or older), married – his wife would be expected to play her part as, for example, teacher of needlework, resident in the adjacent master's house, and until very recently a communicant member of the Church of England. He would be aided by one or two certificated assistant teachers. The term 'supply teacher' does not appear before 1893. This set-up worked well on the whole, although there were ructions leading to resignation or dismissal in 1858, 1883 and 1941. The 57 years covered by the logs saw 18 heads come and go, with an average tenure of three years and two months. Of the six vicars of that same period, one ministered continuously for 35 years.

From 1846 provision was made for training pupil-teachers (PTs) out of government funds, and certificated teachers were paid for supervising their on-the-spot experience. Limited in number to three per certificated teacher, PTs had to be aged 13 or over, give 'criticism lessons' to the master out of school hours (7.15–8.15a.m. being a favourite period here), and teach not more than 25 hours a week while serving a four- or five-year apprenticeship during which they would sit annually graded exams. The successful ones would get an annual grant, and perhaps a Queen's scholarship, entitling them to up to three years' training at a Teachers Training College of their respective denomination. A PT could then expect to graduate to an 'Assistant Teachership' elsewhere.

Meanwhile the period of apprenticeship was one of close social supervision, as the log shows:

1876 2 May Fred Pitfield the male P.T. has done his work in a very careless manner all the week, the time of dismissal seeming to be all he cares about. On Wednesday morning just before 9 o'clock he was throwing stones at the ducks in the river opposite the school. Some of the children telling him the master would not like it, he replied that 'he didn't care, for the master had nothing to do with the ducks'.

2 June Three or four of the elder boys, headed by the male P.T. (F. Pitfield) have set the master's authority at defiance, and the consequence is the lack of discipline. The master spoke to him on Wednesday with regard to his want of energy in teaching, the only effect of which was insolent laughter and increased apathy.

Fighting in the playground on Friday morning, Pitfield was reported to the management committee and by them to his father, 'and an immediate improvement in the boy's manner was manifest'. Again:

1892 5 July The master is using every effort to get the P.T.s to work harder at their studies. Mabel Paulley's progress is satisfactory and she works conscientiously; E. House, the male P.T., appears very dull in taking hints, while Bessie Mitchell spends too much time in walking about the streets during the evenings.

With regards to teaching method, under the Bell system the central area of the classroom was to be filled by groups of children standing in open squares to receive instruction by monitors (later PTs) while the outer area was occupied by desks three deep facing outwards to the walls, where other pupils would be writing. A second set of desks formed a 'gallery' for oral instruction. It is likely, however, that this textbook plan was modified in local practice; and in a diocesan report of 1840 the inspector recommended that all pupils should face inwards. In practice, the adult teacher was more of a superintendent than anything else. Lessons of dogmatic content were instilled by relentless repetition, involving recitation in unison or rote learning of a catechetical pattern. For example:

Q. What is an epoch?
 A. A remarkable point in time.
Q. How many years was the Flood before the birth of Our Lord?
 A. 2348

As to curriculum, expectations were modest, even among certain of the higher clergy themselves. The basic subjects taught continued to be scripture (including prayer-book and catechism – though after 1870 dissenters might absent themselves from these), arithmetic, history, and, for the girls, needlework most afternoons.

Singing was also a grant-aided subject and could be pursued when it was too dark to do anything else. Geography, drawing and basic science were added later. But the government's adoption in 1861 of Robert Lowe's principle of 'payment by results' (of examination and inspection in basic subjects) militated against a variety of non-basic pursuits. For the younger children there were 'object lessons' to improve their powers of description.

Book-keeping appeared in 1885. There were talks on the electric telegraph and the steam engine. In 1892 a school library was begun and in 1899 a museum. In 1902, at the inspectors' request, physical exercise was regularly performed and a variety of dumb-bells, bar-bells and fencing sticks laid on. The year 1911 saw the first cookery class, 1919 the first nature study walks. In 1923 horticulture appeared on the syllabus and gardening tools arrived; in 1925 woodwork commenced in the chapel schoolroom. Playground and out-buildings were expanded spasmodically. Homework, introduced in 1870, had a mixed reception from parents but was persisted in.

How did children and parents respond? Bell, like Lancaster, was against compulsory schooling: draw the children with 'cords of love', he urged, not 'drag them in chains of iron'. This accorded well with the legal situation – non-compulsory attendance until 1876, and the great majority of children nationwide leaving by the age of 11. Even when, in 1893, the minimum leaving age was raised to 13, wide exemptions were made for rural areas. As late as 1919 the Cerne master reported boys working in the fields during compulsory school hours, and that 'all protests against this practice appear useless'. When the average agricultural worker's wage was only 6 or 8 shillings a week, whole families needed to be at work and seasonably mobile from Lady Day onwards. The summer holiday was quite frankly called the harvest holiday and was sometimes prolonged into September if the weather had held up the gleaning. (Not until 1944 did the county standardise its school holiday periods, and night school always followed its own patterns.). Yet 'payment by results' required attendance for a minimum number of days in the year, perhaps 170–180, before the school could claim its capitation tax (then 6 shillings per boy and 5 shillings per girl). So a very careful record had to be kept week by week of the numbers actually present.

Besides being 'wanted in the fields' or 'having cows to manage', children proffered the commonplace excuses for non-attendance: 'did not get up in proper time', 'all family away', 'wanted a washing',

School certificates of 1904 and 1906.

'boots broken', 'mother wanted him/her', 'broken slate', or (until this item was abolished in 1891) 'lacked school pence'. Then there were the festivals - the Forester's Fête, the Temperance Fête, the Police Sports, royal occasions, Empire days, and always the school and Sunday-school outings. A not untypical entry for 13 July 1891 reports: 'nearly 50 children are absent today, some having gone with a trip to Swanage, others are employed in hay-making, the rest are unwell'. Attendance officers varied in diligence, and the conscientious master might spend his lunch hour doing the round of the missing. True, a few paragons are recorded as having attended without intermission for up to five years, encouraged perhaps by the rare prize or medal. During the 1850s 'The Dorchester, Weymouth and Cerne Association for the Improvement of the Labouring Classes' offered prizes for the best articles fashioned by labourers' children at school. On a higher level the Salisbury Diocesan Prize Scheme, administering its own syllabus in conjunction with the schools' religious teaching, examined at three different age levels and made its awards in the course of an annual public prizegiving.

More comprehensively, natural disasters dictated the numbers answering the roll:

1882 26 October   *On Tuesday the neighbourhood was visited with a thunderstorm accompanied with excessive rain. By nine in the morning the water had so accumulated in the mill pond & the hatches all being down the bank gave way & in a short time this street was a roaring flood & and the school was inundated to the depth of ten inches. Fortunately no children had arrived owing to the heavy rain, & for the rest of the week the school was too damp to have school. Fires were well kept up but with no very good result owing to the damp state of the atmosphere.*

1916 21 December   *Registers had been called once, when a messenger came to inform us that Bridge Street was being flooded, and, if the children were not sent home immediately, they would be unable to walk or wade through, so the attendances were cancelled & school dismissed.*

When children had to come on foot from as far away as Middlemarsh, the elements naturally took their toll. The school itself at times registered extreme heat or cold, and sanitation was a constant problem. And then the constant liability of epidemics - mumps, measles, scarlet fever, whooping cough, diphtheria, and something called 'the breaking out'. Typically in 1885 scarlet fever necessitated the Rural Sanitary Authority's closure of the school for over three months from early August. Six girls died of it. The children lost so much ground educationally that

the year's standard work had to be begun all over again, only for a fresh outbreak of the disease to arrive in late November. Not all of the verminous came from the Union workhouse. The first school dentist visited in 1917 and started treating 40 children, some under anaesthetic, over two or three days. As late as 1967 some 70 per cent of the pupils needed dental treatment.

As to discipline, coping with up to 160 seething scholars in a small space was not made easier by a basic conflict of attitudes. On the one hand, most parents supported on-the-spot chastisement, objecting to their children being detained during hours when their help might be needed afield or round the house. Bell's system, on the other hand, was opposed to corporal punishment, instances of which were to be entered for the management committee's scrutiny in the master's logbook. From the latter we therefore select only a 'worst case' scenario: that involving Alfred Green the butcher's son, whose misfortune –and the school's – it was to live next door:

1887 9 September   *The people of Cerne care very little for the regularity and discipline of their children at school. Mr Green, a butcher here, generally causes a row with the Master if they are corrected by corporal punishment, or tasks, & detention, &c.*

1889 10 May   *Mr Green, butcher of this place, has kept Alfred at home for a day & a half because the Master corrected him for telling tales.*

1 July   *Mr Green comes to the School and demands Alfred because he heard Miss Scard (a P.T.) quietly correcting him in the playground. I allow him to take the boy but if he repeats the operation thereby affecting our discipline, the Managers shall be informed and decide about the boy being retained in the School on the report of the Head Teacher.*

1892 7 July   *The Master told Alfred Green for the fourth time to work his sum, he still paid no attention, and on being slightly corrected used a lot of impudence before the whole School, using the words:- 'You shall not hit I'. The Master calmly told him to say 'me', when he commenced calling out other impudent words; then he was sent home accompanied by his sister who testified to his bad conduct. Time 12.10p.m. On the Master seeing the Mother, she took the part of the boy completely, to the great disgust of the lover of order and obedience.*

18 July   *Alfred Green is kept at home simply because the Master required an apology for his rudeness. The parents encourage the boy in his bad conduct.*

1894 11 May   *On Tuesday of this week, Alfred Green, the son of the butcher here, aged 14, with*

Digging for victory in the school garden, 1915. Left to right: Miss Powell, Mary Bird, Charles Cornick, Winnie Marsh, Willie Harris, George Vincent, Bert Fox, Ivy Trim, Barbara Vincent.

the consent of the Managers, was expelled from the School, owing to his long and continued bad conduct consisting of impudence to the Teachers, refusal to work at his lessons and bullying smaller children &c. The boy's parents would never submit to the present and past Master's correction of any nature, without causing a disturbance.

On the calibre of the master, supported as he was by only the minimum of adult staff, the tone of the school depended almost entirely. Over the decades some degree of fluctuation seems to have been apparent and this to be expected. At the turn of the century the master wrote:

1900 23 November It is pleasing to note the increase of kindliness and consideration of the scholars for the teachers. The old spirit of inconsideration has virtually died out. The order is also of a much higher standard & a healthy emulation is evident.

But when the First World War brought temporarily to the helm a visiting supply head he found morale locally at a very low ebb:

1916 23 June After a week's work in this school I wish to say that the work of the children

in Standards I-VI is very far below the average in every subject. The behaviour is very bad also, for in hardly any of the children does honour seem to have any consideration. All the children's exercises are done in a very slovenly manner and no order seems to have been maintained.

The children apparently stayed home on any and every pretext and a week later he resigned. Yet by the autumn of the same year the visiting diocesan inspector could report:

1916 10 November The improvement in discipline and general religious atmosphere of this School is most remarkable; the more so in that the new teacher has only been at work for about two months. It is not only that the general tone and character of the instruction is better, but that the children seemed to me for the first time to be in sympathy with their teacher and not simply kept down by fear.

The inspectors' reports vary likewise, most evidently as a result of having to wrestle hard with the impenetrable Dorset speech. Overall, head teachers' comments in the log - the keeping of which must sometimes have had a therapeutic effect - display something of a ratchet pattern. On appointment the new head typically comments on low achievement and bad order. Before he leaves he registers his impression of a general improvement in standards. Only occasionally is a deeper explanation of failure considered:

1922 30 May Dr Mackintosh conducted a medical inspection here today. He expressed the opinion that we have an extraordinary number of very dull children.

This is worthy of notice as it coincides with the expressed opinion of members of staff. There is an inertia, a failure to realise the seriousness of low attainment, and a want of desire to improve, which nothing seems to alter. This is particularly noticeable among some of the older children, several of whom are reported to have held the same attitude throughout their entire time at the school.

To the community at large the school was most visible on its celebratory occasions, chief of which was the annual 'National Schools Day', combining prize-giving with public junketing. An account of that occasion in 1868 may stand for any such, as reported in the local newspaper of 13 August:

Unfortunately the weather was unpropitious, and to a considerable extent interfered with the proceedings. The children, numbering about 140, were regaled with tea and cake in the afternoon in the schoolroom, which was tastefully decorated with evergreens, flowers, ferns, floral devices, wreaths, stars and crosses. The walls were covered with mottoes, conspicuous among which we noticed the following. 'God bless our Vicar', 'Thanks to our teachers', 'Thanks to our subscribers', 'Peace and Plenty', 'Faith, Hope Charity', beside which were some beautifully illuminated texts and a cross surrounded with graceful wreaths of ivy and flowers made for the occasion... After tea the children were formed in procession and, carrying their banners, and accompanied by the Cerne Drum & Fife Band, they marched through the town to Mr W.H. Clark's field... Here sundry games, sports and pastimes were indulged in until about 7 o'clock, when the children returned to the schoolroom and received a second supply of plum cake. The Revd. A.H. Bull then delivered a short address, and read out the names of those boys and girls (10 in number) who had passed satisfactory examinations, at the same time he distributed to them the usual diocesan school Certificates of merit. The large number comparatively of prizes won by the scholars of the Cerne schools, reflects credit not only on the recipients, but on the master and mistress whose efforts have been thus far crowned with success.

The schoolroom itself was, apart from the church, the village's only roomy venue for evening meetings, lectures, visiting speakers and performers, and general sociability. Here, too, the schoolchildren themselves were assured of regular public attention on occasions which combined entertainment with exhortation:

1884 14 April   The children gave a second concert to a good audience of Parents and Friends. The programme consisted of Dialogues, Recitations, Solo Songs, School Songs &c. and was gone through creditably... Between the parts the Master addressed the Audience dwelling on the question of Regularity and Attention to Homework. The Vicar in proposing a vote of thanks to the Master and children enforced his advice and also strongly urged the necessity for the Parents supporting the Authority of Teachers instead of listening to and making a grievance of the oft-time frivolous complaints against them.

On a November night of 1911 a disastrous fire burnt out The Prince of Wales Inn abutting the north side of the school, and with it the kindergarten section. Though reimbursed with insurance, A.E.L.F. Pitt-Rivers held his hand until the outcome was known of

School outing to Eype under the watchful eye of J.J. Strawbridge, 1930s.

Above: *Cerne school group, 1956. The headmaster is Hugh Reynolds, and the teacher Jean Congram.*
Below: *Notice for the sale of Cerne properties, 1919.*

By Direction of A. E. L. F. PITT RIVERS, Esqre.   September, 1919.

CERNE ABBAS AND MELCOMBE HORSEY
DORSET

Particulars with Plans and Conditions of Sale
of the Valuable

Residential, Agricultural, and Sporting Properties

OF
CERNE ABBAS

with the Abbey House, fine old Western Gate, numerous Residences, Shop Properties, Licensed Houses, Cottages, Farms and Small Holdings, together in extent about **3,000 acres,**

AND

THE PARISH OF MELCOMBE HORSEY

with fine old Tudor Residence, Sets of Farm Buildings, Deep Pasture, Fertile Arable and Good Woodlands, forming an ideal Residential, Agricultural, and Sporting Estate of **1,716 acres,**

TOGETHER EXTENDING TO AN AREA OF ABOUT

4,700 acres

TO BE SOLD BY AUCTION BY

MESSRS. SENIOR & GODWIN

AT
THE TOWN HALL, DORCHESTER, DORSET,
on Wednesday, September 24th, 1919,
at 1.30 o'clock precisely.

Printed Particulars, with Plans and Conditions of Sale, may be obtained of—
Solicitors :
Messrs. FARRER & CO., 66 Lincoln's Inn Fields, LONDON, W.C. 2.
Advising Land Agent :
J. M. WOOD, Esqre, West Rudham, King's Lynn, NORFOLK.

a bill then before Parliament under which 'single-school area' schools would pass to county councils at what was felt locally to be derisory levels of compensation. Until this was defeated, up to 126 children – the 'recognised accommodation' maximum – were for many months on end educated in the unpartitioned main room which had survived the fire.

By 1919, when Alexander's heir sold the Pitt-Rivers Cerne estate (*left*), a generous arrangement had been worked out whereby the school premises were deeded in trust to four named trustees. The National Society then helped with £40 towards the £360 raised mostly by local endeavour, to improve playground, heating, lighting and sanitation. But another ten years were to pass before electricity was installed; and by 1935 parents were in the mood to compile a comprehensive table of discontents. Traffic was too noisy; the earth closets were only 12 yards from the main building (no separate lavatory existed for the staff); no transport was laid on for children coming a distance; there was overcrowding, underheating and no drying facility; the single hand-basin relied on rainwater (a mains water supply not to arrive until three years later).

What should be done? Build a new school here? Transfer the youngest to Lord Digby's school at Minterne? The county authority's proposal struck at the heart of local patriotism – transfer the older students, i.e. those above the age of 11, over the hill to a central school at Buckland Newton, to be enlarged at an estimated cost of £6000. A request for £146 to be raised in the village as Cerne's contribution met with a derisory response. A round robin of objection was signed by over 80 ratepayers and, with Lord Digby's encouragement, a letter was dispatched to the President of the Board of Education.

What scotched this unpopular scheme, however, was not so much its rocketing costs, as the onset of the Second World War. Evacuees from Southampton, Bristol and London, their poor scriptural knowledge a matter of grave concern, swelled the 70 or so native children to well over 100. Hot dinners were provided at Giant's View (the old Union workhouse). The evacuees were housed. Teaching staff were temporarily increased to four and the schoolroom served for ARP (Air Raid Precautions) classes and TA (Territorial Army) training.

Out of international conflict came national plans which demanded standards – alas, unachievable locally. An attempt to improve sanitation with a septic tank was balked by Mr G.T. Green's refusal (despite a letter from the management 'appealing to his patriotism and love of children') to allow an easement over his land – an echo, could it be, of the old school/butcher feud? But this difficulty paled in comparison with the prospective cost of meeting the requirements of the 1944 Education Act.

Minterne having resisted an amalgamation proposal in 1947, that small and virtually private enterprise was closed, and its books, furniture and apparatus transferred to Duck Street without (such was the complaint) its manager's authority. The Cerne management, faced therefore with rebuilding on a site estimated at that juncture to cost £14 400, bowed to the inevitable. In February 1949 Cerne Abbas School became a C-of-E-Voluntary-controlled one under a newly-constituted Board of Management, and its senior students were detached and sent down the valley to Dorchester. For those remaining, a new school was projected in the village, so far, however, fruitlessly.

Some extension of the existing buildings has been effected and in 1952 the County Education Committee leased to Cerne Parish Council the land opposite, levelled and grassed, and at last adequately drained, as a playing field.

In its surviving form the school, with an attendance around 50, thrives, even if, from time to time, the vicissitudes of government policy towards village schools of this marginal size arouse some anxiety in its management committee.

Above and left: *The school in 2000. At the time of writing it has three classes, Year 1 and Year 2 and a junior class and Years 3 and 4. There is a small hall, a headteacher (Jean Riley) and there are four part-time teachers as well as three learning-support assistants.*

103

Dressed in their best for the school photo, 1898.

*Another photo taken soon after. Those in the front row are the children of the Burt family.
Left to right: Daisy, Florrie, George, Fred, Mabel and Lily. Lily belonged to an older group, but
Mabel would not stay put without her! Lily brought up the family after their mother died.*

Mr Upward the headmaster with Group III, 1906. The lady on the left may be Mrs Upward.

Mr and Mrs Upward with Group I, and possibly Catherine Granville, 1910.

School group, 1920. Left to right, back: Bill Hart (the postman), Charlie Loder, Bill Allot, Sid Crawley, Fred Curtis (husband of Ethel, District Nurse and midwife), Jim Belt; 3rd row: Alfie Webber, Ivor Green, Tom Amey, Bill House; 2nd row: Ella Whitemore (later Mansell), Dulcie Fox, ? Uffin, Olive Short, Bob Vines; front: Edie Tyrell, Nellie Biles, Padge Fox, Jessie Pitman, Violet White, Doris Marsh.

Things are improving. Junior Group, early 1930s. Second from the left in the second row up is Eric Fox. On the far left of the middle row is Mione Elliot, now Mrs Fox.

School football team, 1932/3.
Left to right, back: Mr Monk, Eric Fox, Roy Harvey, Ernie Moxtom, Joe Marsh;
middle: Cecil Watts, Tom Legg, Tim Billet,
front: Bill Upward, Henry Old, Normon Fox, Ivan Vincent, Ted Ingram.

Sports Day, 1932.
Left to right, back: J.J. Strawbridge, D. Philpot, G. Way, A. Yard, Miss Plane, Wally Blades,
Mrs Strawbridge, ? ?, Mr Jones;
middle: K. Fripp, E. Mabb, M. Hallett , D. Bishop, D. Fripp, C. Biles, G. King;
front: K. Dennett, R. Norris, ? Thomas, W. Way, W. Wills, C. Watts, T. Billet, E. Fox,
D. Strawbridge.

School group, 1956. The headmaster, Mr Reynolds, with teachers Jean Congram (on his right) and Miss Barthop (to his left).

The school pantomime, 1963.

Cerne C.E.V.C. First School, 1996. Left to right, back: Emily Cooper, Samantha Baxter, Elizabeth Walden, Tobey Williams-Ellis, Natalie Williams, Charles France, Adam Clarke, Edward Duke, Timothy Mortensen, Robert Swatton, Alexander Evans, Jennie Legg, Nicole Carpenter, Dean Tite;
3rd row: Natasha Garrett, Patrick Best, Alex Aldworth, Esmerelda Watts, Jemma Dunn, Leanne Garrett, Charles Mortensen, Jeremy France, William Aldworth, Garry Ross, Sam Percy, Ryan Dunn, Lucinda Swatton, Philippa Aldworth;
2nd row: Miss Goldsack, Sarah Percy, Timothy Popkin, Emily Amey, Mrs Draper, Isobel Williams-Ellis, Ryan Tundley, Emma Baxter, Brienne Fillingham-Bathie, Mrs Searle; front: Jennifer Rowland, Edward Cooper, Alexandra Williams, Sophie Copson, Joelle Gready, Rachael Hughes, Richard France. (Fern Griffiths not in photograph)

Cerne First School, 1998. Left to right, back: Rachael Kellaway, William Aldworth, Esmerelda Watts, Patrick Best, Jemma Dunn, Ryan Dunn, Emily Hobson, Jeremy France, Emma Baxter;
3rd row: Jenny Rowland, Alex Aldworth, Sophie Copson, Edward Cooper, Rachael Hughes, Tim Popkin, Brienne Fillingham-Bathie, Isobel Williams, Ellis, Richard France, Hepzibah Watts, Ben Hobson, Alix Williams, Garry Ross, Leanne Garratt;
2nd row: Jenny Draper, Dominique Brown, Leanne Elkins, William Kirby, Nikita Brown, Freddie Higgs, Kier Garratt, Lauren Downton, Carl Hornyak, Rae Pugh, Stephanie Nicholls, Jane Mockridge; front: Delia Batt, Joshua Stiles, George Peck, Dylan Morley, Thomas Brown, Bobby Miller, Carrick Fillingham-Bathie, Gemma Ross.

Above: *The Antelope, where Piddle Lane and Alton Lane enter Long Street. The brick house on the right was the home of the Northovers, and to the right of that lived Mr George Fox, the baker, whose daughter married William Chamberlain, landlord of the New Inn.*

Above: *The forge behind the Antelope, c.1880s. Carriage repairs were undertaken here as well as shoeing.*

Right: *Memorials in the church to victualling families the Farrs and the Foords.*

Chapter 10
The Inns and Taverns
of Cerne Abbas

'More famous for beer than any other place in the country' (Bishop Pococke in 1754)

In the 10th century, St Dunstan advised King Edgar that there should be no more than one tavern to each settlement; but taverns were to play a major role, not only in the community life of settlements but also in financing the realm, and in 1747 Cerne had some 18 licensees. When tea, coffee, squashes and the like were not on the market, when eau potable did not flow from a tap and water sources were often polluted, when work was largely manual and thirst-making, people drank beer, ale, mead and cider. Anything brewed was healthier and tended to supplement a poor diet.

Cerne Abbey itself was established in a place where the water and surrounding agriculture made for good brewing. There are no records for quantities here, but at Beaulieu Abbey monks had an allowance of one gallon a day. From the 12th century Cerne had markets and fairs. These would have brought in buyers and sellers largely on foot – all thirsty work – and taverns clustered around the market-place (nine within 200 yards) and lined the tracks into the village. Regulation of such an essential service offered rulers an obvious opportunity for raising revenue, and surveys of alehouses were commissioned for tax purposes. In 1577, when Dover Harbour was decaying and Queen Elizabeth I needed money for repairs, as Spain was menacing England, a tax on the 1700 alehouses in the country was deemed more profitable than reducing the number of brewers and tipplers. Records do not detail who ran the alehouses or their location, but as names persist when records are available, it is clear that families ran 'victualling' businesses for many years. Perhaps it

With the war over, Mr Fox, Mr Ryland, Mr Chubb and Mr England prop up the bar in the Royal Oak, entertained by Mr and Mrs Crocker pulling the pints.

is permissible to suggest that the Jacobs, who were taxpayers in 1523, property owners in 1617 and landlords of the New Inn in 1725, having held a licence in 1714, were all along inn-holders.

In 1596 Elizabeth I leased to the Devenish family the Shambles in the market-place with tolls and profits of the market, this being the area of the Royal Oak (built in 1540). In 1891 Lord Rivers sold the 'backsides' of the Royal Oak to a Devenish – the family were still brewers and licensees. The Symonds family held the Nag's Head for at least 50 years. Then Ann Symonds married Richard Barnwell and the Barnwells held it for 70 years.

Clues as to who was where occur in the Rolls when depositions were taken in the public houses – at the Greyhound in 1651, 1688, 1690 and 1693, 'the home of Nathaniel Ryall', and at the Nag's Head in 1690 and 1704, 'the home of John Symonds'. Then the Coombs took over at the Greyhound (they are recorded in 1711). These records not only name names but also show that the taverns were important establishments and their landlords more than simply barmen. Petty Sessions were held in licensed premises until the Court House was built in 1860.

Licensees are sometimes recorded as having had an additional occupation, but that victuallers were prosperous figures in the town is borne out by a glance at the memorials in the church and burial ground: the largest tombs bear the names of the victualling families – for example the Coombs from the Greyhound, which stood at the Sydling crossroad until it was demolished for road widening in 1960. In 1740, when the new Almshouse was to be built, it was the victuallers Thomas Farr and Thomas Coombs who assumed responsibility. William Jacob at the New Inn was a churchwarden in 1747.

Clockwise from above: The Elephant & Castle on the right and The Prince of Wales, the last visible house on the left of the road beside the school. This pub burnt down in 1911, photo 1892; The Crown, now a private house, was at the east end of the market; the Nag's Head, now Barnwells. In the 1920s it was home to Joseph Benwell Clark, artist; Once 'The Inn' but the last landlord died in 1692. Was it after that date that 'The New Inn' got its name?; The Red Lion facing the Market Square, and the Bell with its shutters down, early 1900s. One of the cottages on the right was at some time the Bull; Giant's Head on the top Sherborne–Dorchester road, now a caravan park but a long rough road for the police to traverse from Cerne a century ago; The Greyhound, which stood out into Acreman Street until it was demolished for road widening in 1966.

Commercial services included accommodation for travellers: the New Inn, the Antelope (closed and demolished early in the 1900s) and the Royal Oak all had forges providing re-shoeing for horses and some coach repairs. While the coaches ran through Cerne and agriculture and commerce depended on the horse, these services (while the humans refreshed the inner man) would have been well used, as also were the stabling and storage for goods in transit provided by the larger inns.

Once the coaches ceased to run through Cerne and the horse was displaced by the bicycle for club outings, the New Inn and the Red Lion advertised 'good accommodation for cyclists'.

But of course the basic need in the village was for drink and also for somewhere to go. Dwellings were small and the public houses had good fires and tobacco - village gardens are full of bits of clay pipe - simple games and (mainly male) companionship in the evenings. In the morning, men going to work in the fields would call at the Union Arms for their 'ploughman's' - their bread and cheese and the 'owl' of beer or cider.

Because the Inland Revenue looked to the brewers and the pubs for a large part of the Treasury's trove, rules and regulations were always applied. Beer was taxed at source and at outlet. In the 18th century a licence cost £10 with two guarantors at £5

each. Licensees frequently signed up to support each other. In 1747 the conditions of a licence read:

We, His Majesty's Justices of the Peace for the said County of Dorset... do allow and licence... to keep a common Ale house or Victualling House, and to utter and sell Bread and other victuals, Beer, Ale or other excisable Liquors, by retail in the same house wherein he dwelleth, and not elsewhere... for the space of one whole year... and no unlawful games, Drunkeness or any other disorder to be suffered in his House, yard, garden or Backside, but that good order and Rule be maintained therein.

To sell without a licence incurred a fine and if a constable knew of an individual selling without a licence and failed to report it, he in turn was fined - all very lucrative. The fines were usually put to poor relief. As a result there are innumerable reports of selling after hours; of selling at times of Divine Service and so on. The Giant's Head on the top Sherborne-Dorchester road was a particular pain to the police, who had to trail up Alton Lane to inspect, knowing full well that the tipplers would return after dark.

By 1872 the church was again protesting. At a public meeting in the school the vicar, lamenting the great evils arising from intemperance, viewed with

1. The Antelope
2. Northovers' Brewery
3. The Crown
4. The Royal Oak
5. The Red Lion
6. The Old Bell
7. The New Inn
8. The Greyhound
9. The Union Arms
10. The Prince of Wales
11. Elephant & Castle
12. The Inn
13. The George
14. The Bull

Above: *In the 1900s with Charlie Fox the landlord, and Mary Ann Bull the 'Reddle Woman'. The cob cottages beyond crumbled in the 1930s.*

Lot 58
(Coloured Yellow on the Plan).

The BEER HOUSE called

"THE UNION ARMS"

with Residence, etc., 2 COTTAGES with GARDENS and 3 PADDOCKS, ORCHARDS, etc.,

Situate in Acreman Street, with back approach through Haysend Drove.

The accommodation is :—
No. 11 :—Living Room, Parlour, Pantry, 2 Bedrooms. Tenant, Mr. J. Sprake with other Lands.
No. 13 :—Living Room, Parlour, Pantry, Wood House, 2 Bedrooms, tenant, Miss Bowring.

THE BEER HOUSE

No. 14—Kitchen, Living Room, 2 Bars, Cellar, Wood House, 3 Bedrooms, and Loft ; 2 Piggeries, Stable for 4 Tenant, Mrs. Jane Canterbury.

The Tenants claim Iron of Trap House, Partitions in House, and Fowl House.

The area, in the whole, is about **2a. 1r. 29p.**

SOLD £360

SCHEDULE OF TENANCIES.

NO. ON PLAN.	TENANT.				TENANCY.
163 pt.	Cottages, as above	..	..	..	Sept. 29th
125	Hall and Woodhouse	..	..	..	Sept. 29th
126	Miss Bowring	..	..	..	Sept. 29th
127	Mrs. J. Canterbury	..	..	..	Sept. 29th

Notice to terminate the tenancies of Nos. 126 and 127 have been served to expire September 29th, 1919, and of No. 125 at March 25th, 1920.

The Timber is to be taken at £11 5 0
The Land Tax is £1 8 3

46

Above: *The landlord and landlady of the Union Arms in the 1880s. It was sold in 1919 for £360.*

Left: *Details for the Union Arms from the sale of Cerne, 1919.*

The Glove House, which would have been the first inn encountered by travellers on their way in to Cerne from the north. It was demolished by the order of Mr Broadhead when he purchased UpCerne.

astonishment and deep regret the presence of as many as 13 public houses for his parish of 1160 souls. He said that he was not an advocate of total abstinence, but the Congregational Minister, on the other hand, Revd D. Thomas, 'avowed himself a total abstainer on principle'.

Times were very hard. Houses were still small and lacked piped water, and the coaches having ceased their regular run and the markets having become less important, the village grew less prosperous and more pubs closed. Early in the 1900s the Bell closed, then the Antelope and the Union Arms. The Prince of Wales burned down in 1911. The Nag's Head became, like the Bell and Union Arms, a private house. The last brewery closed in 1883. The Greyhound was demolished for road widening in 1960 and the Elephant & Castle ceased trading in the 1970s. Today the New Inn, the Royal Oak and the Red Lion survive but food is now the staple. When drinking was local, a man could usually walk home (some finding the white line down the centre of the road quite a help!) or if one had further to go, a horse would know the way. Now homes are bigger and the TV keeps people at their own firesides. The car at the end of the day is a liability rather than an asset, and the tax on drink goes up and up. St Dunstan may yet win the day!

LICENCES GRANTED IN 1747:

Robert Nutt	Antelope
Richard Dowding	
Elizabeth Morris	
John Sturmey	
John Cockram	
Richard Curme	
John Farr	
Stephen Farr	Bell
George Romayne	The George
Catherine Coombes	Greyhound
Thomas Trevitt	
James Peatty	
William Jacob (churchwarden)	New Inn
John Symonds	Nags Head
William Dominy	Red Lion
Robert Summers	
Jacob Coward	
William Hassell	

* Other public house names, some already mentioned, included: The Prince of Wales, the Ram's Head, The Shovel, The Calcraft Arms, The Sun, The Stocking, The Cooper's Arms, the Glove, the Bull and the Union Arms.

Right and below: *Portraits of William Samuel Chamberlain, landlord of the New Inn, 1898, and his wife Alice Annie Fox, daughter of George Fox, baker of Long Street (and grand-daughter of Thomas Fox of the Elephant & Castle).*

Right: *Notice of Petty Sessions at the New Inn.*

DORSET
SUBDIVISION OF CERNE.
PETTY SESSIONS,
For the Year 1809
WILL BE HELD
At the New Inn, in Cerne Abbas,
ON

4th of JANUARY,
1st — FEBRUARY,
1st — MARCH,
29th — Ditto,
26th — APRIL,
31st — MAY,
28th — JUNE,

WEDNESDAY

26th of JULY,
23d — AUGUST,
20th — SEPTEMBER,
11th — OCTOBER,
22d, — NOVEMBER,
20th — DECEMBER.

N. B. The Meeting for the Appointment of Overseers of the Poor, will be held on the 26th Day of APRIL.—For Authorizing and Empowering Persons to keep Common Inns, Ale Houses, or Victualling Houses, on the 20th Day of SEPTEMBER. and for Appointing Surveyors of the Highways, on the 11th Day of OCTOBER.

Magistrates Acting in the Subdivision.
SIR JOHN WYLDBORE SMITH, BART. *Sydling St. Nicholas.*
REV. CHARLES PHELIPS, *Piddletrenthide.*
FRANCIS WILLIAM SCHUYLER, Esq. *Woolland.*
REV. GEORGE SAXBY PENFOLD, *Pulham.*
THOMAS MEGGS, Esq. *Piddlehinton.*

Commissioners of the Land, Assessed, and Property Taxes, Acting in the Subdivision.

LAND AND ASSESSED TAXES.
SIR J. WYLDBORE SMITH, BART.
RICHARD BINGHAM, Esq.
THOMAS MEGGS, Esq.
REV. SAMUEL BEREW.
REV. HUMPHREY EVANS.
FRANCIS WILLIAM SCHUYLER, Esq.

PROPERTY TAX.
SIR J. WYLDBORE SMITH, BART.
REV. CHARLES PHELIPS.
REV. GEORGE SAXBY PENFOLD.
REV. HUMPHREY EVANS.
HENRY SHERREN, JUN. GENT.
RICHARD BINGHAM, Esq.
FRANCIS WILLIAM SCHUYLER, Esq.

JOHN WILTSHIRE, *Clerk, Cerne Abbas.*

ASSIZES.
Dorchester, Thursday March 9th or 16th.—Thursday July 20th.

QUARTER SESSIONS.
Blandford, Tuesday Jan. 10th. | Shaftesbury, Tuesday July 11th,
Sherborne; April 11th. | Bridport. Oct. 3d.

G. Frampton, Printer, Dorchester.

The New Inn, c.1920.

Above: *The Royal Oak, built 1540, in the Market Square.*
To the left of it is the Market House, originally the Guild Hall.

Right: *The Royal Oak in the 1930s. Included in the picture are Mr Yearsley, 'Shep' Davis and Jackie Paulley enjoying a pint, a pipe and a good coal fire.*

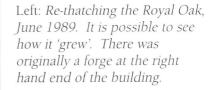

Left: *Re-thatching the Royal Oak, June 1989. It is possible to see how it 'grew'. There was originally a forge at the right hand end of the building.*

Mr Seward, bailiff of Barton Farm, with the milking team, early 1900s.

Mr Seward and Jim Old delivering faggots. Mr Sprake of Barton Farm supplied five bundles of faggots cut from Cerne Park copse to all of his employees each week. Villagers also cut furze from Black Hill for extra firewood in the early 1900s. Now it's electricity and the oil tanker!

Chapter 11
Bought and Sold:
Decline of the Land

What we can learn of the immediately post-Dissolution Cerne, we must glean from an undated suit at law, probably of the 1560s, brought by the son of one Henry Vanwylden to whom (alleged the plaintiff) had in 1540 been granted the Abbey by the Crown for 50 years. He in turn divided his interest between two sub-tenants, and from there matters proceeded through a series of lessees, each one simply concerned to raise as much money as quickly as possible from the sale of demolished Abbey materials. So things continued into the 17th century until the land reverted to the Crown in the persons of James I's heirs, as part of the Duchy of Cornwall, whose interests in West Dorset continue to this day.

Two other lawsuits of this period, concerning rights of access to the old Abbey burial ground, educed evidence from an ex-monk and a former Abbey servant as to the rapid demolition of the Abbey and the monastic premises, excepting the Abbot's gateway but including his brewery and the sale of stone, timber and lead. Later the south gate was torn down by 200 rioters protesting against further enclosures under Edward VI.

There followed for the little town many years of depression, poverty and unemployment. To the outward eye commerce continued – the Wednesday markets and thrice-yearly fairs on mid-Lent Monday, Holy Tuesday and St Matthew's Day (21 September). But that its heart and morale were lost with its raison d'être is evident from a survey of mid-1617 conducted by the well-known surveyors, the Nordens father and son:

There is within the towns an auntient and spatious towne howse called the Guildhall wherein the Courts of the Manor and libertie have bene usuallie kepte untill the howse fell into such decaye and is now in that ruynous estate as none dare to sitt in it And either it must be spedelie repayred or it will fall to the ground. [Their estimate follows]

It is to be considered that there are under this Guildhall manye shopps and places convenient for many uses twochinge the Market whether they may be proved within the general graunt of the shopps and shambles and profits of the market I know yf soe they be I take it fit that the fermer of the same shoulde repayre them at his coste receyveinge the profits of them wch is to be considered.

Among the properties described in the survey are a tenement in Cerne newly built near the Shambles in the market-place and a parcel of land in the east side of the same tenement, held by John Stickland by the grant of John Eldred and William Whitmore, 'contractors', for 50 years after the death of Julyan Alridge, and 'all the shambles or shops in the market place and the profits of the market', held by Edmund Devenish by letters patent. But the dereliction was not merely outward and physical:

To the govermt of the towne are appoynted a Constable and a Tything man under whom the towne is most unorderlie governed as uncivillie as if there were noe magistrates for the officers are weake men for they that inioye the principall howses of the towne dwell from them and let them to a manie of base people meere mendicantees

As namelie one Mr. John Notley hath a fayre house but noe competent under tenant Mr Lovelace also a fayre howse full or poore people One Mr Fowell Mr Devenis and one John Williams wch last hath a fayre howses & hath put nere a dozen lowsey people in it and yet these howse stande in the principall parte of the towne market place.

* P.R.O E36, vol. 157 ff. 113–123, reproduced in Somerset & Dorset Notes & Queries xxviii (1978) ff. 5,6, with commentary by Mr G.D. Squibb.

Nor did Cerne escape the scourge of Dorset towns in subsequent centuries: fires in 1644 and 1740 afflicted a community which, judging from the hearth-tax returns of the former date, was much of a size with Sturminster Newton or Corfe.

Main picture: *Cows wander down Long Street, 1900.*
Inset: *Colin Hallett drops off at The Stores, 2000.*

Main picture: *The Folly in the 1920s. The road needed constant patching, the ditch on the left was in need of cleaning. Mrs Paddick and Mrs Old can be seen getting their faggots.*
Inset: *The scene in 2000.*

...nd left: *Charles Hart and Billy Miller near the alternative watering place in the Folly, 1910s; Lou Fox with Rock, Prince and Flower in Abbey Street after watering at the Town Pond in the 1930s. Inset: No longer for horses, but the ducks on the Town Pond have delighted generations of Cerne people. They are now sadly diminished in numbers, but we hope they will re-establish.*

Right: *Joe Marsh starting the way he was to go on. He and his brother ran Barton Farm for many years* Above two: *Barton Farm in the 1980s, now a 'Beechcroft' housing estate. Some 3000 acres of arable land are farmed by three tractor drivers and a shepherd.*

Main picture: *Olive Dunn with her Canterbury grandparents haymaking in 1933 behind the Union Arms where the Canterburys were landlords. Olive is a professional dressmaker.*
Inset: *John Butcher haymaking in 1989 - a lonely business.*

Left: *Jim Old and George Warren harvesting rabbits as well as oats in the 1930s.*
Inset: *All those lonely acres, 1987.*
Above: *Muriel Marsh in the oats at Barton Farm, 1960s.*

Harvest Home at Tucking Mill Farm c.1910.
The farmer John Guppy and his wife Elizabeth are on the right
and their daughter Daisy is centre left in the dark dress.

By then there were hints of prospective stability. Vanwylden, first in the gallery of post-Dissolution absentee speculators, had in the 1540s bought also the manor of Little Bredy, but in 1584 sold it to Robert Freke of Iwerne Courtney. Then, in 1630, another member of the Shroton family, Sir Thomas Freke, already owning the manor of Burton Bradstock, bought the village of Cerne. Between his and the Holles family possession of manor and land alternated through much of the 17th century, before passing in the late-18th, to the Pitt-Rivers.

Under this comparative stability of ownership and control the township had flourished somewhat, its population sharing the country's general rise during the first half of the 19th century, its own numbers actually doubling to 1343 by 1851. Yet the loss of its monastery had doomed the community not only to a succession of short-term owners and governors: it exposed it also to the harsh winds of national economic forces, to the fortunes of war or peace, to surplus and scarcity, and to cycles of boom and depression, such as any mainly agricultural economy must be expected to face. We look first at the community's base in land, its produce and then its ancillary and dependant trades.

The century closed in war against Napoleon. After his defeat it was reckoned that one in every four males in England was engaged in agriculture: yet this pursuit was no longer perceived as the backbone of national prosperity save in the rhetoric of the 'landed interest'. About a quarter of the people's bread was being imported but a revival of protectionism was not politically feasible. Enclosure of common lands and waste was virtually complete, involving much dislocation of the labour force and polarisation between the enterprising tenant farmer with a little capital and the landless labourer, perhaps working less than 30 acres and hireable by day, now bereft

even of his customary rights of pasturage and fuel. In the enclosing process, as Arthur Young protested, the latter had often been grossly injured. The former, the small tenant farmer, held customarily in Dorset until after the First World War by lifehold, copied in the court rolls, i.e. on the life of the claimant and two others' lives. Admission normally involved low rent offset by numerous 'fines' (notably the heriot, a payment in kind or by cash when a new tenant took over).

Thus, on the one hand access was easy for the newcomer with ready money; on the other, failure of the tenant to renew (as in the case of Hardy's 'Nelly Sargent') left the landlord free to dispose to the highest bidder. As to wage levels, it is generally agreed that the Speenhamland system had led to a fall in the employer's contribution and correspondingly to a demoralising reliance on relief to save the worker from starvation. In the year after Waterloo, poor relief expenditure in England peaked at £8 million.

Hence the 19th-century Dorset labourer, it has been said, became a byword for poverty and degradation. A series of House of Commons special committees, from 1834 to 1895, heard first-hand witnesses testify to the depth of the depression; to which several voices added powerful individual pleas; from Arthur Young, Sir Frederick Morton Eden, Rider Haggard and Thomas Hardy himself. Government and public had no excuse for ignorance; and we here have no pretext for repeating the dismal tale.

During a brief mid-century interlude, known as the 'high farming', the picture was brightened by a combination of new factors: better fertilisers and foodstuffs, novel machinery, better irrigation, wider marketing and banking and a more systematic approach to the farmers' problems. But all too soon the decline was resumed and this time it enveloped not only the workers but the land-owners also.

RULES—Continued.

5.—No Tenant shall work on any Allotment on the Sabbath Day.

6.—No Cattle shall be tethered or fed in the Allotment field. Any Tenant so offending shall forfeit his or her Allotment.

7.—Every Tenant is required to keep the Roads and Paths opposite and belonging to his or her Allotment in good order, and the grass properly trimmed. The South Path belongs to those Allotments which run from East to West, and the West Path to those Allotments which run from North to South, and shall be kept at a uniform width of 18-ins.

8.—The Tenants shall be the Labourers or Artizans and residents in the parish. The Committee reserve the power to let Allotments to Resident Tradesmen, if there are no other applications.

9.—Each Tenant shall be supplied with a copy of the Rules, and a Card on which shall be entered the numbers and size of his or her Allotments. All payments shall be entered on the Card, and signed by a Member of the Committee.

10.—All questions and matters in dispute shall be referred to the Committee of Management whose decision shall in every case be binding and conclusive on all points. All previous Rules rescinded from this date.

Dated

H. DOMINY, Chairman.
A. BILLETT, Clerk.

ING. PRINTER, DORCHESTER.

CERNE PARISH COUN

RULES

of the

Cerne Abbas Land Allotment

ESTABLISHED IN THE YEAR 1844

1.—No Tenant will be permitted to exchange, under-let, or give up the possession of his or her Allotment, or any part thereof, without the consent of the Committee of Management.

2.—Every Tenant to manure at least one-third of his or her Allotment yearly, and to keep the same in a neat and proper state of cultivation.

3.—The Allotments shall be let from January 1st to December 31st. No Allotment shall be let for less than one year. The year's rent to be paid on the third Tuesday in February at the Schoolroom, at Seven p.m. If not paid by the third Tuesday in March the Allotment shall be considered vacant, and the Committee will meet at the Schoolroom at Seven p.m. on that date, and re-let any such Allotments without further notice.

4.—If any Tenant shall place any manure or rubbish on the roads or paths adjoining the Allotments, or shall commit any wilful damage on any Allotment, or shall damage or misplace the number of any Allotment, or omit to keep his or her own Allotment numbered, such Tenant shall forfeit the Allotment or be fined at the discretion of the Committee.

Above: *Chescombe became allotments, photographed here in 1892.*
Left: *Rules were certainly strict.*

Above: *One gardener working at his allotment in 2000.*
Left: *What is now the school playing field was once used to grow fruit and vegetables. Photograph, 1920s.*

Right: *Jackie Warren with his beehives behind his home in Acreman Street, 1920s.*

Far right: *J.J. Strawbridge with a swarm in his garden behind the schoolhouse, 1930s.*

Below: *Hives in a thicket, 2000.*

Main picture: *The sheepshearers move in, c.1880.*
Inset: *Lambing at Watcombe in the 1980s.*

DEPRESSION AND DECLINE

At first sight the fall in Cerne Abbas' population (from the 1851 peak of 1343 to the 643 of 1901) may appear as the mirror image of its doubling in the earlier period foresaid peak in only 30 years – a simple symmetry, no more. But appearances are deceptive. For one thing, in its earlier rise Cerne Abbas was sharing in the overall increase of the entire UK: the later period revealed Wessex as bucking the general tide – an alarming exception.

Several factors had caused this relatively local ebbing, some more obvious than others: a sequence of bad harvests in the late 1870s; the steady, relentless importation of cheaper produce from overseas; corn from the boundless, but no longer virgin, Middle West which reduced wheat prices by two-thirds in less than 40 years; refrigerated meat and dairy produce from Canada, South America and the Antipodes, the latter's wool in particular drastically shrinking the profitability, and therefore the acreage, of the ubiquitous Dorset sheep farms. A second characteristic differentiated the years of decline from those of the ascent of 'high farming'.

The earlier period had borne especially heavily upon the labourer and small tenant. But now depression engulfed not only the landless but the landed, their employers and patrons. Because Dorset appears as an area of small-to-medium-sized stately homes, with no equivalent of Woburn, Chatsworth or Castle Howard, it is tempting to regard the 'landed interest', whatever its composition, as being correspondingly dwarfed by that of other regions. That this was far from the case, a kind of latter-day Domesday survey was about to reveal: the parliamentary inquiry and returns on land ownership conducted during 1872–3 was to disclose that 17 per cent of Dorset's total agricultural area (excluding waste) was occupied by estates of 1000 to 3000 acres (as against a national average of 9 per cent). If the category were extended to 10 000 acres the percentage doubled. In the aristocratic or squirarchical batting order, Dorset came either 9th on the first count or 3rd on the second, exceeded only in concentration of ownership by Rutland and Staffs. Statisticised another way, 32 per cent of the green county was owned by two dozen great families, some of their foundation fortunes going back to the 16th century but hitherto possessing great capacity for survival (see F.M.L. Thompson, *English Landed Society in the 19th Century*, London, 1963). Their peripheral holdings went under the hammer first. There is some irony in the circumstance that it was upon the very verge of this collapse that Cerne passed into the hands of its last, most distinguished, perhaps most enlightened, secular land-owner.

Upon the departure of the Frekes, the Pitt-Rivers had already secured a foothold in the locality

through the properties (see *Somerset & Dorset Notes & Queries* xiv (1915, pp.130–31) held by George Pitt, 1st Baron Rivers (1721–1803), owner and rebuilder of Wellington's Stratfield Saye. In the spring of 1867 Lord Rivers' fourth and only surviving son followed his three brothers to the grave, victims of a wasting disease (their memorials are in Tollard Royal Church, their family vault at Stapledon). The heir, Henry Peter Pitt-Rivers, being minor, the estate passed to his uncle, Horace Pitt, son of the 3rd Baron; but on his dying childless in 1880 it passed not to a cousin, George Lane Fox, but to a descendant of his sister (Marcia Lane Fox) who adopted the Pitt-Rivers name. This was none other than the distinguished General and archaeologist, 'father of scientific archaeology', already disturber of 40 important sites, and inheritor of the 3500-hectare Rushmore/Farnham estate on the Wiltshire border.

A new landlord on this scale naturally implied a new allocation of lands, buildings and occupancies, in the biggest shake-up of tenancies since the immediate post-Dissolution years. Of such enclosures made in the early-19th century, about half were by private Acts of parliament, about half by local agreements at a public meeting between the lord and his lessees/occupiers.

NOT ALL ANCIENT SKILLS ARE LOST.
Top: *Hedgelaying is coming into fashion again. The hedge laid, not slaughtered.*
Above: *A recent hedgecount carried out by members of Cerne Historical Society dated some hedges back 1000 years: Maureen Hartley, Janet Bartlet and Helen Smith on the job.*

The Pitt-Rivers enclosure process was by local agreement at a public meeting on 8 January 1795, recorded (DRO D396) as between on the one part George Lord Rivers, and on the other the Hon. Robert Digby of Minterne, Thomas Cockeram of Cerne Abbas, Thomas Coombes and Gale, 'Gents all of Cerne Abbas' and other signatories being copyhold tenants, lessees for lives or lessees for years determinable upon lives, signed also by Francis Webb of New Sarum and William Jennings of Puddletown plus a third Commissioner selected by them. Lands were to be allotted, chalk and gravel pits to be set out. Surveyors of roads were to be appointed and rights of commons extinguished.

For disposing first of their holdings in Cerne Abbas (together with Melcombe Horsey and its park) the Pitt-Rivers' great sale day was Wednesday 24 September 1919. From 1.30p.m. onwards in Dorchester's Town Hall, under the hammer of Messrs Senior & Godwin, they disposed of 4700 acres of 'residential, agricultural and shooting' properties in 77 lots. From surviving copies of the illustrated schedule we learn the details. Lot I, realising £7600, included the Abbey grounds, Abbot's Porch and Guest House. At the other end of the scale some cottages went for less than £100 apiece. It was a sad sign of the times that it was considered by the vendors an inducement to stress that 'a large proportion of his existing arable land can be grassed down with advantage'. Also included were some leases on surrounding areas and some water meadows in Duck Street, nowadays, after much draining, a children's grassed play area.

So, erstwhile tenants became small householders; some indeed took the opportunity to acquire more than one cottage, thus becoming, to a limited degree, rentiers. The full economic consequences of this transformation would not become apparent until post-Second World War inflation had sent up the housing market and native householders were found to exceed in wealth the supposedly nouveaux riches intent on buying into the village (of which phenomenon the present writer nurses a rueful recollection). A whole small world had been turned upside-down and had to recover its new footing. Futhermore, the withdrawal of private land-owners from the scene left the inhabitants of the village directly exposed to the brunt of state economic policy configured at a distance. Local magnates, though still present on the county agricultural committee, were no longer a buffer between them, and the impact of decision to be taken in Whitehall and Westminster, an intervention which had long been abhorred.

Evaluating the Pitt-Rivers family as landlords is not a straightforward exercise. In the matter of housing their record is comparatively poor. Despite an

Sheep dipping in the 1930s.

obvious need to attract and retain tenants on arable land, they displayed no encouragement in that matter, their records showing badly beside the pioneering in housing design pursued by neighbours to the north and east, viz., Ismay (White Star) at Iwerne Minster or Debenham (drapery) at Briantspuddle, yet themselves capable of realism about rents as when annually they announced an abatement of 5 per cent or more at their January dinner for principal tenants at the New Inn. On the other hand, the family, however patriarchal, was compatible with its context and far from representing the new industrial wealth displayed by, for example, the Guests (Dowlais iron) at Canford. Nor did they design to convert their patrimony into a huge hunting ground like the Draxes (West-Indian sugar) at Bere Regis. On the contrary, they often worked within the familiar rural context to bring important benefits – the new school buildings and the Chescombe allotments in the 1840s – whose coming was greatly expedited by a sponsoring 'angel'. Less specifically, the village benefited during the succeeding century from the benign proximity of the Digby family at Minterne, yet has never felt itself to be in a condition of dependency. Indeed in very recent years it has flourished in the absence of any identifiable 'headman' at all.

But in any event, well before Cerne's 1919 sale its morale had touched rock bottom, with a condition almost reminiscent of 1617. We must now see how and why.

Main picture: *Mount Pleasant, 1921. The centre cottage of the three was a laundry – did they have to get their water from the well on the left? The thatched roofs to the right are Francombe Farm.*
Inset: *This is now the main road past Cerne.*

Main picture: *One of Cerne's many leather traders, the Hodges family claim to have made Sir Walter Raleigh's buskins when he lived at Sherborne and the first hard shoes for the infant Princess (later Queen) Victoria. They lived here in Abbey Street (first house on the right).*
Left: *This stone marks the Hodges' house at the south end of Abbey Street. The house came down in 1910.*

Chapter 12
Trades and Industry

Turning now from work upon the land itself to local trades and industry, one would expect, from the foregoing pages, to detect a contrast in rates of decay as between those occupations closely related to farming and those relatively independent of it. This prediction is not, however, entirely borne out. It is rather as though the same depression, when it came, blighted land workers and artisans indifferently and uniformly. On second thoughts, though, this uniformity of impact should not surprise us. For through much of the village's history, agricultural work and bench work were complementary – two sides of the coin or two strings to the bow – a prudent insurance policy. As Arthur Young noted in 1805: 'there often appears among farmers a great disposition to

Above: *Jane Way, daughter of Charlie Way, the last landlord of the Antelope, outside her shop with her parents and sister, early 1900s.*
Below: *Billy Miller delivering outside the stores in the 1930s.*

embark in various species of trade, manufacture and commerce!'

Some such recognition of balance has prevailed ever since, as when, in the 1790s, Pitt-Rivers' agents drew up his schedule of rentals (or 'admeasurements' as they quaintly called it) (DRO D396) taking care to match a rental of grazing or arable against a proportionate allocation of messuage (dwelling house).

Hence for the most part, in assessing how such and such trade or industry flourished or declined, only a few general observations can be attempted here. Firstly, here as elsewhere in Western Europe, from early times and for centuries thereafter, we note how the division of labour has been mirrored in the derivation of surnames, reflecting the wide variety of

pursuits and their location within the community's boundaries. In Cerne's case we are able to go back to 1327 and Edward II's last attempt at non-feudal taxation of moveable property (the clergy's excepted) to meet the needs of national defence or the contingencies of royal administration. Thanks to a modern edition we can discern, despite a bastard blend of dog Latin, Norman French and Middle English, the names of the forerunners of those who ply their trades here today and, as the collector worked around in sequence, perhaps some hint of their locations:

Le Brewere	Le Schephurde
Le Bakere	Le Pottere
Le Skynner atte Welle	Le Thecchere (Thatcher)
Le Webbe (Weaver) atte Brigge	William Tipecok
Le Hayward attewode	Wilhelmo Carpentario
Le Muleward atte Knolle	Chapman/Chipman

Let us now look at their descendants in village trading and manufacture. Taking the principal modern equivalents in turn:

Brewing Until recent oil exploration Cerne's only subterranean asset was its water, whose quality was such that the itinerant Richard (later Bishop) Pococke could, in the 18th century, describe it as 'more famous for beer than in any other place in the county'. If innkeepers were at the apex of the social pyramid, its base consisted of innumerable small

APRIL 17TH, 1913

CERNE ABBAS.

DEATH OF AN OLD INHABITANT.—Mr. James Northover, a member of an old Cerne family, and who formerly carried on business as a brewer and latterly as a farmer, passed away on Tuesday, the 8th. Mr. Northover had for the last 15 years held the office of Inspector of Nuisances under the Cerne District Council. He was the oldest member of Court "St. Austin," A.O.F., and a number of members attended the funeral on Friday.

Above: *The Strawbridges and Elliotts go dandelion picking for wine in the 1930s.*
Inset: *The last brewer in Cerne dies in 1913.*

brewhouses, all linked to an extensive malting business. Last of the more substantial brewers, operating until 1883 on the site of what is now Chescombe, was James Northover (d.1913).

Silk Also beholden to the rivers of Cerne and Silley, but for water power, were the factory-centred industries of tanning, silk weaving and glove making. Cerne's silk trade was really an off-shoot of William Willmott's more extensive Sherborne manufactory, although he himself managed his Cerne branch for ten years (1772–82) in person. Thereafter, management here passed to a Mr and Mrs Smout. Whereas Willmott recruited his Sherborne labour force from children of the local schools and workhouse, the Smouts' attempt to recruit from farther afield evidently led to some friction. For this or some other reason, Cerne's silk industry, always more focussed on throwing than on preparing the raw material, had by the mid-19th century shrunk to a single building in Duck Street, for which the churchwardens collected rent.

Gloving too, although it involved some outworkers, also required a central workplace, of which until quite recently the village possessed solid surviving evidence in the prominent building along the Sherborne road. This original glove factory was erected by John Frampton, but by 1844 was described as 'decayed... and in a dilapidated state, for sale leasehold with freedom to convert'. In that year a 99-year lease was taken by one John Batten 'who intends to carry on a brewing and baking business and make an Inn'. It was as the Glove Inn therefore that the property was in September 1860 put up for auction with garden, factory, stores, livestock and five acres of land, two of them arable, but still 'with every convenience of water power'. That sales notice is important in that it gives us the fullest possible description of the room-by-room interior, furnishing, fittings, stores and stock. In 1886 the insolvent tenant, T. Dunning, sold to John Groves of Weymouth this historic building which in the 1960s was demolished by that same landowner who virtually obliterated a great part of the village of UpCerne.

Textiles Also demolished at the same juncture was the old Tucking or Fulling Mill operated in the 18th century by John Davies, woolstapler, and in the 19th by George House. Some trading also took place, in leaner times, in dowlas, hessian, linsey-woolsey and other, similarly cheaper, cloths. Only at the leanest would cottagers be driven back on buttony – grinding work and minimally paid. Silk winding at least could secure them 1 shilling a lb for the making-up and about 6d. per pair for ordinary woollen gloves.

Milling and More Among other mills, the grist or flour mill in Mill Lane, whose grindstone can still, with some persistence, be viewed there, never lacked for proprietors or operators, the last of whom, William Holland, retired in 1933. By then its machinery was of some sophistication: in 1908 George Derriman had fitted a 10.6-hp turbine of 14-inch diameter.

If the gradual decay of these Dorset industries, whether in brewing or textiles is attributable, at least in part, to customers being drawn to bigger centres outside the county, can we infer that a lack of a rail-road system was to blame? A clear-cut answer is not easy to give. Even the coaching trade in its latter years had tended to bypass the little town's heart, pre-ferring to use as a stage stop the Giant's Head Inn on the hilltop to the east, thus avoiding the steep gradi-ent into and out of the community's centre. As to assured markets, Cerne's better quality products did not lack them: the real defect was, in the absence of a viable system of mid-county waterways, one of distribution. The farmers in particular needed an accessible railhead for collection and outward trans-port of perishable produce. Maiden Newton, a settlement of comparable size, which had accepted the railway, began thereafter to overtake Cerne, hitherto pre-eminent in stock marketing. Yet even that village in the end succumbed to decay, which the railway had postponed but not ultimately averted.

In the other balance, moreover, must be weighed 'greenness' and 'quality of life', both of which would have been threatened by the practical bisection of a community by the steam-driven polluter. In calculat-ing the advantages of commerce versus tourism and 'heritage' the ultimate net gain could not be assessed until the century that lay ahead.

By the mid-19th century, however, there were already certain signs that village life was to be offered some degree of elevation or refinement which went beyond the mere possession of a tea-caddy. A Mr Snook was proposing lessons in dancing and deport-ment; a Mr Minifee opened a perfumery at the west end of Long Street. In April 1871 the following advertisement appeared in the local newspapers:

Abbey Street. Cerne Abbas. H. HOWELL Tailor & Noted Trouser Maker respectfully informs the PUBLIC that he has COMMENCED BUSINESS as a PRACTICAL TAILOR. Obtaining his experience in the West-end of London, he trusts that he shall receive a fair support of their Patronage. All Goods bought for Cash in the largest and best Establishment in London. A good stock of West of England Cloth, Waterproof Tweeds, Trousering, Meltons, &c, suitable for all weathers. An immense saving will be effected by giving an Order, as every garment will be cut by H.J.H. and made under his supervision. ladies' Mantles, Cloth, Velvet and Silk Jackets and Children's cloth-ing to order, and all orders executed at the Lowest prices. No slop or Inferior Goods will be made at this Establishment. Good serviceable Trousers from 16s.6d. A waterproof Tweed Coat One Guinea. Orders by Post punctually attended to.

Alas, there were few takers, and within a year Mr Howell had removed his business to No.35 High West Street, Dorchester. More ominously, only 18 months thereafter, Mr William Bragg Tibbs, supplier of the village's work-a-day wear, had gone bankrupt with indebtedness of £1600 and removed his busi-ness ('draper, tailor, hatter and tea dealer') from its prime site at the junction of Long and Duck Streets.

Clock- and Watchmaker Another type of specialised skill, which no community could do without, was that of clock- and watchmaker, also described as silversmith; and every such practitioner required ample light. Hence three such craftsmen succeeded one another in the premises (one almost said, in the windows) of what is now the Old Market House. They were Thomas Johns (c.1750–1800), Robert Clarke (c.1800–60) and Ferdinand Jesse Everett (born c.1890). The latter, together with his collection of precious timepieces, indeed achieved some fame beyond Dorset. He was reputed to have learned to drive at the age of 72, graduating from pedal to motorcycle in the course of his itinerant countywide repair duties.

Market House – workroom to clock makers.

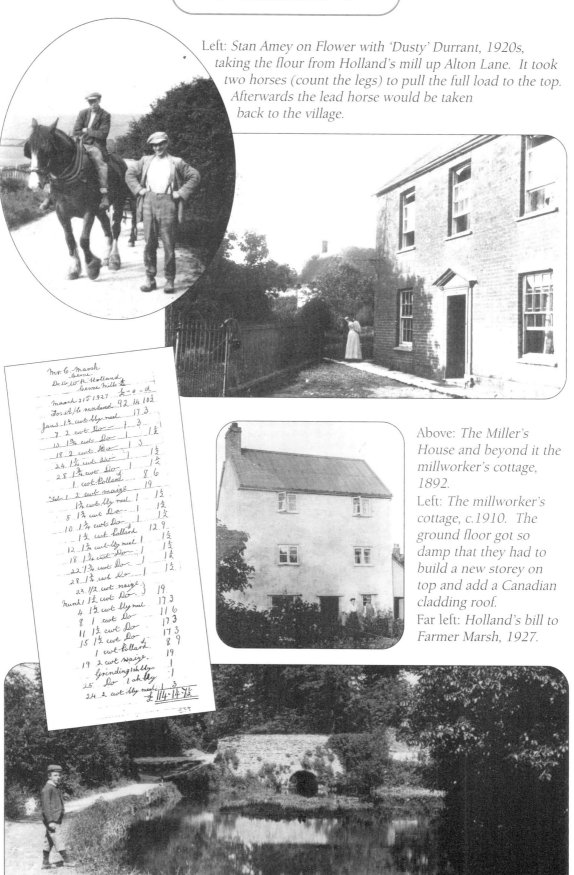

Left: *Stan Amey on Flower with 'Dusty' Durrant, 1920s, taking the flour from Holland's mill up Alton Lane. It took two horses (count the legs) to pull the full load to the top. Afterwards the lead horse would be taken back to the village.*

Above: *The Miller's House and beyond it the millworker's cottage, 1892.*

Left: *The millworker's cottage, c.1910. The ground floor got so damp that they had to build a new storey on top and add a Canadian cladding roof.*

Far left: *Holland's bill to Farmer Marsh, 1927.*

The Mill Brook at Kettle Bridge, 1880s.

❀ BUTCHER ❀

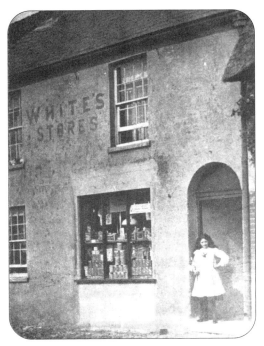

Above: *White's Stores, early 1900s, in Acreman Street. Tom White was pork butcher and grocer. Lily Rayson his niece is in the doorway. The ladies who live here in 2000 make excellent cakes!*

OLDEST SHOP?

IT would be interesting to know which is the oldest butcher's shop in Britain but certainly one of the oldest is that of 86-year-old Mr. George Thomas Green, Duck Street, in the ancient Dorset village of Cerne Abbas, a few miles from Sherborne.

This thatched building has been continuously used as a family butcher's since it was built in the year 1784 and that date is to be seen embedded in the brickwork.

Mr. Green himself is now bedridden but the business in the picturesque raftered but otherwise up-to-date shop is carried on for him by his son-in-law, Mr. Thomas Charles Dunn, and by his grandson, 23-year-old Mr. Thomas Edward Dunn (Mr. Dunn's son) with the aid of Mrs. Dunn, Mr. Green's daughter.

Mr. Green's father, Mr. George Green, was there as a butcher before him but who sold meat in the old building before *his* time is not known. The building consists of two cottages which long ago were made into one and on the premises are such relics of the old butchering days as an ancient poleaxe and an old-fashioned wooden meat "trough" of the kind once carried on the right or left shoulder.

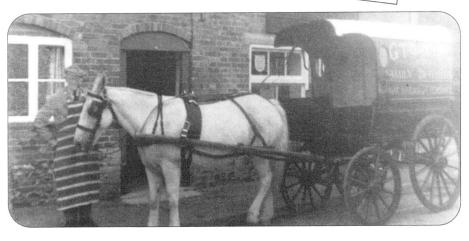

Top: *Cutting from* The Meat Trades Journal, *1960.*

Above: *Mr G.T. Green used to help his father when they poleaxed an animal by lantern light and their wonderful meat was delivered by cart or boys on bicycles over a wide area. The butcher's closed in the 1980s.*

Left: *Walter Fox and Alfred Webber outside the shop, possibly 1930s.*

Top: *The last saddlery closed in the 1930s. Jim Pride on the left, Percy Burge on the right and 'F. Pitman' (who held Francombe Farm) on the box.*

Above: *The Old Saddler Boutique in 2000 with Mrs Lamin and her daughter Susie Thorpe. They design and make lovely clothes and sell a variety of souvenirs.*

Right: *Extract from Paulley's bill to Farmer Marsh, 1923.*

CERNE ABBAS.

Dᵉᶜ 1923

Mʳ C. Marsh

Dr. to H. W. PAULLEY,
SADDLER, COLLAR AND HARNESS MAKER,
HORSES CAREFULLY FITTED.

REPAIRS OF EVERY DESCRIPTION.   FARMS ATTENDED AND CONTRACTS TAKEN.

Above: *The first Post Office was in Acreman Street 1876-78. Mr Cornick moved to Abbey Street in 1878 and was there until 1919 when the Pitt-Rivers sold the village and he moved to Long Street. This picture shows the shop in Abbey Street.*

Right: *The Cornick family, c.1911. Left to right, standing: Alfred George (1899-1975), Alice Mary (1891-1918), Dorothy May (1901-77), Beatrice (1894-1944), Albert Henry (1898-1952); sitting: George William Cornick (1864-1951), Charles Stanley (1905-92), Ellen Cornick (1866-1932) holding baby Norman (1911-30).*

Above: *The Shop in the Square, 1990, incorporating the Post Office. Janet and Arthur Mason in charge. The windows do not match because an American Army vehicle backed into it during the 1940s.*

Right: *Andrew Farrow in the doorway of the invaluable stores, 2000, the successor to Derriman and Waygood.*

'Tiger' Curtis second from the left with little Jackie Devenish and Charlie Hart behind him, probably 1920s.

The Forge in the 1980s. It closed in 2000.

VERSATILITY OF SKILLS

As a general proposition it may be maintained that the more highly skilled the artisan, the more versatile he could prove himself in response to the economic demands of his time. Thus a skilled joiner like Mr William Mitchell in his Mill Lane workshop could prosper as cabinet maker when the gentry could afford him, or execute a commission such as the oaken doors at St Mary's west end; alternatively he could function routinely throughout the year as coffin maker and funeral director; or more roughly as wagon maker to the village carrier (to say nothing of functioning on occasion as dowser and well digger). Lower down the skill scale, on the other hand, cruder workers had in hard times to hire themselves out at piece rate, with switch bills and axes, to local farmers for 'hedge carpentry' and ditch digging. Likewise, even an ordinary leather worker could, as circumstances might require, turn out various products at different levels of refinement, from footwear such as the Hodges reputedly made for Raleigh and the young Queen (when Princess) Victoria, to aprons, and from saddles down to whips.

Commonly it has been said that those who upped and went were mainly the young, active and enterprising adults. But historians should look at this again. A glance at the school population figures reveals that these did not conclusively fall until the First World War, which seems to imply that villagers of childbearing and child-rearing age stayed put. On the other hand, numerous newspaper reports suggest that ('natural wastage' apart) departers were seniors confident of possessing mature skills which would secure them a living anywhere. This was at a time when the kind of publicity exhibited would attract just such men - as, for example, when the Allan Line took the Village Hall for an evening to exhibit the beauties and opportunities of Canada. If so, this would have had serious consequences for the balance of maturity remaining in the village.

Another instance of repetitive occupation of the same premise is afforded by the wedge-shaped, double-fronted shop at the junction of Long Street and Duck Street. Originally known as Hellyer's Corner, it may today rightly be placarded as either Paulley's or the Old Saddler, since it was occupied intermittently by generations of the Paulley family, of that profession, up to 1937. One particular area, too, was frequented by the butchers - East Street, adjoining what may well have been the pillared ground floor of the old Guildhall, hence naturally come to be called the Shambles.

At the other, more delicate, end of the professional spectrum, the surviving tawers (skin strippers) and parchment makers - skills that cease to be recorded in the directories after 1849,

where the last such professional appears as 'parchment-maker and cheese factor' - huddled together most years in Abbey Street. Usually, however, and even in that 'classy' thoroughfare, the residential pattern is one of all trades and professions co-existing in close proximity, indeed even interlocking where convenience of access was in question.

Above: *The home and bakery of C.J. England was next door to the Constabulary. With the first wireless in Cerne, locals came to listen in the evenings in the warmth of the bakehouse. While delivering bread during the war Mr England arrested a couple of German airmen whose plane had been shot down over Sydling Hill.*

Top: *Post in action. Left to right: Norman Cornick, William Cornick (postmaster), Bert Smith (postman), Bert Cornick on the motorbike, Jack Warren on the bicycle and Winnie Mowlem and her brother Leonard.*

The Post Office moved into Long Street in 1919 but when Mr Cornick died in 1952 it moved again to the shop next door.

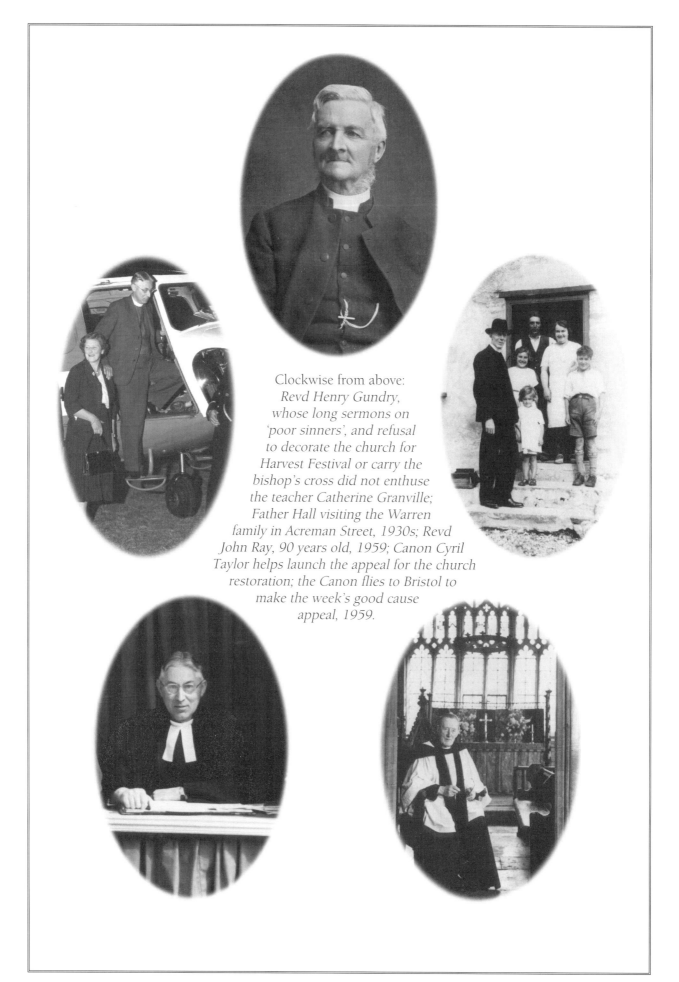

Clockwise from above:
*Revd Henry Gundry,
whose long sermons on
'poor sinners', and refusal
to decorate the church for
Harvest Festival or carry the
bishop's cross did not enthuse
the teacher Catherine Granville;
Father Hall visiting the Warren
family in Acreman Street, 1930s; Revd
John Ray, 90 years old, 1959; Canon Cyril
Taylor helps launch the appeal for the church
restoration; the Canon flies to Bristol to
make the week's good cause
appeal, 1959.*

Chapter 13
The Church
in the 20th Century

St Mary's welcomed in the new century through a brand new pair of oaken west doors, the handiwork of William J. Mitchell, carpenter, wagon-maker and water diviner (in which capacity his skills were much in demand for locating suitable well sites) at the junction of Duck Street and Mill Lane, whose initiative had done much to raise the necessary subscriptions. In 1910 the 57 years of faithful service of Henry Hodges as Parish Clerk were commemorated by his grandson, J. Earle Hodges of Weybridge, with a memorial window in the south aisle depicting St John's vision on the Isle of Patmos and executed by Nathaniel Hubert Westlake, esteemed author of *A History of Design in Painted Glass*.

In 1914 Alexander Pitt-Rivers leased at peppercorn rent a residence in the old market square as a church and parish house, roomy enough to accommodate dances such as were held during the subsequent First World War for the Blue Cross in aid of the wounded. Though that building and its neighbour were burnt down in 1933, something called a 'parish room' was still being referred to five years later. During the war itself 'hospital Sundays' continued to be observed, though shorn of much of their ostentation. A special 'Titanic Sunday' service had been held in 1912.

Post-war St Mary's moved into the age of improved hot water radiation and electric light. Technology reached its climax in 1953 with a television relay in the church of the coronation service: to mark that occasion. Lord Digby presented some of the material used in Westminster Abbey to form a frontal for our north-aisle altar.

VICARS AND VICARAGE

But this piecemeal account has already run ahead of a considerable constitutional change in parochial administration and control. In accordance with Parliament's Enabling Act of 1919 the Church Assembly in 1921 merged the old vestries with the new parochial church councils. Henceforward the historic Vestry would operate, if it operated separately at all, only as a curtain-raiser on the latter's activities; a five-minute forum to make choice of

wardens where there was likely to be little dispute. The potential of the vicar, on the other hand, was undiminished and perhaps relatively enhanced. To his office and power base we must now turn, albeit that the record here is somewhat sketchy.

Though a medieval distinction persisted between Rectory and Vicarage, the patrons of both were then the abbots of Cerne. After the Dissolution, the rectorial tithes of corn, hay, wool and lamb, together with the advowson of the Vicarage, were granted to private purchasers who by the second half of Elizabeth's reign had come to be the Freke family; and later to the Pitts. To the same families went also the poorly endowed vicarial patronage which by the mid-18th century yielded the incumbent only £8 per annum. A more detailed picture is given by a terrier compiled in August 1612 by the Revd Humphrey Nutt. His churchwardens and their sidesmen owned:

> *Imprimis a Mansion House with a Hall parlour Buttery Kitchen Chambers and Garden and Orchards and one Acre of Meadow by estimation to the same adjoining on the south side of the House.*
>
> *Item all the same Tithes of the Town of Cerne excepting the Tithes of Corn Hay Wool and Lamb with the Offerings of the Church and Weddings and purifying.*
>
> *Item a pension of five pounds nine shillings and four pence by the year payed from the proprietory of the Rector of Cerne aforesaid.*

A deed exists of 1741 executed by the surviving trustees for George Pitt junr and setting a yearly rent of £60 for a 'parsonage or rectory' plus barn, plus pasture in Cerne Park, but, apart from these scanty facts, little light is shed on the parson's accommodation. However, a second terrier drawn up in May 1785 during the incumbency of the Revd Richard Daubeney by his curate (and son?), William Daubeney, describes (1) an abode of 24ft by 16ft undergoing internal refurbishment:

> *... in a field of 2 acres bounded on ye E by a field of Isaak Dominy on ye S by a Field belonging to ye*

The Vicarage. Henry Dickinson Gundry and his wife on the lawn, c.1892.

Farm on ye West by a Field belonging to Levi Groves on ye N by ye Highway.

(2) a Modus Tithe of Horned cattle 8d for a Cow 4d for a Heifer 2d for a dry [barren] Bullock.

(3) Tithes of orchards and gardens

(4) twopence a head for Easter offering for all people above fourteen years of age.

fifthly a Churchyard about one Acre with ye Church and Churchyard Fees.

A marginal scribble appears to estimate the notional cash value of those assets for that year at £219.7s.6d. but their net worth at only £22.4s.2d. It will be noted that the location described would be compatible with that of the present Vicarage, dated 1711. Some 66 years later the 1851 Census of Places of Religious Worship gives the value of the living as about £80 a year from the small tithes, to which the patron Lord Rivers adds £30 p.a.

When, in the 20th century, the valley from Minterne down to Godmanstone became a single parish, the central location of Cerne's Vicarage doubtless saved it from the selling-off which had befallen too many other church properties of that size and quality. Despite destructive fires in the stables in 1950 and again in 1993, it survives as an indispensable centre of activity incorporating the village's only 'parish room'.

Of the incumbents themselves, a few have achieved some small notability on one ground or another. Samuel Watson (1654-72) of whom all we know is on his memorial in the south aisle, was sufficiently adaptable to survive in office through Commonwealth, Interregnum and the restored Charles II: his misfortune, and Mrs Watson's, was to lose two children on successive days and a third in less than three years. We have already noted the exceptional generosity of James Hay Waugh

(1842-45) - which may have included some contribution to the refurbishment of his Vicarage - and of Augustus Howie Bull (1866-75) in bearing the cost of reshaping St Mary's interior. 'Of the Evangelical school', they said of the latter when he died in office, 'but no bigot, and always open to conviction'. Of unusual length (1878-1913) was the ministry of Henry Gundry, of the Bridport family, seemingly the last Cerne incumbent to lack formal academic qualification. Through 35 placid years he saw his parochial population almost halved.

The succession of Henry's son Hugh, already a curate at home and with experience in the mission field overseas, was observed to signal 'a great awakening of church life and interest which is welcomed by the parishioners', accompanied by a 'progressive spirit that is slowly but surely invading the parish'. 'Deservedly popular with all', Hugh Gundry had the misfortune to collide with his Vestry in 1916 over the handling of moneys he had collected in his drive for church restoration. On the one side the Vestry men asserted as a principle:

... that all contributions and collections made in the Church for whatever object should be handed to the Churchwardens who Wd. be responsible for the disposal of the same.

The vicar denied (not altogether without precedent):

... that funds raised for the Church Restoration Fund were in any way under the jurisdiction of the churchwardens, as they were raised by his personal efforts.

After he had absented himself from several successive meetings the Vestry resolved unanimously 'that the Bishop be asked to hold an enquiry'.

At the following meeting Mr Gundry reappeared, to present his special account showing a balance of £20.14s.6d. which he said 'was in the hands of the Bishop'. He also gave notice of his intention to quit the living in three weeks' time, having accepted another Dorset benefice also in the gift of Lord Rivers. For some months his place was temporarily filled by the Revd E.S. Moss.

Of inter-war pastors the Revd Arthur Dobie also met with blank opposition from the Vestry in 1918/19 to his democratic proposal 'that the ordinary seats in the nave and aisles of St Mary's parish church are free and unappropriated for the common use of the inhabitants of the parish'. Some other difference, however, of a private and personal nature, seems likely to have prompted the startling motion at the Easter Vestry of 1923: 'that the vicar had forfeited the confidence of this council and, it is believed, of the parishioners as a whole and that therefore he be asked to resign'. Eight named voters splitting evenly, the matter was dropped and Mr Dobie remained to minister in Cerne for another two years.

Charles Frank Hall, preferring (it is said) to be known as Father Hall, brought with him in 1925 some practices higher than his parishioners had been accustomed to, such as installing a rood over the choir screen. When he left after ten years, bequeathing to the church a fine collection of vestments but taking his rood with him to West Moors, 'it was unanimously agreed to ask for the appointment of a Moderate man with no Extreme Views'. The Revd Sinclair Burton may have fitted the bill but left after less than four years to become General Secretary of the Church of England's National Schools. There followed John Ray, over 70 years of age, who saw his parish faithfully through the Second World War, but whose PCC (Parochial Church Council) minutes thereafter plumb the depths of monotony. For whatever reasons, his candid record of typical church attendance during the autumn of 1950 makes depressing reading:

Morning Service Sundays - (a) a Sunday mid-Sept. - 8 in the congregation, (b) a Sunday mid-Oct - 12 in the congregation. While the attendance of the Choir (14) and of the Children's Church (35-40) was extraordinary, the Acts of Communion averaged 16 per Sunday... The estimated population of Cerne was 547 - therefore allowing 100 to the Congregational ch., 47 RCs etc., 100 mothers, 40 very young children, 50 cattlemen, 90 invalids and the aged, there are still 120 who could be in Church...

When in 1958, therefore, Canon Cyril Tayor was inducted as (such had been the progress of pluralism) 'Vicar of Cerne Abbas with UpCerne, Rector of

Minterne and Godmanstone and Perpetual Curate of Nether Cerne', a heavy task of spiritual revivification awaited him. Very soon it became evident that this would be complicated by physical reconstruction too.

INCUMBENTS OF ST MARY'S CHURCH, CERNE ABBAS

1317   Robert de Muleborn
Richard de Stoke
1348   Thomas de Hull
1399   John Corby
1418   William Bracer
1419   Walter Archer B.Can.L.
John Boner B. Can. L
1422   Nicholas Mille
John Wareyn
1445   John Osey
1452   John Lombe
Walter Bryant
1515   Henry Alambryke
1538   John Conized
1576   Robert Fludd
1576   Richard Griffin
1580   Humphrey Nutt B.A.
1629   Henry Lamb B.A.
1654   Samuel Watson V.A.
1672   John Ball B.A.
1711 John Derby B.A.
1736   John Veneer B.A.
1751   Charles Hughes M.A.
1765   Richard Daubeney B.A.
1803   William Davis B.A.
1812   John Davies B.A.
1842   James Hay Waugh M.A.
1845   Thomas Colingwood Hughes B.A.
1849   Alexander Williams M.A
1857   William Henry Davies M.A
1866   Augustus Howie Bull M.A.
1875   John Hosegood M.A.
1878 Henry Dickinson Gundry
1913 Hugh Gundry B.A.
1917   James Williams A.K.C
1917-1918   Stanley Moss locum tenens
1917   Arthur Dobie M.A.
1925   Charles Frank Hall O.B.E
1935   Arthur John Sinclair Burton L.Jh.
1935   John Thomas Bernard Ray
1958   Cyril Vincent Taylor M.A. Canon of Salisbury
1969   Hugh Roger Mumford M.A. Canon of Salisbury
1979   Derek Jackson M.A. Emeritus Canon of Salisbury
1993   Ted Longman M.A.

[Source: Mr George Drewry Squibb]

RESTORATION IN THE 1960s

The great problem, at first believed to be the sole problem, was the nave roof. Work done there early in the preceding century, mainly the bolting of wrought-iron plates at the rotted ends of the tie beams, had long ceased to be satisfactory; as had been evident when, in the 1930s, and against professional advice, the then vicar (the Revd Hall) had had the flat plaster ceiling removed in the hope of revealing something handsomer and more antique underneath. In the early 1950s the parish had raised some £2000 to renew the lead on the chancel and south-aisle roofs: since when the fabric had been under the care of a local architect whose report of 1957, although unfavourable, had given no inkling of the extent of renovation required.

That extent became all too clear when in 1959 Mr Robert Potter of Messrs Potter & Hare (later the Brandt Partnership) of Salisbury was invited to make a survey of the whole church every five years. From this it was at once evident that not only was £7500 required straight away for a new roof, but that there was dry rot – heretofore known only in the north-aisle roof and the south side of the chancel but now also apparent in the wooden flooring, the pews in the north aisle, and spreading into the nave. So in addition there would be needed (save in the chancel) a completely new concrete base over which could be laid a woodblock floor or, for the aisles, pavors of artificial stone. This need became all too apparent when in the following spring (1960) the old nave floor, joisted and boarded, collapsed under scaffolding. Thenceforward regular measurements had to be taken of the arcade pillars to ensure that the main structure itself was not shifting.

The new roof, it was decided, should be of a plain 15th-century style but with reinforced concrete beams. To manoeuvre these into position a helicopter, subject to cross winds, was deemed too risky and the operation was entrusted to a tower crane, from Woolaway Construction, Bridport, which on 1 May 1960 lay the length of central Long Street before being erected to commence its delicate hoisting the following day.

The opportunity afforded by such major work was seized upon to make interior changes, too. A narthex was formed behind the west screen and a processional passage from the south door. The 13th-century font, restored to use in 1932, was moved out of the vestry into its present position and given a cover designed by Mr Kenneth Wiltshire, the partner most directly concerned with the ongoing works. The organ was once more shifted back diagonally from the south-east corner to the north-west, where it may be hoped that the venerable machine may be allowed to end its days, and a store created behind it.

A modern, small-bore, low-pressure oil-fired heating system was installed to run controlled convector units. Messrs Jewell and Norcombe completely rewired the electrics. The old pews were replaced by 150 chairs, a generous gift of the church congregation at Tamworth-in-Arden, Warwickshire.

From March 1960 to May 1961, therefore, St Mary's worshippers suffered disturbance. As Canon Taylor put it:

We were excluded gradually from the church, moving east to west, till we went out of the west door into the Congregational Chapel, where we nearly reached an impasse because we brought the hassocks with us!

Left: *Hodges memorial window next to the south porch.*
Below: *The church chandelier*
Bottom: *The organ in its present position showing the new seats.*

Above: *The roof exposed and in need of replacing during the 1930s and* (left) *finally off during the restoration three decades later.*
Below right: *The plaque in the south porch.*

In return the exiles paid the full running expenses of their hosts during the period of occupation, with a donation to their organ fund.

They returned on Whitsunday, 21 May, to a fanfare of trumpets from Sherborne schoolboys and a splendid service of thanksgiving (now commemorated by a plaque in the south porch) followed by tea for all on the Vicarage lawn. In the procession, beside the appropriate ecclesiastical dignitaries and behind a new processional cross, were representatives of all the various bodies who had subscribed to the restoration. These included the Morris Fund of the Society of Antiquaries of London, the Dorset Church Building and Restoration Committee, the Dorset Historic Churches Trust, the Pilgrim's Trust, the Historic Churches Preservation Trust, and the Dorset Trust Incorporated Church Building Society. With them walked two outstandingly generous individuals – Lord Digby and Mr George Squibb.

The financial effort had indeed been great. From an original estimate of £7500 the cost had risen to nearly £14 000, of which the parishioners themselves had raised £8400 (as well as shouldering two interest-free loans). On regular 'gift days' the vicar had sat opposite the church under the shell porch of Mr Squibb's Old House. One notable exercise in

fund-raising, on an October Sunday in 1959, deserves particular mention. In order to broadcast a 'Week's Good Cause Appeal' from the Bristol studios of the BBC, Canon Taylor and his two churchwardens, their harvest festival concluded by 5p.m., had led the whole congregation to the school recreation ground behind the music of the Pipe and Drums Band of 15 Training Battalion, RASC, Blandford, to the tune of 'The De'il amang the Tailors' (punningly) and 'Will ye no come back again' (perhaps apprehensively). Awaiting them was a helicopter, due to take off before 5.45p.m. because it was forbidden to be in the air later than half an hour after sunset: summer time had ended that very day.

Financially exhausted, for another year or more the Parochial Church Council put no further large works in hand, although some minor embellishments are noteworthy. The south-chancel window was unblocked and the adjacent mural paintings (*see page 144*) restored by Mr Peter Courtney under the supervision of Mrs Eve Baker: a further fragment (possibly of an Ascension) was uncovered above the chancel arch. The restored texts in the nave were completed with a matching modern cartouche celebrating the occasion. A name-board of past vicars, or priests-in-charge, was compiled by Mr Squibb and executed by Mr Wiltshire. In the tower, inspected from a bosun's chair, the floor of the ringing chamber was renewed and a new clock supplied by Applegates. The fine chandelier, reputedly of 18th-century Dutch origin, was electrified. During March 1963 John Hall & Sons of Bristol undertook the very draughty operation of reglazing the west window, last glazed in 1862 in memory of James Bragg, and went on to the north and south aisles where they 'de-Victorianised' the Hellyer windows by removing stained glass and edgings.

A return to bigger and more costly undertakings was evident when in 1966 Messrs Webb & Ford restored and reglazed the great east window, renewing or re-pinning many crumbling mullions in the process. Under the guidance of Mr Squibb the PCC decided that not only should the fragmented arms be restored, but the gaps in the two lines of shields filled in. Mr Squibb's description of the completed work may be studied on the back of the chancel screen.

The Church in Cerne Abbas thanks God for the many gifts whereby this place having been closed for restoration in March 1960 was by May 1961 made fit again for his praise

Interment beneath the church floor - at 6s.8d. supportive of her finances though not of the building's foundations - seems to have been discontinued around 1830. Charges for breaking the ground for churchyard burials are, as we have noted, recorded in the accounts alongside pew rents. In 1875 maintenance of the churchyard and the curtilage of the building was put out to contract. Until then sundry payments are noted for the carting away of 'robbel' and 'rubbage' and for repairs to the hedge; and although the parish maintained no flock of its own, reliance seems to have been placed mainly on sheep to subdue the grass.

1735 April 30 Pd.Robert Gillingham & John Stickland for Cleansing the Church-yard & Carrying 10 Load of Dung from thence 12s.4d.
1755 Paid Charity Stickland for weeding ye church doors 4d.
1756 paid John Stickland for 3 days work about ye Churchyard 3s.0d.
for Beer 10d.

On 8 April 1858 the Vestry resolved 'that a sum not exceeding Five pounds be granted to James Northover junr for taking a survey of the Churchyard & making an Index of the grass therein', which he duly did for that sum the following year. By 1871 there were so many graves that the Vestry was obliged to debate whether an overall levelling was the only solution. Sheep were eventually to be superseded by regular cutting and more evergreen shrubs were planted. Children were no longer to be allowed to play there, a walk leading to the south-east corner of the area was closed, and charges for interment raised.

Soon, however, 'the churchyard was declared to be very full and it was considered desirable to apply to the Lord of the Manor for an additional area'. A further nine years passed before application was made to Mr Creech, Lord Rivers' steward, and a further six before it was reported that:

... a piece of ground presented to the Parish by Gen. Pitt-Rivers was consecrated by Dr. Wordsworth, Bishop of the Diocese, on Saturday October 16th. 1886. This piece of ground is situated to the south of the churchyard and was given as an additional burial ground for the Parish.

From the 1820s to '60s an annual rental of 2s.6d. was charged to various persons for 'use of the road adjoining the church', presumably either for access or as the site of a market stall. In 1919, with Hodges' bootmaking premises derelict, the Vestry passed a resolution deploring the state of the ground adjacent to the south side of the church and asking the Lord of the Manor, as landlord, that this too be handed over to the keeping of the church officers, who subsequently raised the war memorial there. As part of the big restoration of St Mary's interior in the early 1960s a 13th-century stone coffin and lid were moved outside into the south-east corner of the walls.

After six years' work by our Historical Society during the 1990s, there is now a complete and detailed record of the 763 gravestones and other inscriptions in the burial ground, made under the supervision of the late Mr John Turner. This information, checked against burial and parish registers, is lodged with the Parish Clerk, our historical society and the County Record Office.

Wall paintings revealed when the church was restored in 1959. The cartouches have now been reworked.

THE BELLS

It now remained to reinstate what should be the church's crowning glory, the peal of bells virtually silent for 50 years during which only tolling could be risked. Like the clock, these had always been a cause for anxiety and expense, as had even the simple alternative, hand-operated chiming mechanism: '1647 September Pd. Jo Bartlett & Edw. Pettibone for mending the horologue, 8s.0d.' At his own expense Mr H. Derriman renewed this piece of apparatus as late as 1904, but it was out of order again in less than ten years. In 1633 the re-casting of four cracked bells and the making of a new fifth were entrusted to Roger Purdie at Maiden Newton. The total and individual weights of these bells were recorded the following year. From time to time attempts were made to restrict their routine use to certain authorised persons by a kind of farming-out not always profitable to the latter:

1717 April 7 At a Vestry held 'tis agreed by the Inhabitants of the Town that henceforth no Bell or Bells shall be rung or raised at any Funerall but by the Clerk or his Agent for which Ringing he shall be impowered to demand two shillings upon the Consideration that if ye Bell should be overturned at any time by ye sd. Clerk or his Agents he shall forfeit three shillings and fourpence to be paid to ye Church wardens towards ye maintenance of ye sd. Bells.

1719 April 28 Received of Thomas White 3 times overthrowing ye great Bell each time 3s.4d.

Maintenance had, by the 18th century, become a contractural matter for the wardens. For example:

1726 November 12 Received of Mr. Richd. Shephard & Mr. Richd. Trott Churchwardens of Cerne Abbas Three Pounds for putting in Repair their Town Clock and Chimes, and I doe hereby promise the said Churchwardens and their successors that I will yearly during my life from henceforth Repair and amend the sd. Clock & Chimes as often as they shall be out of order for the yearly sum of five shillings without putting the sd. Churchwardens or their successors to any expense abt. the same. John Biddlecombe.

It. Spent when we bargained for ye Clock 6d.

1744 December 6 Agreed with John Boyse of Pedle town to keep ye Church Clock and Cheems In Repair for the sum of five shillings yearly During his Life without Putting the said Church Wardens... or their successors to any expense about the same During my Life. Given under my hand. Joh. Boyse.

The great whirlwind of 31 October 1731, which carried away the New Inn's sign into the neighbouring street, necessitated repairs the following spring to pinnacles, battlements and Richard Barnwell's weathercock. New bells were cast, transported, hung and tuned in 1747, 1755 and 1762, the last being a particularly busy autumn in the tower:

October 14
Pd. Mr. Belbie for making three Bells £27.16s.3d.
for 48 pound of new mettal at 1s. £2.8s.0d.
for 3 new clappers £1.1s.0d.
pd. Mr. Combs for 9 days labeling of Mr. Belbie & beer for him and all the workman £1.11s.0d.
pd. Mr. George Andrews bill for 9 days work for taking down & drawing up & chipping of the bells 18s.0d.
Mr. Sam. Thorne for boxing the 4 Bell clapper 1s.0d.
Pd. Mr. Jn Thorne for 2 days for taking Down of the Bells 2s.8d.
Mr. Jn Dominy's bill for a Cheem rope & Bell ropes £1.3s.6d.
Pd. Mr. Tos.Wiltshire for beer about the bells & Payment to others in beer & beef 5s.0d.

Clock dials needed renewing or repainting about every 30 years. The winding of the clock and chimes is noted as part of the Parish Clerk's duties in 1865; as part of the Sexton's – his wife washing the surplices and communion linen – in 1897.

Liturgical routine apart, what occasions of village life prompted the ringing of the bells? A great variety are recorded: coronations, royal deaths, births of heirs apparent, the failure of attempts on the monarch's life, visits of bishops or the return of local heroes from the war... and of course victory in battle – excellent ground for many peals. The Seven Years War, for instance, introduced to the churchwardens' accounts many an exotic name:

1758 August 21 Gave the ringers on taking of Louisburgh 7s.6d.
1759 May 29 Gave the Ringers when prince Ferdinand Defeated the French in jarmony 6s.0d. Gave the Ringers when Quebeck was taken 5s.0d.
1762 June 14 Gave the Ringers at the taking of Bellisle 7s.6d.
June 24 Gave the Ringers at the victory in Garmany & at the taking of Pondicarry & Domyniche 10s.0d.
Sept.22 Gave the Ringars and others by order 1/2 Hd. Beer & 1/2 a Crown at Every House Coronation Day £1.7s.0d.
1763 May 29 Gave ye Ringers upon Som Great News 5s.0d.

Ringers at the ready, 1976. Left to right, standing: Ray Wareham, Frank Hamblin, Sarah Hamblin, Jack de Caberet, Peter Grantowskis; kneeling: Mrs Bradford and Mrs Hall (?).

The bells leaving St Mary's in 1975, watched by, from left to right: a young Mumford, Revd Hugh Mumford, C.W. Paul, Miss Benson, Mrs Moore, Mrs Bradford, and Mrs Mumford.

There may be some alive who recall the most humdrum use of all - the ringing of a single bell at 1 p.m. on Sundays to warn those concerned that their dinners were ready for collection from the Bakehouse for the sum of one penny.

After the First World War an attempt was made to revive an obsolete practice. The minutes of the PCC for 26 July 1920 contain the following entry:

The Chairman brought up next the question of the Death Bell and it was unanimously decided that according to the Canon Law of the church as soon as the Sexton receives notice of a Death he should then repair to the Church and pass the Bell as follows. For an Infant three strokes For a Woman three strokes - a pause and then three strokes. For a Man three strokes - a pause - then three strokes - a pause - then three strokes… and that when these strokes were knelled out then a stroke for every year of the deceased and this reviving of old customs would gratify Cerne parishioners.

Evidently it did not gratify the sexton, for two years later his failure to toll on every such occasion ('a specific duty… whether separately paid for it or not') was deplored. Whether or not raising his salary to the level of the organist's, £12 p.a., persuaded him to comply is unrecorded.

In 1897 Queen Victoria's 60 glorious years had been marked by the purchase of a daily winding clock, its substantial oak dial made by Mr Mitchell and engraved in gold. In 1949, with the return of peace to the world, a new electric-impulse clock was installed, its face no longer placed asymmetrically as had hitherto been necessary while the Hodges' house had stood between tower and market-place. (Four decades later, incidentally, the date stone of that house - 1576 - was reincised.). But a full peal of the bells had not been regularly rung since 1902. The Whitechapel Bell Foundry, called in in 1928, had reported that the ringing frame was unsafe. Summoned again in 1973, they found the three trebles, recast in 1762 by Thomas Bilbie of Chewstoke, all heavily indented and in need of retuning, as was the 4th, fashioned in 1747 by Wm. Knight of Closworth. The 5th and largest (tenor, of $14^1/_2$ cwt.) was very badly cracked and almost toneless. It was recast, the other four were dismantled and re-hung in a new Iroko frame and a new treble made to bring the peal to six. Then it was decided to recast the second treble too. Adding in the cost of ancillary work to the tower, VAT, and the effect of rapid general inflation, the final bill of 1975 came to £10 200 - nearly twice the initial estimate and the equivalent of nearly half the cost of the whole church restoration of the previous decade.

THE WASHINGTON CONNECTION
by Jean Turner

Set into the floor of the central aisle of Cerne Abbas Church are brass plaques in memory of two John Notleys, father and son. There were several Notley families in South Dorset in the 16th and 17th centuries, especially in Winterborne Came and Winterborne Monkton. At least two members of these families emigrated to Maryland, a Catholic colony established by charter in 1632. One was Walter Notley of Winterborne Monkton, who went to Maryland in 1638 and obtained a land grant from the proprietor of the colony - Cecil Calvert, Lord Baltimore. The other was Thomas Notley, who emigrated to Maryland in 1662 at the age of 28.

Thomas Notley's family was established in Winterborne Came. The Came Manor Court Roll shows that on 9 September 1550 one John Notley obtained the tenancy of some 38 acres from Sir John Meller, the major landowner there. Notley's son, another John, took up further acreage in 1564, but in 1579, then 39 years old, John senr moved to farm Meller land in Cerne Abbas, leaving John junr on his plot in Winterborne Came. By the time of his death in 1612, John Notley senr had established himself as a respectable yeoman farmer in Cerne Abbas. John junr succeeded him and took over his lease of land, dying there in 1626. These are the two John Notleys whose memorial plaques appear in the church floor.

A later John Notley, son of the John who died at Cerne in 1626, had four children - John, Charles, Katherine and Thomas. This Thomas, born in 1634, was he who emigrated to Maryland in 1662. Little is known about his early life, but when he arrived in America he was a practising attorney, so he must have had a sound basic education, probably at Dorchester School, and legal training at one of the Inns of Chancery attached to the Inns of Court in London. Possibly it was his sojourn in London which gave him the opportunity to cultivate the friendship of Charles Calvert, who in 1661 had succeeded his father, Cecil, as Governor of Maryland.

Be that as it may, Thomas Notley became a successful attorney in the Maryland courts, as well as a planter and merchant, eventually attaining the position of Deputy Governor. At some stage, he acquired a plot of land close to the original fort in St Mary's City, which he offered to the use of the county shortly after he became Deputy Governor. This was the land which in 1934 was chosen as the site for the reconstruction of the 1676 State House. Thomas also owned Basford Manor, a property of 1500 acres, probably on the eastern bank of the Wicomico River (conveyed to Col Rozier shortly before Thomas's death).

In November 1670, Thomas purchased 1800 acres of land from George Thompson, who had received them by deed of patent from the proprietor, the second Lord Baltimore. The price was 40 000lbs of tobacco. These lands stretched northwards from the Annacostia River and encompassed all of what was then called Jenkins' Hill and is now Capitol Hill. They had been occupied at an early date by the Powhatans, a sub-tribe of the Algonquin Indians, whose Council House was then located at the foot of the hill. On 1 March 1671, by certified deed of patent, Thomas Notley united his three patents from Thompson, comprising Duddington Manor and Pasture and New Troy, into a single manor which he called Cern Abbey Manor, after the ancient ruined Benedictine foundation in his native Dorset village.

Dying child-less, probably in 1678, Thomas willed all of his 'tract or parcel of land called Cern Abbey Manor, lying situate and being in Charles County' to his godson, Notley Rozier, son of Benjamin Rozier. Notley Rozier married a Jane Digges and their only child, Ann or Eleanor Rozier, became sole owner of the lands that today include Capitol Hill and much of south-east and south-west Washington DC. Ann Rozier married twice. Her first husband was Daniel Carroll of Annapolis, whose father, an Irish Catholic lawyer, had come to Maryland in 1680 following his appointment as Attorney-General of the colony by Lord Baltimore. Their son, Charles Carroll, inherited Duddington Manor in 1759 and eventually bequeathed the property to his eldest son, Daniel. Ann Rozier's second marriage was to Benjamin Young, by whom she had another son, Notley Young, to whom in 1761 Ann made over all the Cerne Abbey Manor holdings except Duddington Manor, which remained in the Carroll family.

As inheritors of Ann Rozier's lands, Charles Carroll and Notley Young became the most considerable land-owners in the area. Charles Carroll planned to develop a port town at the mouth of the Annacostia River, but it was never much more than a 'paper town' and very few lots were ever sold. His own house, located near the present Navy Yard, was one of the earliest in the Annacostia area and was built in 1759, when he acquired the property. Charles' sister, Mary, married Ignatius Digges, whose family estates included the land opposite Mount Vernon, where Fort Washington was later built. His cousin, another Charles Carroll, of Carrolton near Baltimore, was a signatory of the 1776 Declaration of Independence.

After the War of Independence, the question arose as to the possible location of a capital for the new Federal Government. Both Maryland and Virginia originally ceded territory and on January 22 1791 President Washington appointed commissioners 'to survey and by proper metes and bounds to define and limit' the area of the city within the experimental boundary lines of the District of Columbia. One of these commissioners was Daniel Carroll of

Carrolton, Maryland, the cousin of Daniel Carroll of Duddington. The area selected for Congress House was on Jenkins' Hill, owned by Daniel Carrol, who became the leading spokesman for the interests of the Carroll family and other neighbouring proprietors.

Two months later Daniel Carroll and Notley Young joined with other proprietors in signing the agreement of March 30 1791 which established the Federal City, making their lands over to the Federal Government 'in consideration of the good benefits which we expect to derive from having the Federal City laid off from our lands'. The division of land between Government and proprietors was by alternate lots or by areas of equal value. Carroll was quick to see the possible advantages of his situation. He built a large house on the south side of Capitol Hill, formerly Jenkins' Hill, and in 1799 began building a tavern on his most northerly lot, facing First Street. When Congress arrived in Washington in the autumn of 1800, the tavern was completed and became a popular hostelry with congressmen. Notley Young remained in the old plantation house he had built in 1756 overlooking the Potomac River. James Kent noted in 1793 that 'Notley Young's old brick house where I dined... had a fine view down to Alexandria even to Mount Vernon'. In the Young Chapel the first services of the Roman Catholic Church in Washington were held and it was the custom for everyone to stay for dinner after Mass. The house remained on the site until it was demolished in 1856. According to John Cotton Smith in 1800:

There appeared to be but two really comfortable habitations... within the bounds of the city, one of which belonged to Daniel Carroll Esq., and the other to Notley Young... former proprietors of the land appropriated to the city, but who reserved for their own accommodation ground sufficient for gardens and other useful appurtenances.

Carroll and the other proprietors of lands in the area assumed that the selection of the Potomac site for the new Federal City would make them all rich men. However, as Daniel Carroll wrote in 1837, recalling those times, the results were other than expected:

I perfectly remember that the general opinion was that so great was the gift that the citizens never would be subject to taxation for the improvement of the streets having relinquished every alternate lot to the Government. Indeed, some were so wild as to suppose... that the Government might pave the streets with ingots of gold or silver. After nearly half a century the result is now fully known: the unfortunate proprietors are generally brought to ruin and some with scarcely enough to buy daily food for their families.

Chapter 14
Two Wars and A Festival

Readers with lively recollections of 1939-45 will scarcely credit what comparatively little impact hostilities made upon the local domestic scene of 1914-18. True, Cerne's war memorial bears the names of those dozen saluted every November by our branch of the Royal British Legion who, during those five years, lost their lives in duty abroad. But, apart from the formation of a Ladies' Rifle Club and something called the Duty and Discipline Movement, that national emergency was still merely the occasion for material and collective support of those engaged in distant actions. Thus, the British Red Cross Society's Blue Fund for the wounded took the place of the Transvaal Fund of a decade earlier. There was a Baccy Fund as well as some Kitchener's Day collections in furtherance of the great man's Socks-for-the-Boys appeal, which raised over ten dozen pairs by local manufacture or purchase, a fillip for local outfitters. A small government subsidy was available for the gathering of blackberries, the boiling of jars and the making of jam in the 'Church Room'. Negatively, between 6a.m. and noon, licensed premises were closed against soldiers and sailors and at all times against the blue-uniformed, hospitalised wounded.

In its multiple impacts the Second World War could hardly have differed more strikingly from its predecessor. Besides the influx of a new race of evacuees, and in addition to the unfamiliar processes of registration and rationing, the prospect of military conflict itself could not be discounted by civilians in advance. Not for nothing has it been dubbed 'The People's War'.

In contrast, during the years of peace, outside events found only a pale reflection within the village. On 25 April 1912 worshippers observed 'Titanic Sunday', and on another Sunday in August of that same year were gratified with their first glimpse of an

Short of labour, Lord and Lady Digby took to delivering the milk from the farm themselves. Mrs England receives her pint, 1946.

aeroplane overhead reassuringly 'proceeding steadily in a northern direction'. Mechanisation advanced; long-established blacksmiths like Dick ('Tiger') Curtis disappear from directories as smithy and forge were displaced by garage keepers and motor mechanics; the first school child was run over in Duck Street by a car on its way to a Dorchester Show of such automobile marvels. Years were still to elapse, however, before the full implications for personal mobility of the internal combustion engine were realised.

War, as always, accelerated change. Yet even in peace time Cerne's petrol-driven journey into modernity was proceeding apace. This transformation can best be followed by extrapolating along the lines of the 'improvement' in services and sociability we began to trace in chapter 8. Thus, of mains services, electricity arrived in the 1930s, water and sewage drainage had to wait another generation until the 1960s: thereafter it was no longer possible for mischievous lads to operate the millstream sluice-gate so as to literally discommode, indeed unseat, those in mid-session at their ablutions! Not all wells, though, were converted into soakaways; some, with their historic wellheads, have survived here and there to embellish a private garden. Too often, however, water has been the enemy, which has required taming, and flooding the recurrent calamity such as that recorded typically in the autumn of 1882:

November 2: The storm that visited most parts of the county broke over this parish between 9 and 10 o'clock in the morning of Tuesday last week, doing considerable damage to the roads, bridges and trees. The millstream burst its bank, making a breach about 40ft. wide and about 25ft. deep, bringing down a great number of trees and washing the allotment gardens clear of everything into Duck St. The torrent rushed down into Long

St., filling the houses some 2 foot and others even 5 ft. deep in water, Messrs' Norman's tannery suffering considerably. At the Glove Inn a sow and 4 young pigs were drowned. The county bridge leading to Minterne was also washed away...

In the (very) long term, permanent 'flood alleviation' required no less than grant-aiding by the Ministry of Agriculture and Fisheries, with whose support the County Council in November 1986 engaged contractors from Exmouth to erect a substantial dam on the north side of Kettle Bridge. This seems to have been effective, although some Duck Street residents still retain sliding cills slotted into the bases of their doorways as relics of a torrential past.

A rescue operation of a very different nature was required for the village stores, inundated by bank debts – in this case by a priming of the pump when a group of public-minded villagers turned to and restocked the shelves. As to developments in public transport it would be a mistake to assume that no third alternative existed other than either buying a private car or suffering at the mercy of a rigid and under-funded bus system. The latter, in fact, was to offer a good deal of experimental flexibility. By the 1950s there was a seven-day-a-week service to Dorchester utilising a number of double-decker vehicles. In addition Southern National ran a summer service to Weymouth from Yeovil, and Western National one from Taunton. After unsuccessful trials of other companies in the mid 1990s, a conditional five-year contract was awarded to Southern National, subsidised by the Rural Development Agency, which has proved stable and basically adequate.

Of other services earlier noted, it remains to record the growth, in size and sophistication, of the medical. From the skeletal post-war service, split between Cerne Abbas and Pulham, consolidation and expansion have been made possible by a greatly enlarged physical premises at Alton Lane, its expertise radiating out from a five-member core under a practice manager to auxiliary services which entwine with the health roots of an area reaching from Charminster up to the Caundles and embracing health visitors, district nurses and a broad counselling system.

Turning next, as we did in Chapter 8, from the administrative framework to those informal, but vital, groupings arising out of spontaneous sociability we

Edward Young, one of Cerne's casualties. The following of Cerne also gave their lives in the First World War: Charles Damen, Charles Burt, Horace Collier, George Curtis, Hamilton Diment, Harold Hunt, William Miller, Frank Paulley, Albert Way, Thomas Williment, Harry Derriman, James Lake, Reginald Vine and John Henry Strode Batten (UpCerne).

note more gain than loss. After 75 years of life, alas, the Women's Institute wound itself up in 1994, pleading an intolerable burden of bureaucracy. From its ashes arose the 94 Club, meeting much the same needs. Thus did the ladies acquire their own equivalent of the Men's Discussion Club, formed when (now the late) Sir Jack Longland, County Education Officer, defied the long dark nights of the Second World War by gathering in his residence, the Old Bell, a fortnightly group of not more than 30 males. Older traditions, too, were revived, as when a new Cerne Abbas Society for Horticulture reinstated the traditional annual prize-awarding exhibition of flowers, fruit and vegetables, now in the Village Hall – itself an enlightened private bequest of the 1930s. Likewise a Cerne Abbas Dramatic Society now carries on the good work of the Cerne Players, whose memento is the big lectern Bible in St Mary's. At the same time a theatre-going club keeps us in close contact with professional drama in Salisbury, Bath and elsewhere. Out of doors each mid June some 1500 weekend visitors will view about 25-30 open gardens. This event was first held in 1976 to raise funds for the church and then raised about £150. It has proved so popular that as an annual event it has since then raised some £50 000, much of it now going to charities outside the village. Visitors, also, beholding our plethora of posters, detect a continuous rumble of low-grade sociability; of plant sales, 'hunger lunches' and coffee mornings there is seemingly no end.

All this growth of activity has been mirrored in a simultaneous physical expansion. The 1960s and '70s saw relatively huge developments of domestic housing respectively to the south and west of the village centre providing accommodation for old and young, all of whom help to justify the continued existence of essential services. Even so, a population of some 800 now makes one wonder how 1300 lived when the village was half its present size.

Always willing to mark a special occasion, as it did for the victories and Queen Victoria's jubilee, Cerne has found numerous excuses for celebration, and the commemoration in 1987 of the millennium of the Abbey (founded in AD987) provided the opportunity to bring together all of the local talent (of which there is a great deal) in a true multimedia festival where all the arts were represented and displayed.

THE HOME FRONT, 1939-46

Unlike the First World War which claimed young men of Cerne as casualties but seems not to have greatly changed village life, the Second World War made a considerable impact. Mrs Elliott listed the ways in which the villagers took an active part and fortunately her simple record survives. Now the older generation tend to reply to requests for memories with 'but I wasn't here. I was in the Army/ Navy/Airforce' or 'I was nursing/elsewhere', so it is those who were at school who can flesh out the picture.

There were airfields at Warmwell and Yeovil. There was a torpedo works not to mention the Navy at Portland, and German bombers overflew on their way westwards, frequently dropping bombs and incendiaries on their way. Cerne had searchlights - first on St Catherine's Hill to the east, and later moved closer to the village. Some 22 barrage balloons flew over the Giant.

When invasion threatened, a Home Guard unit was formed, and night after night men watched on the hill using a shepherd's hut for a few hours kip, two at a time. Those on duty reported every passing aircraft and thump and the village patrol reported every chink of light from unsatisfactory blackouts. On one occasion when a plane came down over Sydling to the west, Mr England (the baker) went to arrest the German airmen. He took his rifle then discarded it remembering that he had no ammunition anyway! One of the Germans came quietly but the second - who had his parachute caught in a tree - was not so pleased about his capture.

The Home Guard trained like the territorials even after invasion scares were past, and others trained as firemen. Some men were reserved for essential agricultural work and urged to produce more food. Farming went on. Horses had to be shod and vehicles kept in working order. Children had a six week 'holiday' allowance, to be taken when their assistance was needed on the land. They had a card to be marked when they were out of school and were paid 3d. an hour.

Not only men and boys were put to it. The women served as nurses at Minterne which became a naval hospital. There Mr Curtis, in charge of the greenhouses, became a blood donor and was called in from the grounds to give direct transfusions whenever there was an emergency!

The WI, long campaigning for decent sewers to make the school's outside toilets less horrendous, accepted that 'the money had gone to munitions' and communicated with Mrs Roosevelt, wife of the US President, for seeds to grow vegetables from. They worked the allotments and utilised the produce; they knitted and sewed and looked after servicemen billeted in the village.

The butcher, who had once poleaxed his beasts as they quietly dozed in their field at night to satisfy customer demand, was now required to send his animals to Dorchester so that the meat could be fairly rationed. Both meat and bread were distributed over a wide area from Cerne.

Slit windows for snipers were inserted in the south walls of houses on the Dorchester Road, and the owners of petrol pumps were given 'some sort of steel wool' which would have enabled them to put the pumps out of action should an invading force hope to find a local supply of fuel. Soldiers were billeted all over the village and were fed in the Wesleyan Chapel Hall, now long gone, while the canteen provided additional refreshment.

Once preparations for D-Day were afoot there were soldiers everywhere, and Mr Shutler who ran the village newsagents found himself delivering newspapers to the US Army. He parked his van at the entrance to the camp while he walked to the mess and always found his petrol tank full when he got back to it, no questions asked. But one day a US serviceman backed his truck into the shop window and for many years the left side windows contained long panes of glass hastily put in, not matching the square panes on the right side of the door!

In many ways, however, life went on as usual; there were numerous complaints about lights at the Village Hall when there were dances and whist drives. Eventually peace was celebrated. Muriel Marsh says that she danced right through a pair of shoes that night.

Right: Mr Shutler, Cpl in the Home Guard, outside the pig shed at the back of the Post Office.
Below: The British Legion parade at Bovington, 1947.

Firefighting was updated, the Cerne Team, 1940s.

The Home Guard of Cerne Abbas, UpCerne, NetherCerne and Godmanstone.
Left to right, back: the present Lord Digby, Messrs Cornick, ?, Yard, Claxton, Bowditch, Hunt, Bull,
Napier, C. Notley, ?, Hart, Drake, ?, Gill;
3rd row: ?, T. Dunn, L. Squib, G. Read, Green, T. White, Woodsford, Napier, B. Belt, Fripp, Copp, B.
Drew, H. Drew, Roberts, ?, Curtis, T. Whittle;
2nd row: Tomkins, Lake, Chubb, Hurworth, Lamb, G. Way, Morgan, Bald, E. Fripp, Best, Iles,
Maidment, Legg, F. Moxom, Herbie Davis, Pile;
front: Harvey, Legg, Shutler, F. Gray, S. Notley, Lake, ?, ?, N. Warren.

The Dramatic Society in 1955. On the left is Betty Marsh with the broom. Jean Congram, Bob Stenhouse, Mrs Congram (?) and Mrs Shutler are seated.

A Tale of Cerne, *1987.*
Left to right: Chris Harris, Norman Watts, ? Murrin, Nick Hill, Bob Prowse (white smock), Phiol Hallett (in front of Bob), another Murrin, Ben Prowse, Chris Murrin, James Field (holding target).

Left: *George V Jubilee, 1935.*
The procession reaches Long
Street.

Right: *Cricket in the 1920s.*
Left to right, back: Joe Clark,
Monty Moore, ?, Revd Hall;
front: Mr Richards (?), Erne
Roberts, Dr Dalton, Vincent
Dalton (?)

Left: *The coach collects the Theatre Club and*
Graham Baker and Duggie Howel let the
ladies on first.
Below: *The street party put on to celebrate the*
wedding of Charles and Diana.

Musically, St Mary's resounded with four concerts by contrasted choral and instrumental groups (the Tallis Scholars, the Martin Best Ensemble and the Bournemouth Sinfonietta Choir). Visually, the church also housed an exhibition of local art and displayed a magnificent set of communion kneelers embroidered in Celtic pattern, dedicated at a special service following a Whitsun procession through the village headed by an ex-Bishop of London.

In the Village Hall a succession of lecturers presented aspects of the Benedictines and their work from respective viewpoints. The drama front went from the sublime to the ridiculous; at one level was a production in the Tithe Barn of Christopher Fry's *The Boy with a Cart*, at another, the stable court in Piddle Lane entertained a good-humoured burlesque in the form of an unofficial history of Cerne in sketch and fable.

Around the fringe were the Wessex Morris Men, a ramble and a street fair, in addition to the annual 'open gardens' weekend. With more permanent consequences, an exhibition in the school of Cerne's historical memorabilia with many photographs set going a movement which, as more and more material came to light, acquired a big archive and, in a very short time, the need for a Cerne Historical Society to conserve them... which, in turn, naturally drew to itself an annual programme of visiting lecturers, a further exhibition in 1993 and, eventually, this volume.

Finally, a millennial pilgrimage starting south from Wells merged on 15 August with a great gathering of folk in the field called Beever (Belvoir) to hear Eucharist celebrated – truly the perfect culmination of all other observances, the complete merging of our sacred with our secular; and here indeed, within eyeshot of the original Abbey site we sensed the identity of our ends with our beginnings.

Top: *Bill Bown and Jack de Carteret lead the walk up through Park, 1987.*
Above: Whitsun procession through Duck Street, 1987.
Right: *The Morris Men atop the Giant for Mayday morning, 1987.*

EPILOGUE

Epilogue and, in spite of all those dire prognostications, not an obituary! *Country Life* discovered Cerne in 1955 and reported it to be 'a jewel in a perfect setting.' Similarly, in 1979, *The Field* declared: 'Cerne Abbas stands in such an attractive setting and is so pretty people come from all over the world to see it'. When estate agents search for words these days Cerne becomes 'one of the most attractive and desirable villages in Dorset - lovely rolling countryside and yet in no way isolated', in fact 'one of Dorset's most sought-after villages', all of which is of course disastrous for house prices! But once here you can ramble in that lovely rolling countryside, join societies catering to many tastes, take your place on the boards of many groups such as the Dramatic Society, serve teas for 'Open Gardens' visitors, work in an allotment, and still - so far - go hunting. One thing you should not come here for is a quiet life!

At the turn of the new century Cerne has taken on a festive air. In May 2000 there was another street party and other junketings. During August local artists exhibited their paintings in the church and the Historical Society staged a large exhibition in the school. A 'Parish Map' was also being embroidered by ladies in the village. The church tower was floodlit and the Giant survived yet another scouring!

Children enjoying the sunshine and a Punch and Judy show at the millennium street party, 2000.

SUBSCRIBERS

Mr and Mrs David Adams, Cerne Abbas, Dorset

Ruth M. Adams, Cerne Abbas, Dorset

Walter (Stan) Stanley Amey

Mr and Mrs B. H. Atkinson, Cerne Abbas, Dorset

Graham E. Baker, Cerne Abbas, Dorset

June and Eugene Balbinski, Cerne Abbas, Dorset

Margaret Balmer, Winchester, Hants

Kristina Barber, Derbyshire

Janet and Gordon Bartlet, Cerne Abbas, Dorset

Wendy D. Bazzell, Puddletown, Dorset

Rosemary Beasley, Shrewsbury, Shropshire

Hugh and Karen Bellis, Cerne Abbas, Dorset

Mr and Mrs S. Beresford, Cerne Abbas, Dorset

Mrs B. Billings (née House), St Albans, Herts.

Mr Hibbert A. H. Binney, Sherborne, Dorset

Mrs Janice Birch, Landlady, The Royal Oak, Cerne Abbas

Mr David Birch, Landlord, The Royal Oak, Cerne Abbas

Hazel Bird, Yeovil, Somerset

Chris and Ray Bowden, Cerne Abbas, Dorset

Margaret Bown, Cerne Abbas, Dorset

Margaret Boxwell, Cerne Abbas, Dorset

David Brown, Wellington, Somerset

Michael Brown, Gairloch, Wester Ross

David and Elizabeth Brown, Braishfield, Hampshire

Elizabeth M. Brown, Cerne Abbas, Dorset

Tanya Brunt-Murphy, Chippenham, Wiltshire

David C. Burgess, Buckland Newton, Dorset

Janet and Keith Burt, Buckland Newton, Dorset

Cindy Chant, Sherborne, Dorset

Andy, Hilary and Alex Charlesworth, Minterne Magna, Dorset

Rowena J. Cherry, Michigan, USA

Patricia F. Chorlton, Cerne Abbas, Dorset

Michael Clark, Cerne Abbas, Dorset

Jill and John Cole, Cerne Abbas, Dorset

Keith and Amanda Cole, Cerne Abbas, Dorset

Mr Edward Michael Octavius Collins, Cerne Abbas, Dorset

Gill and Adrian Coombe, Cerne Abbas, Dorset

J. Cooper, Frampton, Dorset

Mrs Jenifer Cooper, Cerne Abbas, Dorset

Doreen M. Cooper, Upton, Aylesbury, Bucks.

Colonel and Mrs A. E. Cornick, Camberwell, London

J. S. and N. M. Cotton, Back Lane, Cerne Abbas, Dorset

Dr John D. Cox, Cerne Abbas, Dorset

Mr C. Crocker, Buckland Newton, Dorset

Max and Clare Crosbie, Cerne Abbas, Dorset

Miss C. Dally, Cerne Abbas, Dorset

Orpha Davenport (née Puckett), formerly of Cerne Abbas, Dorset

The Lord Digby

Margaret Doncaster, M.B.E.

Mr and Mrs Peter Downton, Cerne Abbas, Dorset

Lee, Tracey, Rebecca and Katie Drage, Cerne Abbas, Dorset

Mr Stuart Drake, Cerne Abbas, Dorset

Mrs Dunford

Olive Anne Dunn, Cerne Abbas, Dorset

The Dunn Family, Cerne Abbas, Dorset

Mr Edward H. Durrant, Dorchester, Dorset

Mathilde Edward, Cerne Abbas, Dorset

Phyllis Edwards, Cerne Abbas, Dorset

John England, Cerne Abbas, Dorset

Stephen M. England, Cerne Abbas, Dorset

Michael and Ann Evans, Chetnole, Dorset

Viv and Brian Evis, Cerne Abbas, Dorset

David and Roselyn Forrester, Cerne Abbas,
    Dorset
Bob and Sue Foulser, Cerne Abbas, Dorset
Anthony Edward Fox, Romsey, Hants.
Malcolm Clive Fox, Cerne Abbas, Dorset
William Edwin Michael Fox, Southampton
Eric and Mione Fox, Cerne Abbas, Dorset
Geoffrey Fox, Stour Provost
E. Shirley Francis, Cerne Abbas, Dorset
R. P. Fraser, Cerne Abbas, Dorset
Anthony Clive Frater, Cerne Abbas, Dorset
A. E. H. and Mrs G. Frost, Buckland Newton,
    Dorset
Mrs Alison S. Gardner, St Albans, Herts.
Roy R. Gibbs, Newbury, Berkshire
James Gibson, Cerne Abbas, Dorset
Mrs P. Golding, Yeovil, Somerset
Mrs Dorothy W. Goodsell, Yeovil, Somerset
Olive E. Goodwin, Back Lane, Cerne Abbas,
    Dorset
Mrs C. G. Goodwin, Cerne Abbas, Dorset
Ursula E. Grantovskis, Plymouth, Devon
Peter John Grantovskis, Dorchester, Dorset
Anneliese Grantovskis, Cerne Abbas, Dorset
Kenneth S. Griffin, Cerne Abbas, Dorset
Pat and Harry Groves, Sherborne, Dorset
Dorothy C. Hall,
Colin Hallett, Cerne Abbas, Dorset
Henry J. T. Hallett, Cerne Abbas, Dorset
Frank C. Hamblin, Cerne Abbas, Dorset
Caroline A. Hart, Cerne Abbas, Dorset
Maureen and John Hartley, Cerne Abbas,
    Dorset
Richard and Clover Hartley-Sharpe, Cerne
    Abbas, Dorset
Wendy J. J. Harvey, Cerne Abbas, Dorset
Jeanne Head, Cerne Abbas, Dorset
Nancy Lady Henley, Cerne Abbas, Dorset
Joanna M. Higgs, Cerne Abbas, Dorset
Dilys M. Hill, Winchester, Hampshire
Shelagh Hill, Sherborne, Dorset
Edward J. and Maureen J. Hitt, Cerne Abbas,
    Dorset
W. H. Hodder, Cerne Abbas, Dorset
James House, Oxted, Surrey
William F. House, Oxshott, Surrey
Jeanette House, Edinburgh, Scotland
Major Tim House, The Devonshire and
    Dorset Regiment

Donald and Jill Hudson
Cdr and Mrs G.W.G. Hunt, Cerne Abbas,
    Dorset
G. (Roy) Hunt, Born 6 Ackerman Street 3.9.1919
Bob Johnson, Speen, Bucks.
Mrs Helen Judge, Minterne House, Minterne
    Magna, Dorset
Clare and John Killinger, Cerne Abbas, Dorset
Faith and Neville Lamb, Dorchester, Dorset
Christopher Langston, Bridport, Dorset
Justine F. Langton, Cerne Abbas, Dorset
E. Mary Long (née Yearsley), Bridport, Dorset
Joanna Longland, Bakewell and London
Revd and Mrs Ted Longman, Cerne Abbas,
    Dorset
Dr Gordon Lush, West Moors, Dorset
Stuart and Roz MacLean, Duck Street,
    Cerne Abbas, Dorset
Air Commodore Maurice and Mrs Elizabeth
    Mahoney, Cerne Abbas, Dorset
Cdr and Mrs A. Mancais, Cerne Abbas, Dorset
A. W. Mansel, Cerne Abbas, Dorset
Edward G. Markey, Cerne Abbas, Dorset
Mrs Muriel Marsh, Cerne Abbas, Dorset
Janet and Arthur Mason, Cerne Abbas, Dorset
John and Leonora McDonnell, Cerne Abbas,
    Dorset
Professor George McNicol CBE, Cerne Abbas,
    Dorset
Rosemary and Frank Mears, Cerne Abbas,
    Dorset
Alan Miles 1944-55, Now Aylesbury
Jane Mitchell, Oakland, California, USA
Maureen Mitchell (née Cornick), Dorchester,
    Dorset
Mrs M. B. Molony
Alan and Sandra Morrell, Cerne Abbas,
    Dorset
Frances Margaret Mowlem, Shrewsbury,
    Shropshire
Martin Mowlem, Tibberton, Shropshire
A. J. Muirhead, Cerne Abbas, Dorset
Simon Mumford, Dorchester, Dorset
Mark Mumford, Dorchester, Dorset
Hugh and Margaret Mumford, Dorchester,
    Dorset
James Mumford, Dorchester, Dorset
Robin and Daphne Nayler, Cerne Abbas,
    Dorset

Pat and Peter Neate, Godmanstone, Dorset

Sarah Nichols, Marlborough, Wiltshire

Charles Nicholson, Cerne Abbas, Dorset

Phyllis Nicholson (Nikki), Cerne Abbas, Dorset

Nicola Noakes, London, SW15

Mary Norman, Dorchester, Dorset

Mr Robert Northover, Chilthorne Domer, Somerset

Bev and Christine Nunn, Cerne Abbas, Dorset

Winifred M. Nurse, Cerne Abbas, Dorset

Gerald, Christine T., Heather, Christopher and Wendy Oakes

Alec and Peggy Palmer, Weymouth, Dorset

Melanie Patt-Corner, Cabin John, Maryland, USA

Sylvia Pearson, Minterne Magna, Dorset

Bidsy Pearson, Cerne Abbas, Dorset

Angela M. Scard Peck, Ferriby, E. Yorkshire

John and Josephine Pentney, Taunton, Somerset

Mrs Harry Percy, Cerne Abbas, Dorset

Richard K. Pilcher, Cerne Abbas, Dorset

Roger A. Pile, Cerne Abbas, Dorset

Gerald H. D. Pitman, MBE, FRSA, Sherborne, Dorset

Lisa J. S. Poole, Solihull, West Midlands

Andrew K. Popkin, Thimble Cottage, 3 Long Street, Cerne Abbas, Dorset

Bob and Linda Prowse, Cerne Abbas, Dorset

E. K. Pulliblank, Cerne Abbas, Dorset

Margaret Rehahn, Poundbury Village, Dorset

Robin Rendell, Bedfont, Middlesex

Jill Reynolds, Cerne Abbas, Dorset

Mark and Sarah Richardson, Cerne Abbas, Dorset

Ralph Herbert Riffer, Cerne Abbas, Dorset

Mrs Gillian Riggs, Cerne Abbas, Dorset

Irene E. Riglar, Cerne Abbas, Dorset

Ann Robson, Cerne Abbas, Dorset

Dr and Mrs Eric (Ted) Roebuck, Cerne Abbas, Dorset

Pamela E. Ross, Christchurch, Dorset

Elizabeth Russell-Gaunt, Cambridge

Peggie Sargent, Holnest

Michael A. Scard, Hastings, Sussex

Stephen and Stella Scott, formerly of Cerne Abbas, Dorset

Mr Douglas G. A. Simmonds, Cerne Abbas, Dorset

Drs Stephen and Debbie Simpson, Cerne Abbas, Dorset

Miss K. Slocum, Cerne Abbas, Dorset

Helen and Jim Smith, The Old Market House, Cerne Abbas, Dorset

Mrs Averil Stevenson, Middlemarsh, Dorset

Dr David J. Strawbridge, Bridport, Dorset

Noel and Pauline Sullivan, Cerne Abbas, Dorset

John S. Sutherland, Cerne Abbas, Dorset

Mr Christopher Talbot, Cerne Abbas, Dorset

Mr S. W. Taylor, Cousley Wood, East Sussex

Dr T. H. Taylor, Goose Green, Cerne Abbas, Dorset

Mr H. W. Taylor, Margaretting Tye, Essex

Jessica Thomas, Barnes, London

Philip Thomas, Barnes, London

A. J. P. Thorne, Ringwood, Hants.

Mrs Jean E. Turner, Cerne Abbas, Dorset

John F. W. Walling, Newton Abbot, Devon

Barbara West, Cerne Abbas, Dorset

Donald H. Whistance, Cerne Abbas, Dorset

Janice M. I. Whitfield (née fox), Southampton

D. R. J. Whitty (Barnes), Dorchester, Dorset

Nick and Ginny Williams-Ellis, Cerne Abbas, Dorset

Mr and Mrs Patrick Woodford, Cerne Abbas, Dorset

John Young, Charminster, Dorset

ALSO AVAILABLE IN THE SERIES

The Book of Addiscombe, In Celebration of a Croydon Parish • Various
The Book of Bampton, A Pictorial History of a Devon Parish • Caroline Seward
The Book of Bickington, From Moor to Shore • Stuart Hands
The Book of Brixham, Portrait of a Harbour Town • Frank Pearce
The Book of Chittlehampton, A North Devon Parish • Various
The Book of Cornwood and Lutton, Photographs and Reminiscences • Compiled by the People of the Parish
The Book of Creech St Michael, The Parish and Its People • June Small
The Ellacombe Book, A Portrait of a Torquay Parish • Sydney R. Langmead
The Book of Grampound with Creed • Amy Bane and Mary Oliver
The Book of Hayling Island and Langstone • Peter Rogers
The Book of Helston, Ancient Borough and Market Town • Jenkin with Carter
The Book of High Bickington, A Devon Ridgeway Parish • Avril Stone
The Book of Ilsington, A Photographic History of the Parish • Dick Wills
Lanner, A Cornish Mining Parish • Scharron Schwartz and Roger Parker
The Book of Lamerton, A Photographic History • Ann Cole and Friends
The Book of Loddiswell, Heart of the South Hams • Various
The Book of Manaton, Portrait of a Dartmoor Parish • Compiled by the People of the Parish
The Book of Meavy, Dartmoor Parish, Village and River • Pauline Hemery
The Book of Minehead with Alcombe • Hilary Binding and Douglas Stevens
The Book of North Newton, In Celebration of a Somerset Parish • Robins & Robins
The Book of Plymtree, The Parish and its People • Tony Eames
The Book of Porlock, A Pictorial Celebration • Denis Corner
Postbridge – The Heart of Dartmoor • Reg Bellamy
The Book of Priddy, A Photographic Portrait of Mendip's Highest Village • Various
The Book of Silverton, An Exe Valley Parish • Silverton Local History Society
South Tawton and South Zeal with Sticklepath, 1000 Years Below the Beacon • Roy and Ursula Radford
The Book of Torbay, A Century of Celebration • Frank Pearce
Widecombe-in-the-Moor, A Pictorial History of a Dartmoor Parish • Stephen Woods
Uncle Tom Cobley and All, Widecombe-in-the-Moor • Stephen Woods
Woodbury, The Twentieth Century Revisited • Roger Stokes

SOME OF THE MANY TITLES AVAILABLE IN 2001

The Book of Bickleigh • Barrie Spencer
The Book of Blandford Forum • Various
The Book of Constantine • Various
The Book of Hemyock • Various
The Book of Hurn • Margaret Phipps
The Lustleigh Book • Joe Crowdy and Tim Hall
The Book of Rattery • Various
The Book of Publow with Pensford • Various
The Book of Severn • Various
The Book of South Stoke • Various
The Book of Sparkwell • Pam James
The Book of Stourton Caundle • Philip Knott
The Book of Watchet • Compiled by David Banks

For details of any of the above titles or if you are interested in writing your own community history, please contact: Community Histories Editor, Halsgrove House, Lower Moor Way, Tiverton Business Park, Tiverton, Devon EX16 6SS, England, e-mail:sales@halsgrove.com